As a wartime evacuee to North America I am fascinated by the variety of experiences of other evacuees Michael Henderson has uncovered and the generosity of American families that is revealed."
— JESSICA MANN, crime novelist and author, *Out of Harm's Way.*

"It takes a good storyteller — like Michael Henderson — to capture the spirit that informed the trans-Atlantic floating nurseries in which thousands of British children escaped the fear of a possible German invasion in 1940.
During my years as reporter in several countries — including the United States and South Africa — I came across many of those refugees. Without exception, I found them modest, uncomplaining, and courageous. Michael himself has proved to be a shining example. His new book leaps the years and has assumed special relevance with the plight of political refugees now back in the news.
Michael is a persuasive and persistent reporter who thinks on his feet. Thank goodness he pursued those now adult, eternally grateful refugees whose experiences he wasn't able to fit into his first account."
—KIM SHIPPEY, international journalist and editor in radio and television with the BBC in London and *The Christian Science Monitor* in Boston.

"Michael Henderson's latest book reminds us of the Americans who opened their homes to the children of Britain in need in 1940. These wartime refugees became ambassadors for America and their contribution to our society has been immeasurable. Henderson's exchanges with hundreds of other evacuees have uncovered a wealth of revealing stories from the American Home front in World War II. May we use Michael's stories as a reminder that we again must open our hearts to war refugees in need."
— DONNA ZAJONC, former Oregon State Legislator, author, *Politics of Hope.*

a HARVEST of FRIENDSHIPS

ALSO BY MICHAEL HENDERSON:

The Adventures of Angy, a Red Cross Nurse at Mons

Ice in Every Carriage

Forgiveness: Breaking the Chain of Hate

No Enemy to Conquer

See You after the Duration

The Forgiveness Factor

All Her Paths are Peace

Hope for a Change

On History's Coattails

A Different Accent

Experiment with Untruth

From India with Hope

a HARVEST of FRIENDSHIPS

A story of World War II child evacuees,

American generosity, and British gratitude

BY MICHAEL HENDERSON

Arnica Creative Services
Portland, OR | Los Angeles, CA | Palm Springs, CA

ISBN: 978-09838168-6-7
Publisher's Cataloging-in-Publication Data
PCN: 2015952470

Publisher: Ross Hawkins
Editor-in-Chief: Gloria Martinez
Book Designer: Aimee Genter-Gilmore

 PUBLISHING

Portland, OR | Los Angeles, CA | Palm Springs, CA
ideasbyacs.com

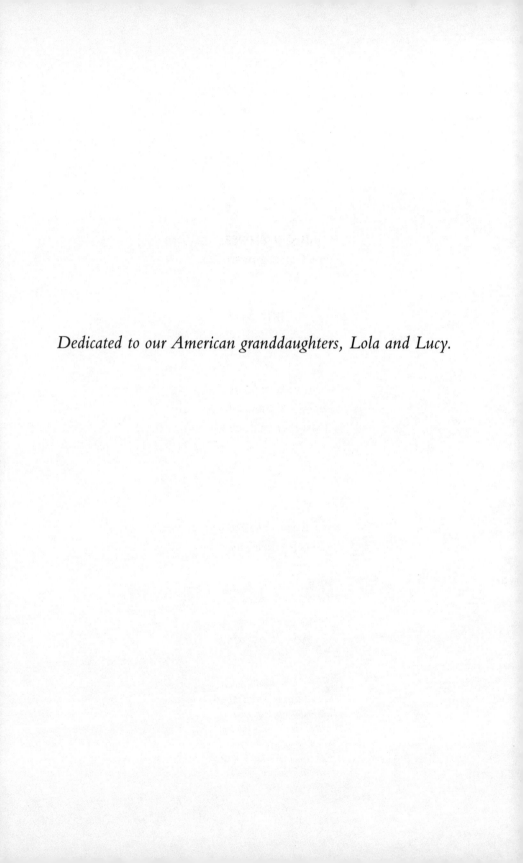

Dedicated to our American granddaughters, Lola and Lucy.

CONTENTS

FOREWORD

THE PUBLICATION OF *A HARVEST OF FRIENDSHIPS:*
A Story of World War II Evacuees, American Generosity, and British Gratitude cannot
be the last word of the experience and impact that changed the lives of both the
World War II British evacuees and their American hosts. Its impact will live
forever in the minds and hearts of not only those who experienced it, but their
descendants for many generations. It will also last forever in the minds of the
people fortunate enough to read this book.

There are touching stories of parents torn with the loss of the company
of their children's growing up, sending them into danger, afraid of how
their lives would be changed, and wondering why some five million
Americans, according to Gallup, were offering their homes and their lives to
be changed by the introduction of children they didn't know. But they did
know that they were raised by people who shared the same values that they
did, the same values that President Barak Obama identified in his speech to
Parliament a few years ago.

In President Obama's address to both Houses of Parliament in 2011, after
the introductory pleasantries, the first point he made was his understanding of
the "Special Relationship:"

> *"Our relationship is special because of the values and beliefs that have
> united our people throughout the ages. Centuries ago, when kings, emperors,
> and warlords reigned over much of the world, it was the English who first
> spelled out the rights and liberties of man in Magna Carta."*

The President of the United States in that stirring address also said:

> *"Our system of justice, customs, and values stemmed from our British
> forefathers."*

FOREWORD

Former Ambassador to the Court of St. James's Honorable Louis Susman's inaugural speech to the Pilgrim Society in London on his first formal address upon his appointment some years ago said:

> *"In war and peace, in prosperity and in time of economic hardship, America has no better friend and no more dependable ally than the United Kingdom."*
>
> *"Our nations are deeply rooted in our enduring values of democracy, rule of law and tolerance; a shared history, culture and language, and a mutual ability and willingness to bring real diplomatic, financial and military assets to the table for joint action to promote and defend our common interests."*

These statements I would argue and the witness to them expressed by those children evacuated are the truths told by the young people who share with us their anxieties, fears, and sorrow of the loss of their families for who knew how long, replaced by unknown, unfamiliar surroundings and people they feared wouldn't give them the 'home' in all that conveys that they were leaving behind.

I've been chairman of the senior 'Anglo-American Friendship Society', the Pilgrim Society, which has as its sole objective: "the furtherance of Anglo-American good fellowship', and have tried to be among the most ardent of those espousing the strength of the bond between the country of my birth and of my choice, now, of residency and nationality. Often asked how I as a loyal American came to renounce his American citizenship and become a British citizen, a subject of the Crown. My answer has been two-fold, that I've chosen to live in Britain for nearly fifty years, a country which has been very good to me, and lucky enough to have received a knighthood. I felt that I should, and equally important, that I cannot conceive of any deeply serious breach of the 'Special Relationship' that would cause me to regret my clear dual loyalties to my two countries. There are in the Pilgrims a number of evacuees even today as there have been since the War, and they are among the most deeply committed and outspoken of their dual loyalties as I am.

A most meaningful chapter is difficult to choose from among several. Some might choose the pages that tell the story of the boys and girls from the Actors' Orphanage at Silverlands, Surrey, who thought they were going to Hollywood instead went together to New York in the chapter entitled Just a little Detour. Another chapter is about the extraordinarily lucky children who arrived at a former private hunting and fishing reserve called Tuxedo Park, an enclave of millionaires who offered to fund the trip over, and haven for fifty

English children, at no cost to their parents still in England.

By the time you read the quotation [2] that "Britain has 3,500 unofficial ambassadors" you will be a believer.

> *"They carry no diplomatic passports, nor do they claim any diplomatic privilege. They work not in the limelight of officialdom, but insidiously in the very heart of the country in which for the time being they are at home. They carry no instructions in sealed envelopes, for their instructions are simple and easy, even for the very youngest of them to remember. 'Be truthful, brave, kind and grateful' are the words written in their hearts... Six simple words accepted with childlike faith as sufficient to enable them to meet any situation they might have to face in the country far from home where they not work for Britain. For these are the children of Britain who during the months of July, August and September 1940 sailed from the threatened shores of our island fortress to the kindly welcoming lands of our great Dominions and of the United States of America."*

These words had deep meaning for me, for my class at J.C. Nichols grade school in Kansas City, Missouri, was joined by a boy named Dennis Brown, who together with his older sister, Jennifer, had come to America, lucky to be able to join his aunt and uncle. They had the benefit of being safe from the ravages of the war, in the Middle West of America, and at the same time, being with family.

The Brown brother and sister were, looking back, the best ambassadors that Britain could have had. They were true 'ambassadors' for Great Britain at a time that the 'special relationship' was vital to the saving of Britain — and democracy in Europe.

— Sir Robert Worcester

INTRODUCTION

A HARVEST OF FRIENDSHIPS HAS BEEN
written as an expression of thanks to the American families who took
in some three or four thousand young British evacuees and looked after
them during World War II. My brother and I were two of them and we
spent nearly five years in New England. In most cases host families paid all
expenses as very little money could be transferred from Britain. If things
had gone terribly wrong, which in 1940 was a real possibility, those homes
might have become our homes for life.

It is also an expression of gratitude to countless organizations who played
their part in donating services, whether it was White Cross and Blue Cross
covering medical expenses, the Gould Foundation in New York and the New
England Home for Little Wanderers providing way stations and sometimes
more for evacuees, Hoover and Kodak taking in employees from their English
counterparts, Yale professors arranging to host children from professors at
Oxford and Cambridge, or private schools reducing or waiving fees. There
were legislators who worked to persuade Congress to amend the Neutrality
Act to allow American ships to sail to England. One could especially mention
the First Lady, Eleanor Roosevelt, and Marshall Field, who headed the US
Committee for the Care of European Children which, with its seventy
affiliated committees, became the legal umbrella and organizational hub for all
arrangements for the young visitors. It was Mrs. Roosevelt who came up with
the idea of an administrative ruling that would allow the children to enter as
temporary visitors rather than immigrants. Doris Kearns Goodwin writes that,
"Mrs. Roosevelt had found her first wartime cause in the movement to open
America's doors for the refugee children of Europe."

This book has been completed as the anniversaries of World War II
give way to those of World War I and fewer and fewer of us are still around
who lived through those momentous years and can talk from firsthand
knowledge. I realize that when I speak to children in British and American

INTRODUCTION

schools it is as if at my school a speaker had come in to talk about the Boer War or the Spanish American war.

It is surprising how little is known about this evacuation let alone the fact that thousands of British children were also sent for safety to Canada, Australia, New Zealand and South Africa. Or if known about, that knowledge is sometimes slight or even inaccurate, particularly when that evacuation gets mixed up with the sending of so-called orphans to Australia as was done with less honorable motives and more disastrous results and led to the terrible abuse for which the Australian government has apologized. The American version of a BBC film about the evacuation of British children to the United States was quite wrongly called *Orphans of the Storm*. I am familiar with the film as I was waiting to record the commentary for it until I heard from the producer: "We have decided to go with a woman's voice."

It is hard today for families in Britain and the United States to imagine why parents would be willing to put their children in the care of strangers in another country and send them across the dangerous Atlantic or for strangers to offer homes to foreign children. It would be less hard to understand perhaps for parents in Syria and other countries worried for their children's future today. Britain in the summer of 1940 was not at that stage. The British were already aware of what had happened when Germany conquered the countries of mainland Europe, although they were buoyed to a certain extent by the rescue of more than 300,000 British and French soldiers from the beaches of Dunkirk; the country was now faced with the possibility, even the likelihood, of a German invasion and doubts about the country's ability to resist. Imagine the feelings of the Jewish families rescued from their countries who thought that they had found safety in England and those British families who were featured on the Nazi black list. Then, in the midst of such worries, came the hope given by generous offers from all over the world, particularly the United States, to give sanctuary to the children.

There were many motivations that overrode the dangers their children would face if sent over an Atlantic patrolled by German U-Boats. For some, the horrors of the Blitz were less worrying than a future where the Swastika flew over Buckingham Palace. Some children were old enough to have talked with their parents about overseas evacuation but most of us had little idea what was going on in 1940.

I hope that this book will also let the American public know of the generosity of their fellow country men and women in those crucial years, and the resulting lifetime friendships that flowed from it. It will also help to explain to readers the answer to the question I am most asked: "How in the world could parents think of sending their children away?"

———————

In 2002, a Rhode Island woman, Mary Beth Kreger, and her husband, Chris, decided to set up a bed and breakfast establishment in a big old house in Narragansett. When she moved in there were only two objects on the walls, a 1905 postcard depicting the water tower outside and a letter signed Elizabeth R. thanking the owners for sharing their home with children from the United Kingdom during World War II. Queen Elizabeth had written, "For all this goodwill towards the children of Great Britain I send you my warmest and most grateful thanks."

Mary Beth wanted to "restore the house to its perfection." She was surprised to find symmetrical holes in the living-room floor and asked her realtor what they were. He said that fifteen children from the United Kingdom had lived in the house during the war and that was where desks had been bolted to the floor for their "school." A little trap door in the floor led to a dirt cellar under the foundation, and on the underside of the floor boards was painted: "Quiet, school in session." More information he couldn't give. This discovery had always intrigued her. A guest in her bed and breakfast, being told the story, decided to Google "Children in War" and up came an interview I had given to the Quincy paper, the *Patriot Ledger*. It was about my five years as an evacuee in the next state, Massachusetts, my book *See You After the Duration* and my website address. She enlisted me to try and track down the family and the school. Now she is able to tell her guests what we discovered. The search helped motivate me to write this further book uncovering other unusual and varied stories and is told in Chapter 5.

———————

In 2000, further north the then executive director of the "Lakes Region Conservation Trust," Thomas C. Curren, described in his newsletter how he was invited to climb one of the lesser-known summits in the region. He found on one ledge a route marked by a unique set of blazes, a series of tin can lids painted orange and nailed into trees along the trailside. Some sprouted rust through fading paint; others sported fresh coats of blaze orange. "I made a mental note," he wrote, "that if we were ever to protect this land, we ought to find a more suitable way to mark the trail."

INTRODUCTION

Thomas asked his guide about the source of the trail makers. Her response, he reported, was something like this: "Before the United States entered the Second World War, my mother and father took in a group of English children whose parents sought sanctuary for them from the dangers of the Blitz. There was one boy who loved the view from those ledges, he used to climb them early every day and spent long hours looking out over the valley... He's the one who put those markers there, and every so often in the ensuing fifty years or so, he would come back to us for a visit and quietly slip away to freshen or replace the old ones. He passed away just a few years ago."

Thomas wrote, "I thought of that homesick English boy climbing up through the forest, hugging his knees on the ledges, and taking what comfort he could in the view of Mount Chocorua. It dawned on me during that same time that the American ambassador to England was former New Hampshire Governor John Winant. Night after night, as the air-raid sirens wailed, John Winant walked the streets of London in a business suit, giving what comfort he could to the British people in the months before Pearl Harbor. I made a mental note that if the Trust was ever to protect this land and if anyone else was ever so dumb as to suggest that those tin can lids should be removed, my response would be: 'Over my dead body, pal.' There are a few things we won't forget about here in New Hampshire... even those of us who were born in Massachusetts."

This "homesick English boy" was Charles Fay, who was my best friend at my Connecticut school. I remember well, at Christmas time toward the end of the war, walking with him on snowshoes over the frozen mountain streams and his insisting that I join the Little Larcomb Mountain Club, which he founded. I can still describe the view from South Tamworth and recall the names of the mountains — Paugus, Whiteface, Chocorua and Mt. Washington.

─────────────

On a more recent visit to New Hampshire I set out to show my wife where, during the war, I had attended each summer a camp, South Pond Cabins, near Mount Monadnock. I found what I thought was the right place but practically no trace of it, none of the old cabins, no sign of the tennis courts, even of the dock where I learned to swim and canoe and sail. The pathway into the property took a different course than I remembered; there were large trees where I didn't expect them. We decided to venture in and ran into the present owner. He had a vague memory of what had been there before and drove us around and down to the lake where I recognized a rock feature. He said he had stashed away some old papers that had been left behind. The first one he produced, to my astonishment, had a photo of me on it! It was part of a leaflet about the camp. I was definitely at the right place.

A school in Rhode Island which was all but forgotten, a trail blazed on a New Hampshire mountain by a "homesick English boy" and a camp which has been all but buried in the woods. We are not talking about an ancient civilization but pretty soon there will be no one around who can supply chapter and verse on what happened all those years ago. It is like that with much of the story of the evacuation of children to the United States in World War II. A number of books have been written on this subject, including my own. The title, *See You After the Duration,* repeats the words I called out to my parents as we said goodbye to them in August 1940. It drew on the experiences of more than a hundred evacuees and had a Foreword by another evacuee, Sir Martin Gilbert, which is reprinted here as an Afterword. So I am not attempting this time to cover the whole story, but to highlight a variety of lesser-known experiences. My latest research has brought me in touch with more than a further hundred evacuees and led to lively correspondence, emails and phone calls with other octogenarians. Each had a story that had many of the same ingredients, an anxious goodbye, a dangerous sea voyage, an introduction to a new country and a new family, a return trip in safer circumstances, for most. But each had also distinctive and unique features, about which little have been written. It was above all, another reminder of the continuing harvest of Atlantic friendships that have spanned the generations.

As an Englishman who has lived nearly a third of his life in the United States, I would like to thank all those who shared their experiences and once again put on record the generous response of the American people to Britain in its hour of need — the response which Queen Elizabeth referred to in her message to the previous occupants of the home that is now a bed and breakfast.

Michael Henderson
Westward Ho!
North Devon, England
michaeldhenderson@btinternet.com

IN LOVING AND PROUD MEMORY OF MICHAEL RENNIE ELDER SON OF THE VICAR OF THIS CHURCH. CHILDRENS ESCORT S.S. 'CITY OF BENARES' SEP.t 18, 1940. REQUIESCANT IN PACE

The sinking of the *City of Benares* on September 17, 1940 must be remembered in any account of overseas evacuation. 256 people died including more than eighty children, of which seventy-seven were sponsored by CORB. This government scheme was ended immediately and private overseas evacuation more or less ceased. This painting in a London church by Walter Starmer remembers Michael Rennie, 23, the youngest official escort and son of the church's vicar, who again and again dived into the sea to rescue children to the lifeboat: "It was a harrowing and spirit-lifting quarter hour. Rennie hauled thirteen of fifteen boys back in this way, wresting them from the water and from the precipice of death." He died of exhaustion just as a rescue ship was seen. His last words: "Hurrah! Here comes the destroyer. Thank God."

CHAPTER ONE

SEE YOU AFTER THE DURATION

THE BOAT ON WHICH I CROSSED WAS ONE OF THOSE IN WHICH ENGLAND WAS SENDING CHILDREN TO CANADA. THE SCENE ON DECK WAS TOUCHING AND AMAZING. A THOUSAND CHILDREN WERE AT PLAY IN THE SUN AROUND THE GUNS THAT PROTECTED THEM. THREE WARSHIPS ESCORTED US.

WHENEVER I THINK OF THAT SHIP I FEEL AS IF I WERE RECALLING A DREAM. THIS GIANT FLOATING NURSERY SEEMED UNREAL. ON DECK HUNDREDS OF LITTLE FOLK, WITH BLOND AND BROWN CURLY HEADS RUSHED ABOUT, LAUGHED, SHOUTED, CLIMBED ON THE RIGGING, HOISTED THEMSELVES UP THE COMPANION STAIRS, FELL, WEPT, THEN LAUGHED AGAIN.... SOMETIMES I WOULD GET UP AT DAWN AND STRETCH OUT ON DECK IN ORDER TO ENJOY FOR A TIME THE SILENT BEAUTY OF THE OCEAN BEFORE THE CHILDREN TOOK POSSESSION....

IN THE SAME CABIN WITH ME LIVED ADRIAN, A LITTLE BOY OF EIGHT, WHO WAS MAKING THE LONG VOYAGE ALONE. THROUGHOUT THE WHOLE TRIP ADRIAN PROVED HIMSELF A RESERVED AND DIGNIFIED COMPANION. EDUCATED IN AN ENGLISH SCHOOL, TRAINED TO SELF-CONTROL FROM INFANCY, HE WAS NEITHER TIMID NOR OVERBOLD. HE TRIED TO DO EVERYTHING FOR HIMSELF.... HE WAS NEAT, THOUGHTFUL AND BRAVE....
—André Maurois, *Why France Fell*

The waters around the Irish Sea were pretty crowded in the summer months of 1940 as convoys formed up with ocean liners and escorting warships to take thousands of British evacuees to the United States and Canada and further afield. There were also ships coming in and out all the time that carried vital food supplies that kept beleaguered Britain alive and German U-boats prowling around for the chance to sink them. My father was at the time with Movement Control at Birkenhead across the Mersea River from Liverpool, the English port which along with Glasgow and the Clyde in Scotland sent off the overseas evacuees.

I like Maurois' description (above). I don't know whether my brother Gerald and I were on the same ship. His recollections in *Why France Fell* underline the crucial difference between "internal' evacuation" and "overseas" evacuation — the broad and dangerous Atlantic which we had to cross whether we were heading for Canada and the United States or further afield. All sorts of ships were involved. I have compiled a list of forty-seven vessels on which evacuees told me they had traveled, some with just a few children, some like Maurois' ship with hundreds aboard, and some of them making several trips in those crucial months of July, August and September. That is why a common question that gets asked when you meet an *internal* evacuee is, 'Where were you evacuated from?' whereas with an *overseas* evacuee, the first exchange is likely to be, 'What ship were you on?' Internal evacuation was a huge upset, with crowded trains taking a million and a half children away from dangers of heavy bombing in cities. Overseas evacuation was in a different dimension, always involving ships and usually convoys. It was not an era where jumbo jets existed or where flying at all was even an option. The one common factor to both evacuations was disruption to family life.

Pre-war government thinking about *internal* evacuation began as early as 1925 and by 1931 meticulous preparations were being made, years before the great exodus of more than a million and a half children under Operation Pied Piper began on September 1st 1939, the eve of the war. The frightfulness of aerial bombing as displayed in the Spanish Civil War and in the most recent German attacks on Rotterdam only increased the concern. *Overseas* evacuation planning, in so far as it involved government, began only nine months *after* the war had begun, in June 1940, with the first ship sailing a month later, in the circumstances an incredible achievement. I write "in so far as it involved government," because *overseas* evacuation in the first six months or so involved largely only private initiatives by families who could afford it or who had relatives overseas that would take the children. The fact that before the war an invasion from continental Europe was never expected is underlined by the fact that many children in 1939 were evacuated to England's south coast where any invasion would start! The fact that eight months later an invasion was expected is confirmed in a recently published book about code breaking, *Colossus*, by Paul Gannon which reveals that in the wake of Dunkirk, the level of fear was such that busses were kept on standby at Bletchley Park, Britain's key code-breaking center, so that its staff could rapidly be transported to Liverpool where they could board a ship bound for the United States."

I was eight and my brother six when we set off for the United States in August 1940. "See you after the duration," I called out to my parents, using the latest grown-up phrase I had heard. "Duration" because no one knew how long the war would last. British parents had no idea in 1940 that the separation would last five years, any more than American hosts could imagine their generous offer of help at a time of Britain's desperate need would be so stretched out. Not many people were as prescient as Harold Macmillan, later prime minister, who, when asked in 1940 how long the war would last, replied: "Twelve months if they win, five years if we do."

Many overseas evacuees went privately or as part of university, company or school arrangements. But few adults in Britain even now know that a British government scheme offered in June 1940 to all families might have led to every eligible child in the country being signed up to be sent overseas. It had been put forward because it was felt to be unfair and politically damaging if the option of overseas safety was only available for those who could afford it. In the first two weeks of it being made public in the newspapers the response to the scheme, known as CORB, short for Children's Overseas Reception Board, was so overwhelming, with 211,448 children signed up to go, that the organizers had to temporarily suspend it. Thirty thousand of those children had their names put down to go to the United States.

The government scheme was unrealistic — one would never have been able to find the ships, the convoys, and the escorts for so many — and it came to an abrupt end with the sinking of the *City of Benares* in September. Only 2,664 CORB children were sent to Canada, South Africa, Australia and New Zealand and none to the United States. The deaths of more than eighty children in the *City of Benares* brought home to the public how dangerous the submarine-infested waters of the Atlantic mid-summer 1940 were and was a wake-up call to parents who were still considering the private option. This sinking, which was a colossal shock to the whole nation, is why in many of the children's accounts the name *City of Benares* features because they just missed being on that ship. Those who left earlier would have known nothing about it and those who left later were too young to have been told at the time. Over the years, however, it has added understandably a dramatic element to their personal stories.

My brother and I were two of the some three or four thousand evacuees who had already arrived safely in the United States.

As is the case with many, if not most families, we never talked after the war with our parents about the decisions taken then. We just got on with life. I am sure that a motivation that my parents shared with others was how they could pursue their responsibilities in defending Britain while still looking after the children.

In 1939 my father, at the age of forty-seven, was already back in the army and my mother was with St. John's Ambulance nursing service. My mother had a particular motivation which drove her as she visited the offices of shipping companies to find spaces for us. It was to get us out of the war zone. She was Irish and Protestant and had grown up in the midst of "the troubles" at the time of Irish independence. She remembered machine gun fights around her Dublin home and soldiers occupying her school. In 1922 her father, my grandfather, was told to leave Ireland by the end of the week or be shot, which was why indeed they escaped to England and I am English. A family home was burned to the ground by Irish nationalists.

Just as Maurois describes it, we sailed with hundreds of other children in a liner, the *Duchess of York*, in a convoy of liners escorted by five destroyers and across from us the battleship HMS *Revenge*. I was particularly pleased to secure the autograph of the battleship's signalman when he was transferred over to us. No wonder that for many of us it was the adventure, not the trauma that is our strongest memory. We did not know the name of the ship when we boarded it. We had only been told, for reasons of security, that it was the SS *Early August*. But roaming all over the ship, as the Maurois children did, we soon discovered the real name poorly painted out. Most of us fortunately were too young to appreciate the very real dangers. On board the *Duchess of York* my brother and I sat on our bunks playing "Battleships" trying to sink each other's ships quite oblivious to the reality that our convoy was a target of German submarines. Jim Baynard-Smith, another evacuee who went as far as New Zealand, told me: "We children didn't mind the discomfort as day after day we played the popular board game, 'Smash the Nazi navy'." For him, too, "It was all a colossal adventure."

For parents it was a different matter. Dr Alan Ardouin, who had been evacuated to Vermont when he was nine, emailed me, recalling that he was very naive at the time. "My mother recalled this naiveté. When we were about to leave our parents, I asked, 'Why is everybody crying?' Then she broke down."

Children on the *Duchess of York*.

CHRISTIAN SCIENCE MONITOR

The author (right) and his brother (left) with Toby and Faith Coghill, a front page photograph in Boston, August 1940.

One father, Ted Matthews, noted in his diary during an air raid on August 10, the very day that four of his daughters sailed for the United States on the same ship as we did, "I feel as if I had committed some horrible crime. There are mines strewn across the oceans, submarines lying in wait to torpedo them, aircraft searching for them to blow them to pieces. Yet I cannot but believe that the crime of exposing them to these dangers is less than the crime of keeping them at home to be the possible victims of an invading army. Every minute that passes takes their ship further and further away from that danger. If ever my children read this, I beg them to forgive me for doing this thing. They have no conception of what it has cost to make this decision. They will never know the agony which I suffer at the thought of them tonight." It was only many years later, after our mother died, that I realized what it had cost her to send us away. A close friend of hers, commiserating on her death, had written me, "Your mother was very brave."

In September 1939 Gerald and I had already been evacuated from London to the countryside away from the danger of bombing. However, by May 1940, with the woods around serving as a camping place for soldiers who had escaped from Dunkirk, the even bigger threat was that likelihood of a German invasion. Offers of all kinds had come in from the Dominions, as the large Commonwealth countries were then called, and other countries to host British children. A Gallup Poll taken that summer indicated that five million American families would be willing to take them. Committees were set up in the United States and Britain to be responsible for coordinating arrangements.

We were invited to live with the Walter Hinchmans, in Milton, near Boston. We had never met them but Mr. Hinchman wrote reassuringly describing his family and home to our parents. They had six children; the youngest was sixteen when we arrived. Mr. Hinchman taught English at Milton Academy and in 1902 had even captained the American touring cricket team, the Gentlemen of Philadelphia. This was at a time when the Philadelphia newspapers devoted as much space to cricket as they did to baseball. His wife, Julia, was English — also a Henderson — but no relation to us, and her brother in the British army had been evacuated from Dunkirk. They met us on arrival in Boston, an event which was recorded in a front-page photo of my brother and me and two other children as we faced the U.S. immigration and drove us to a camp in New Hampshire.

In 1940 young British knew little about life in the United States, in fact few had ever met an American until thousands of GIs arrived in Britain a few years later to prepare for the Normandy invasion. The experience of crossing the Atlantic in a convoy and then being whisked away to a camp on a lake in

Michael and his brother, Gerald, soon after arrival in 1940 with their hosts Walter and Julia Hinchman and their son, John.

the woods, being driven on the "other side of the road" and on the way seeing trains that ran in the streets — what an immediate change of perspective for us that was! At the camp, Gerald and I won first prize in a fancy dress competition. We were dressed, appropriately as "Bundles from Britain."

At the time, a knitting bee had caught the imagination of Anglophiles across the United States and by that summer "Bundles for Britain" was employing 900,000 knitters and support staff, all buying wool from the proceeds of cake and jam sales and sending socks and scarves to Britain.

There was for us youngsters the fascination of the new: new food, like hotdogs and hamburgers and waffles, corn on the cob and donuts, peanut butter, blueberries, cranberry sauce, and twenty-eight flavors of ice cream at Howard Johnson's. There were new sports like American football and baseball and basketball and ice hockey, which I loved.

Our appearance changed as we swiftly got out of short trousers and gartered long stockings and into dungarees or corduroy knickerbockers, while school caps gave way to ski caps, not to mention crew cuts. As the weather changed there were parkas and slickers and sou'westers and even snowshoes. There were different and exciting customs, too, like Halloween and Thanksgiving. We learned that American boys and girls start each day with the Pledge of Allegiance to "the flag of the United States and to the Republic for which it stands" and for some historic reason celebrate the Fourth of July. At the Rectory school in Connecticut which I attended for two years they put up a Union Jack so we English children could face it

GETTY IMAGES

Princess Margaret Rose and Princess Elizabeth, the future Queen of England

when the pledge was said. We enjoyed summer camp and I can still sing the college songs I learned round the campfire. In fact, many years later I nearly caused an incident at a party at the American Embassy in London when I got singing with some Americans their college songs. I can still recite from "Paul Revere's Ride" and from "Barbara Frietchie," and can list the U.S. presidents — but only up to Grover Cleveland because that was where I reached in school when the war ended and I returned home.

There was no television but daily fifteen-minute radio programs like "Jack Armstrong, the All-American boy, brought to you by the makers of Wheaties, 'Breakfast of Champions'" and at the weekend a half-hour of "The Lone Ranger." Princess Elizabeth, later the Queen of England, and her sister, Princess Margaret Rose broadcast to us and we were all given a chance to broadcast to our parents. In our case, there was consternation when the wrong parents were put on to talk to us. It is hard to get across to younger people today that were no iPads and iPods and Skyping, not even computers and the Internet. International telephone calls were difficult, expensive, and rare. Letters were the principal way of communicating and it was wise to number them as many ended up in the ocean.

On October 13, 1940, two months after our arrival in the United States, fourteen-year-old Princess Elizabeth broadcast from Windsor Castle to evacuees in Britain and around the world. It was her first broadcast and the first time her voice had been heard publicly.

A HARVEST <u>OF</u> FRIENDSHIPS

"Good evening. Thousands of you in this country," she said, *"have had to leave your homes and be separated from your fathers and mothers. My sister — Margaret Rose — and I feel so much for you, as we know from experience what it means to be away from those we love most of all. To you, living in new surroundings, we send a message of true sympathy, and at the same time we would like to thank the kind people who have welcomed you to their homes in the country. All of us children who are at home think constantly of our friends and relations who have gone overseas — who have travelled thousands of miles to find a wartime home and a kindly welcome in Canada, Australia, New Zealand, South Africa and the United States of America.*

My sister and I feel we know quite a lot about these countries. Our father and mother have so often talked to us of their visits to different parts of the world. So it is not difficult for us to picture the sort of life you are all leading, and to think of all the new sights you must be seeing, and the adventures you must be having. But I am sure that you, too, are often thinking of the Old Country. I know you won't forget us; it is just because we are not forgetting you that I want, on behalf of all the children at home, to send you our love and best wishes — to you and to your kind hosts as well.

Before I finish I can truthfully say to you all that we children at home are full of cheerfulness and courage. We are trying to do all we can to help our gallant sailors, soldiers and airmen, and we are trying, too, to bear our own share of the danger and sadness of war. We know, every one of us, that in the end all will be well; for God will care for us and give us victory and peace. And when peace comes, remember it will be for us, the children of today, to make the world of tomorrow a better and happier place.

My sister is by my side and we are both going to say goodnight to you. Come on, Margaret. Goodnight, children. Good night, and good luck to you all."

Gerald Cock, who was the North American representative of the BBC in New York, sent a telegram: "Princesses yesterday huge success here. Some stations report telephone exchanges jammed with requests for repeat." In the days following the Princess' first broadcast, the Canadian correspondent of *The Times* of London reported that churches had installed 'wirelesses' in order to hear her speech in Canada and the news agency *Reuters* reported that hundreds of children in Wellington, New Zealand and in the United States tuned in.

The Japanese attack on Pearl Harbor on December 7, 1941 meant that we were all now in it together. We became part of the war effort as we collected scrap metal, saved for war bonds, grew Victory gardens.

Campfire at South Pond Cabins, a camp in New Hampshire which I refer to in the fourth section of my introduction. It no longer exists.

Our mother with sons in the countryside... and father in uniform.

Hinchman cricketer.   Hinchman home.

A HARVEST OF FRIENDSHIPS

I earned my first money weeding Mr Hinchman's garden. Though very young, because I lived near the school I was permitted to spot for planes from the top of the school chapel. Though I cannot imagine how German planes would ever have got to Boston. In 1944 my father arrived unannounced on a mission to Washington. He phoned up unexpectedly from there one evening. When I put down the phone, I apparently said, "Gee, he talks just like in the movies." The year before, I was in Harvard Yard when the British Prime Minister Winston Churchill received an honorary degree. I was waving a Union Jack. There is no doubt that we were all unabashedly patriotic.

As the years went by pressure grew for children to come home, with older ones returning to join the armed forces. The "guest children" became more of a load on host families, for it must be remembered that this was all carried by them. Little money could be transferred from England. Some English parents were worried that their children might be becoming too American or wanted them to share something of the wartime experience at home. Some of the children were eager to do their part. But the Atlantic was still dangerous. Indeed, the losses to U-boats in March 1943 were the highest in the war.

However, by August that year, thanks to long distance air cover, improved submarine detection radar and the ability to break the latest version of German naval *Enigma* keys, the figure was reduced dramatically, and Karl Doenitz, the German admiral, was forced to withdraw submarines from the Atlantic. There were, however, still few spaces available for civilians as weaponry and soldiers were the priority in the build up to the invasion of France.

In May 1945 Gerald and I returned with some twenty other boys on an escort aircraft carrier HMS *Patroller*, again in a large convoy. My school rushed through a graduation certificate so that I could take it with me. The biggest fear of most evacuees and of most parents was that we wouldn't recognize each other. Indeed, we walked straight past our mother. The biggest task, after getting off the grime of two weeks let loose on an aircraft carrier, was rebuilding our family life. Our parents had lived through the London Blitz and the horror of V1s and V2s, German rockets that rained on London in the last months of the war, and would jump at any loud noise. They expected greater obedience than perhaps we gave them. We were constantly comparing life at home with life in the United States. "*We* don't do this, *WE* don't do that" and pretty soon America became known in our family as '*WE-land.*' Like many other young people returning we had to contend with an unfamiliar school syllabus and a return to the complicated arithmetic of pounds, shillings and pence. Some struggled with exams and took time to readjust. I was grateful that my American schools had kept up my Latin needed for British exams. In chapter 13, several evacuees assess the whole experience.

After the war the U.S. Committee for the Care of European Children, the umbrella organization for most evacuees, reported, "In the long run, the 861 British children in the Committee's program turned into nearly that many emissaries of goodwill, who through the personal feelings they developed and provoked added solid substance to the friendliness of British-American relations." It is where a true special relationship resides. Many evacuees have kept up their links with their host families. We have maintained friendship with our host families, even attending the wedding of a great granddaughter in Oregon. We have visited and spoken at our old schools. Among now elderly evacuees to the United States you will encounter little mindless anti-Americanism and a lot of appreciation of that country, even on the part of some of those whose experiences were less happy than ours. Many of us could say, along with Shirley Williams, Baroness Williams of Crosby, one of the high-profile evacuees, "America became my other country."

The U.S. Committee also noted that the evacuation was "an applied lesson in international understanding." My mother's experience growing up amidst conflict in Ireland and our experience separated by war for five years came together in finding a way to contribute to such understanding. In 1947 we attended a conference at Mountain House in Caux, Switzerland. It had opened the year before and we were attracted by our wish to heal the divisions in our family and to see how we could contribute to helping heal the hates of the war. It is a center of reconciliation whose role in helping bring the two enemies, Germany and France, together has been described by eminent historians.

One day an Irish Senator, Eleanor Butler, a Catholic and member of the Council of Europe, spoke about unity in Europe. My Protestant mother was incensed. Who is this woman, she thought, who chucked me out of my country and is talking about unity? But in the spirit of that place, which was that you start with yourself and your country, rather than pointing the finger of blame, she apologized to the Senator for the indifference she and her family had shown to Catholics and they became friends. Eleanor went on to be one of the founders of the Glencree Centre for Peace and Reconciliation, and my mother and my family, with our unity restored, undertook to work for understanding in many countries. In an unusual way my mother's

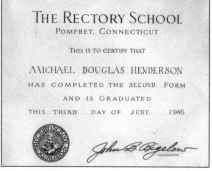

THE RECTORY SCHOOL
POMFRET, CONNECTICUT

THIS IS TO CERTIFY THAT

MICHAEL DOUGLAS HENDERSON

HAS COMPLETED THE SECOND FORM

AND IS GRADUATED

THIS THIRD DAY OF JUNE 1945

Rectory School headmaster, Fred Williams,
presents the author with its Distinguished
Service Award.

Irish origin not only led to our evacuation but after the war led on to my
spending my life working for reconciliation and peace and writing books on
the subject. But that is another story.

On May 2, 2015 the Rectory School in Pomfret, Connecticut, where
the author was in seventh and eighth grades during the war, gave Michael its
Distinguished Service Award. Making the presentation Rectory headmaster,
Fred Williams said, "Rectory's Distinguished Service Award is presented
annually to that member of the Rectory community, be he or she graduate,
employee, or friend of the school, who has embraced across a career or
a lifetime the four words that comprise the Rectory creed: Respect,
responsibility, honesty, and compassion. In a world too full of hatred and
animosity, Michael Henderson has distinguished himself for efforts to
promote reconciliation and encourage forgiveness. He has written about this
in his many titles."

CHAPTER TWO

UNLIKE ANYTHING
THEY HAD EVER KNOWN

SHE ASKED FOR ONE HUNDRED CHILDREN — BUT, AS WAS HER CUSTOM, THERE WERE RESTRICTIONS.
—*Helen Clay Frick: Bittersweet Heiress,*
Martha Frick Symington Sanger

In the evacuation of children to the United States, unlike the case of children evacuated within Britain, much more care was taken to match children with families of corresponding backgrounds. In interviews at Grosvenor House Hotel, Park Lane, London, which became an annex to the U.S. embassy and was where almost all children, including my brother and I were processed. Families were asked searching questions on their income, education, religion and interests. The Sylvia Warren Committee, under whose auspices we came, played a significant role together with the main United States Committee for the Care of European Children. Sylvia laid down the expectations: "It is important to try to approximate the background from which they have come from, the educational and economic point of view, not only for success here, but for repatriation later on." In our case, as I mentioned in the first chapter, we were matched very suitably with the Hinchmans in Milton. Equally suitably matched was my best friend at school in Connecticut, Charles Fay, who had been sponsored by the *Boston Transcript* newspaper and taken on by another teacher and his family. Charles' father, a London judge, wrote congratulating the committee that they could not have found a better match.

There were, as one might expect when a large number of people are involved, some cases where there were mismatches or even abuse. Though fortunately, under the various programs there were regular inspections where cases could be sorted out and, if necessary, children moved. Perhaps the most unusual evacuation story of a mismatch with a happy ending is the case of seven young girls, three of them sisters, who found themselves without great fuss put into the home of Helen Frick who, having inherited $38 million in 1919, was then named "the richest, unmarried woman in America." I spoke to one of the "girls," Valerie Goodwin (Sayers), when she was eighty-five and she told me that they were supposed to be equally matched. Fortunately, she said, before she came she had attended an all-girls English grammar school and so "was sufficiently well brought up and well-behaved not to be put out that Helen Frick had a butler. We took it all in our stride. We didn't come back with any fancy ideas."

These girls came to America, like Charles Fay, under the *Boston Transcript* scheme. This now defunct newspaper set out to find 500 homes for British children. There was a daily appeal as the paper encouraged communities to outdo each other in taking in evacuees. "Your home may save a child's life" was the paper's front-page headline on the eighth of August.

The first four girls, Margot Horn, Sheila Inglis, Molly Stuchbery and Mary-Joy Shuttleworth, all aged twelve, sailed that August 1940 on the *Samaria* in the same convoy Gerald and I did. It was before the bombing had begun in earnest. By the time, however, the three Sayers sisters, Pixie, nine, Valerie, twelve, and Mavis, thirteen, were ready to depart, the bombing had stepped up.

Valerie remembers their departure from London: "With our parents we spent the noisy night of Battle of Britain Sunday in a hotel near Selfridges. The next morning we assembled with dozens of other children at Grosvenor House Hotel trying to be brave as we said goodbye and got on buses for the station. When we arrived in Liverpool there was a heavy raid going on. We were hurried into a warehouse basement. My youngest sister was terrified by the dreadful bombing that went on all night. However, there was no panic in the huge cellar where we were on camp beds row upon row. No breakfast arrived until after 11 a.m. When we left the building it was virtually the one still standing on the street. It was said that of the stick of bombs dropped the one that fell into our kitchen didn't explode."

Valerie wrote me, "None of our parents sent us because of the bombing. We could have coped with that. It was the very real fear in 1940 that England was going to be invaded and that three small girls should be in an occupied country that decided my parents to make the huge sacrifice to part with us. I was old enough to realize that we might never be together again."

A HARVEST of FRIENDSHIPS

They sailed on September 14, on the RMS *Antonia* the day after the *City of Benares* had sailed and before the tragic news of its sinking and the death of eighty children shocked the nation and more or less brought the overseas evacuation to an end. When Valerie's mother heard the news, she managed to see the passenger list and was relieved that her daughters were not on it.

The first arrivals were housed at Wellesley College which became a halfway house for some of the evacuees as children and hosts were brought together. Sometimes evacuees could be linked up with host families immediately but, being wartime, ships could arrive unannounced and everything might not have been prepared, so children stayed for a short time there. The three sisters, and many of the 'Transcriptors' as they were called, were also processed on arrival at *The New England Home for Little Wanderers*.

During the war *The New England Home* housed 255 British children on their way to finding homes. Its newsletter, *Advocate,* reported that summer: "Under the eyes of experienced workers, who treat them as individuals, rather than as a group phenomenon, the children seem happy with the pleasant aspect of their green and quiet surroundings so similar to their own countryside. They are occupied with the rest and diversion to recover from the great emotional strain so recently undergone. In the meantime, their habits, taste, hopes, fears, talents and shortcomings are noted to prepare them for the homes where they will have the greatest chance of affection and success. No less exacting are the requirements for the future foster parents. Unhappy homes or families with grave problems of their own are discouraged and other alternatives for charitable instincts are suggested. Once settled, the children will remain in their new homes with occasional visits from the committee until the war is over. Psychologically these plucky children were well prepared for this sea-change in their lives. The courageous parents who have sent them far away out of danger, but also out of reach, have told them how to behave in a strange land. Contrary to the usual techniques of children as young as six or eight, no criticism or complaint has been uttered of the unfamiliar food or any other new and confusing aspect of their lives."

It is not recorded how the charity prepared, or even if they prepared at all, the girls who were sent to stay with Helen Frick or "Aunt Helen" as they came to know her. It is clear in Valerie's mind that they had not been told where they were going. "Kind people came to collect the children, everybody disappeared, doesn't anybody want us? My sisters and I thought we would soon be the only ones left."

Helen Clay Frick was a most unusual woman with a life-long commitment to social welfare and the environment, and a supreme devotion to the visual

Interviews at Grosvenor House Hotel.

Miss Frick.

The seven girls in 1942. Front row seated left to right: Sheila Inglis (Milliken), Valerie Sayers (Goodwin), Margot Horn (Nicol), Pixie Sayers (Love). Standing: Mavis Sayers (Archer), Mary Joy Shuttleworth, and Molly Stuchbery (Willcox).

arts. A magnificent biography *Helen Clay Frick: Bittersweet Heiress* by her great niece, Martha Frick Symington Sanger, describes how her philanthropy touched the lives of thousands with contributions that included: "...a vacation home for young female textile workers, two wildlife preserves, a Victorian-era house museum, a pre-Civil War historic Mennonite village, a university fine arts department, two art history libraries, and the purchase of many, significant works of art for her private collection, the Frick Collection in New York, the University of Pittsburgh teaching collection, and the Frick Art Museum."

So this was the formidable woman the seven young English girls encountered in the summer of 1940 and who, many years later, still kept in touch with and welcomed on occasions to Britain.

The *Boston Transcript* offer of homes had been publicized in British as well as American newspapers and prompted many responses on both sides of the Atlantic. It was in a British newspaper, another of the girls, Margot Nicols (Horn) told me, that her parents heard about the opportunity of evacuation. Helen also contacted the newspaper, offering to take in one hundred children at her Eagle Rock home. "But," Martha Sanger writes about her great-aunt, "as was her custom there were restrictions, only young girls, no Catholics, and since Helen did not want to take care of boys, no brothers. Her stipulations may have worried the authorities; they reduced her allotment to just twelve children." She also hired a "merry and kind" British lady, a Miss Lindsay, as chaperone. In early August to outfit the dormitories, she transferred to Thissell House, a charitable corporation designed to provide foster homes for British refugee children: "all the family linen from the Westmoreland Railroad car, its Gorham and Tiffany silver and carpeting from the fourth floor of Eagle Rock's demolished wing." Lastly in anticipation of the girls' arrival later that month, Helen enrolled them in the local North Shore County Day School.

In the end only seven girls arrived. She had expected them to be four or five years old and had decorated their rooms accordingly with bunny rabbits and the closets contained beautiful little dresses. However they were seven or eight years older and so "she immediately exchanged the clothes for larger sizes, rearranged their rooms, and in an effort to make them feel as much at home as possible she instructed the Thissell House staff to observe all English customs and serve only English dishes."

They arrived just before the 1940 national elections in the United States and a cousin helped look after them. "It was not an enviable job," remembers Margot, "we could put our foot in it with complete innocence." Helen asked the young girls which of the candidates they were for, Roosevelt or Willkie.

"Roosevelt," they replied. Margot heard a surprised Helen tell the cousin afterwards, "All those children are Democrats." "Of course, we had no idea who Willkie was."

In letters from the girls' parents to Helen, the sadness of parting with their children was conveyed, as well as their gratitude to her. Molly's father, for instance, wrote: "I find it difficult to put into words the feeling of gratitude and relief we feel at the kindness you and other citizens of the states are showing to our children. It was very reluctantly that my wife agreed to part with our only child but in view of the savage attacks made indiscriminately on civilian homes both by day and night Mrs. Stuchbery now is fully in agreement with me that we were fortunate in being able to avail ourselves on Molly's behalf of your wonderful offer of your hospitality extended by warm-hearted people like yourself."

The letters back and forth, except for those lost through enemy action, are now kept in the Frick Art Reference Library in New York City and give some idea of the new world the girls entered into, the integration into American life and also into a unique American life. Over the next four years under Helen's generous nurture, the girls experienced a life unlike anything they had ever known. She was with them and provided for any medical needs, confirmation classes, school vacations, cultural visits and new wardrobes for new seasons. Their first Christmas, in 1940, she spent with them, even sat listening to the King's empire broadcast. In the spring each girl was given a garden to tend and each summer they swam off Eagle Rock's beach and picnicked in the fields. Home movies were sent to the parents.

Helen continued a tradition which started at the beginning of the war of gifts to England which included a thousand blankets and $7000 for the Women's Voluntary Services. The English girls themselves raised money for the five children's rooms in the London underground and railway system they had adopted. They organized, for instance, a dog show with homemade refreshments and prizes for the dog that most resembled its owner, the most obedient dog, or had the shortest nose or the loudest bark. Members of prominent North Shore families supported the event. It was for the English girls an introduction to co-ed schools, American celebrations like July 4th, Halloween, Thanksgiving, and the pledge of allegiance and, as they grew older, to "proms" and formal graduations. "Sometimes, there was not enough control and we misbehaved," says Valerie.

The girls always did everything together. Aunt Helen insisted they all be treated alike. "If they went to a party, all had to be invited. She didn't agree with shopping," says Valerie. "If they needed shoes her secretary

They girls raised money for a London Underground children's shelter.

The three sister (from left to right) Valerie, Pixie and Mavis.

would draw round our feet on paper and they would end up with badly fitting shoes. She was worth a fortune and had her way. ...a strange experience." Yet she was remarkably generous and continued gifts even after the war. Sarah Strong, Molly Willcox's daughter, says her mother remembers Helen as "austere and autocratic" but 'she gave £3000 for her parents' wedding and bought their first house."

In mid-July 1944, Helen took the girls to Long Island to be ready for their return to England. Most of them had completed their schooling. On July 14, Molly Stuchbery, now sixteen, wrote to Aunt Helen, "Although this was the last time we'll see you for any length of time, I don't think you'll ever be completely away from us. If you love people you are always there." On July 25 they departed in the *Rangitata*, a liner which had been converted to a troopship. "We thoroughly enjoyed our voyage," writes Valerie, "all seven of us now very close friends. But of course we did. We were going in the right direction — home. Just in time for 'doodlebugs' (the name given by Londoners for the V1s) and V2 rockets." She was then eighteen, and had graduated *cum laude* from the Horace Greeley High School in Chappaqua, N.Y, and went into war work at the de Havilland aircraft company. Four other girls had graduated from the same high school before they returned. For all evacuees there were challenges in readjusting to life in Britain. Perhaps this was harder for them than for some of us. Relations had to be re-established with families. Her spurt in growth was the first thing that surprised her mother.

Their transatlantic relationships continued unabated. Helen wrote the girls letters and sent birthday presents and when traveling abroad she bought them a good piece of furniture "so each had something nice." Once she had arrived, Margot says, "We were all on call. She kept us together." Valerie remembers in 1947 going up to London to join her at the Savoy Hotel. "She brought her car and chauffeur on the ship plus butter, bacon, huge piles of Andrex toilet paper never seen in Britain and a whole box of cutlery. 'Madam, this is the Savoy,' she was told. I think she felt we had melted everything down for the war effort. She didn't stay there again. She stayed at the Connaught but was asked to leave when she brought sandwiches into the grill. She was extremely eccentric."

Over the years they visited her, too. Mavis, who became a doctor, went many times. When Valerie attended a fiftieth anniversary of their evacuation she stayed with Sheila. She was the only one who had came back to live in America and married Henry Milliken, son of Helen Frick's architect. He emailed me in 2013, "Sheila has dementia. She is still at home. We have been married sixty-five years. Although Helen did not approve of me at first we eventually became close friends." He also told me that Helen had offered to pay for Sheila's college tuition.

"Aunt Helen" maintained her friendship with all the girls until she died in 1984 at the age of ninety-six. "I am grateful for the experience," says Valerie. Where others have been critical of America, she is nostalgic, she says. Margot says she would be the first to say it did her a world of good: When she was in her eighties she told me, "It meant a great deal for me and Molly." Sheila says, "We really had a good time and were treated awfully well."

I wish I had known of this story many years ago while the experience was still fresh. Now many of the seven have died or have memory losses but those with whom I have been able to talk with know what a remarkable, youthful experience they had and are grateful for an unusual, eccentric and generous woman. That of course is also clear from reading *Bittersweet Heiress*.

CHAPTER THREE

PROGRESSIVE AMERICAN COMPANIES

> AT A TIME WHEN BRITISH CHILDREN ARE BEING KILLED AND MAIMED
> ALMOST EVERY DAY BY GERMAN BOMBS, THE EXECUTIVES AND WORKERS
> OF THE HOOVER VACUUM CLEANING COMPANY AND THE EASTMAN KODAK
> COMPANY HAVE SET A FINE EXAMPLE BY BRINGING TO THIS COUNTRY THE
> CHILDREN OF EMPLOYEES IN THEIR BRITISH FACTORIES.
> —*New York Times,* 1 September 1940

One largely overlooked American initiative in World War II was the
decision by the Hoover and Kodak companies to give asylum to children of
their employees in Britain. It was held up by the *New York Times* as "a fine
example" worth studying by other great American businesses. In the event
the Hoover/Kodak examples could not be followed by other companies
because news of a dramatic sinking of an evacuee ship brought home to
the nation and to parents the dangers of the Atlantic and a halt to further
evacuation.

An impressive image of 156 children sitting in rows of chairs in front
of a company headquarters on the edge of war-torn London in 1940 sums
up for me the boldness and the riskiness of this initiative. The children did
not know that they were on the verge of the biggest upheaval of their lives.
They were about to be evacuated to the United States and most were far too
young to understand what that meant. For some it had even been portrayed
as a long summer holiday. It was to be an introduction to an America they
knew hardly anything about, and they would not see their families again for
five years. Neither they nor their parents could know that — or that seventy
years later many of them and their children and grandchildren would still be

close friends with the American families they were about to encounter.

That image also underlines for me how dire the situation must have been for parents to be willing to send their children overseas and away from the threat of invasion. Less than two months later another group of children, eighty of them, were blown to bits by a torpedo, or drowned or frozen to death in lifeboats in the cold waters of the Atlantic. If the news of the sinking of the *City of Benares* had come that many weeks earlier perhaps parents would have been more hesitant — and this story of generous American hospitality might not have been written. At the outset few parents may have grasped how dangerous was the Atlantic crossing on which children were embarking that summer.

In the spring of 1940 as the countries of Europe one by one were taken over and the defeated remnants of the British Army had been evacuated weaponless from Dunkirk, the future of Island Britain was perilous. Many offers had already been received from countries around the world to take in British children. The *New York Daily Mirror* urged: "America must say to England 'Our bars are down to your children. Send them by the thousands, it is our duty and privilege to give them a home.'" Yale University professors offered to take in children of their opposite numbers at Oxford and Cambridge. Other organizations including churches, private schools, even a newspaper, the *Boston Transcript*, now defunct, got into the act.

The *New York Times,* in an editorial on September 1, 1940 wrote:

> *At a time when British children are being killed and maimed almost every day by German bombs, the executives and workers of the Hoover vacuum cleaning company and the Eastman Kodak Company have set a fine example by bringing to this country the children of employees in their British factories. These companies have found a particularly intelligent way of saving large groups of children from the air-raid horrors. Their example is worth studying by other great American businesses which have branch factories or affiliated plants in Great Britain. Today they are assured of good food, good schooling and a certain amount of competent supervision in this country, and they are living in new homes not very different from those they left behind them.*

The paper concluded its editorial: "These children, at least, are safe; but thousands of others who work for American companies in England will hear the scream of the air-raid sirens in the middle of the night. They will live among constant reminders of death and danger, and they may be killed or injured for life if they are not brought to safety here. The pioneer work has now been done by two progressive American companies; it is now all the easier for other companies here to follow their lead."

With the sinking of the *City of Benares*, the British government ended the official government program and the private overseas evacuation petered out. Some other companies like H.J. Heinz, Bowaters and the Ford Motor Company of Canada had brought children over but now it was too late for more to follow the *New York Times* recommendation. Somewhere between three and four thousand of us, including my brother and I and the others described in these chapters, along with 158 children from Kodak and eighty-four from Hoover who had already arrived in Canton and Rochester, had come safely across to the United States. Thirty thousand others who had been preparing to come under the CORB scheme were disappointed or relieved.

This "pioneer work" began with senior figures responding to the urgent humanitarian need. In the case of The Hoover Company, it was Herbert William Hoover Sr. ("HW"), son of the founder "Boss" Hoover who was concerned for the safety of his employees in Britain. He worked with E.L. Colston, managing director of Hoover Ltd. in Perivale, West London, where some 10,000 workers were employed. His own three children were evacuated along with children of salesmen, district and service managers, metal polishers and machine operators. The project, as with my own group, came under the umbrella of the U.S. Committee for the Care of European children, which was chaired by the First Lady, Eleanor Roosevelt.

Hoover's plans to care for the evacuated children were outlined on July 3 to local organizations as well as to company foremen and department heads and two days later the first Meeting for the Care of Evacuated Hoover English Children was convened. It was unanimously decided that Mr. Hoover be appointed general chairman "to use his discretion in setting up the organization and appointing the necessary committees." It was the start of his hands-on commitment that lasted through the war. At the first meeting a Catholic priest asked what consideration was being given to the religious training of the children and was advised that "the most logical procedure would be to place children brought up in the Catholic faith in Catholic homes, and those of Protestant faith in Protestant homes."

Employees showed their willingness to take a child into their homes by filling out an application form that had been drawn up outlining the responsibilities of the would-be hosts and the commitment of the company. Hosts, for instance, agreed to pay all expenses of the ordinary care and maintenance of the children while the company would cover all the

KODAK HISTORICAL COLLECTION/BRITISH LIBRARY

Kodak children on the eve of departure.

HISTORICAL CENTER/WALSH UNIVERSITY

Hoover children and nurse on SS Samaria before disembarking.

KODAK HISTORICAL COLLECTION

First Kodak evacuees arrive.

HOOVER HISTORICAL CENTER

The evacuees at Hoover Camp.

transportation costs and any medical and hospital expenses. The form ended with a pledge of financial assistance. Other Hoover families offered their help in supporting the children in those homes. Most foster parents resided in North Canton and nearby areas.

In the case of Kodak, it was Walter G. Bent, managing director of the Harrow-based Kodak Ltd., who cabled Rochester New York asking if the parent company would be interested in taking British children. Could a haven be provided for a limited number of British Kodak children, five to sixteen years old, he asked. A Rochester Committee was formed and a notice went up on all plant and office bulletin boards. It outlined the critical position of Kodak people in Britain and made it clear that neither the company nor the children's parents undertook to make financial provision for the living expenses of evacuees, if or when they came over. There was a swift, affirmative response from more than 600 Kodak families and a cable went back indicating that as many as 300 children could be taken.

In Harrow the manager of industrial relations at Kodak Ltd. notified the Kodak people in London and after "sometimes agonizing weighing of all the factors" ninety-two families decided to accept the Rochester offer. Both parents had to agree on it; further, they had to absolve their future foster parents of responsibility in case of accident. While in Rochester, the manager of industrial relations, organized to meet "the invasion." Volunteer parents had to be scrutinized. Did the actual facts of their homes, their way of living and their personalities justify the impulse that made them volunteer? Provisional lists of foster parents were made, and the families selected given some preliminary notion of their impending responsibilities, problems and opportunities.

Mr. Rouse of Kodak Australia also said that they would find homes and finance for up to twenty-five children of Kodak employees for the duration of the war. He was thanked for his "wonderful offer" but told that due to transport and other difficulties this suggestion could not be considered "at the present time." Indeed, the shortage of shipping at first threatened the evacuation of all children and a report in the Kodak Works Bulletin in July 1940 announced that the government was temporarily postponing the official scheme: "We however are not stopping in our efforts to prepare everything so that the first children will be able to go on one of the first ships for this purpose…. The children still wait, although the bomb raid and the casualty lists grow more heartbreaking every day. They wait because the British Navy cannot spare warships for convoying British passenger vessels, while we are barred by an unintentional technicality of our Neutrality Law from sending any American ships to the war zone except Red Cross ships carrying food and medical supplies.... The framers of the Neutrality Act never intended it to forbid missions of mercy like the rescue of children. When Congress reconvenes next week they will have an opportunity to amend the law so that this mission, the greatest humanitarian challenge we have yet had in this war, can be carried out without delay."

It was difficult to find a basis on which evacuees would be allowed into the United States. Behind the scenes, Mrs. Roosevelt and the British Ambassador, Lord Lothian, worked for a solution. The First Lady put forward the idea of "temporary residents." On July 14 the *New York Times* could report that the State Department had removed the red tape preventing the admission of refugee children. A new ruling was issued whereby visitor visas would be issued to British children "upon a showing of intention they shall return home upon the termination of hostilities." This was through a "corporate affidavit" which allowed a non-profit organization to guarantee support of a specific number of children and to receive within forty-eight hours "blank visas." These could be sent abroad to be filled in with names of children awaiting exit. Six days after the ruling the State Department issued 1,500 visas.

Praising the State Department's action in an editorial the next day, the *New York Times* went on to plead for Congress' amendment of the Neutrality Act. This act prohibited U.S. ships from carrying evacuees to U.S. ports. Until then evacuees had been carried by British ships to Canada.

Just as my brother and I did, and several thousand other children, all the Kodak and Hoover children — the former were soon known as Kodakids — went to Grosvenor House, London, a Park Lane hotel which became an annex of the American embassy, where they were interviewed and the paperwork was completed. Kodakid David Bateman remembers that "dressed in our best clothes, shoes brightly polished, hair Brylcreemed into some attempt at tidiness, we marched out in quite long crocodiles, gas masks slung over our shoulders, not quite sure what was really happening."

Kodakery, the in-house bulletin was to give a running commentary on the trip to anxious families as did the Hoover equivalent *The Dust Bag*.

Mr. Colston wrote in August to the first group of the Hoover children as they were leaving to prepare them for the new experiences they would encounter. On the question of racial prejudice they might encounter, he wrote, "Remember that a man's colour was given to him by God and as long as he's kind that's all that matters."

The ocean trip features in all the memories of all evacuees. It was something few had ever experienced. I know that travelling with hundreds of children on an ocean liner with other liners and escorted by a battleship and five destroyers was an excitement that helped dispel homesickness. My brother and I, as described earlier, were on the *Duchess of York* and the "Hoover group" was on the *Samaria* in the same convoy. Nearing North America our convoy split with some ships going to Halifax and Montreal and others to New York from which arrangements had been made to get the children to Rochester, New York and North Canton, Ohio. Ruthe Davis remembers a police escort through New York City.

The Manager's page of *Kodakery* in September 1940 began: "The toast is 'our children' and coupled with the names of those kindly people in Rochester, New York, who have offered their homes for the duration and their hearts forever to the children of Kodak, Ltd. By now everyone knows that the youngsters arrived at the other side of the Atlantic in fine shape and that by special train they were carried to the Kodak City. The travelling arrangements clicked to the last detail and it seems in keeping for us to mention the courtesy and attention which these children received from the railway and boat officials and from countless unknown friends who helped to make smooth the passage to America. Above all, we send our heartfelt thanks to the foster parents in Rochester who, we know, will minister to and protect our boys and girls in the truly hospitable manner which characterizes Rochestarians. We over here will not soon forget the generous actions of our colleagues in the States."

In an earlier issue Wrathall Rowe, company medical doctor, described the trip across: "On Sunday afternoon the weather became calmer and everybody cheered up and all the kids started running around again. There are about 800 children on board and the place is alive with them. I suppose there must be about 1,300 people on board altogether. We ran into fog but in spite of it we went cracking along at our 18 knots or thereabouts. The sea has been like a millpond since then, and at times we hardly seem to be moving. On Sunday afternoon we had a service for the children in the lounge, which they practically all attended, and which was a great success. I played the hymns on a tin-pot piano and all the kids sang lustily. The service was conducted by the Padre, who is one of the escorts, and he produced an extempore prayer all about 'God bless our brave soldiers and sailors and airmen who are taking care of us, and please let the war end soon, and God bless our mothers and fathers and keep them safe from bombs.' All the children repeated it line after line, and it was really very effective. There were several other mothers with children in the lounge that did not belong to our party, and the tears were rolling down their cheeks as they listened to all the children reciting this prayer."

The imminent arrival of the Kodak children in Rochester made the front page of the *Democrat and Chronicle*: "The war will be brought home vividly to Rochester when 120 refugee children of Eastman Kodak employees arrive here within the next few days... Exact time of their arrival aboard ship is cloaked in the secrecy that of necessity hides the movements of camouflaged vessels. Even the ship's identity is unknown to Kodak officials."

They came on the *Duchess of Atholl,* which docked in Montreal on August 24. Each child had a large name tag tied to his or her coat with the legend "U.S. Committee for the Care of European children, Kodak Scheme." It was decided that all of them should go, at first, to the Hillside Home — a children's home where the initial shocks of acclimatization could be undergone as a group experience. With all of them together, the necessary checking examinations could be more conveniently made. The Hoover equivalent was to have the children stay at the Hoover Inn and Hoover Camp with its open space, baseball field, table tennis, and movies.

As one report said: "So began a five-year human experiment in human relations. No one expected everything to work perfectly; there were problems of all sorts but, in the main, common sense, adaptability, and the ultimate recession of homesickness produced an amazing degree of content. The Kodakids flourished, they grew fond of their foster parents who, in turn, found it easy to love them. And the interchange of correspondence with the Harrow parents became, for many, the basis of lasting friendships."

Soon after the arrival of the children Mr. Hoover wrote to hosts thanking them for their action and giving advice: "Being English children they have many adjustments to make. They will experience great differences in American home life, food, sports and words used to express thoughts and describe things. Our school system will be strange to them. They will have to find new pals and learn to play new games. Whether they show it or not, at times they will carry heavy hearts, longing for their parents and homes and things most dear to them. As real Britishers, young as they are, most of them will bear up bravely and carry their griefs unannounced. As the children return home think of their reports of all that has been done for them and of the growth of its appreciation into a rich and lasting bond of friendship, which for the rest of your days should serve as a fine added reward for the love and reward for the love and consideration bestowed during their stay with us."

It had originally been intended that it would be one child per home but because of the number of siblings not as many homes were needed so Hoover wrote also to apologize to those who had offered but were disappointed.

Hoover evacuees celebrate Thanksgiving 1943.

British Ambassador Lord Halifax meets the Kodak evacuees.

Evacuees Vi and Sonny Warren with Mr. H.W.Hoover on the train that brought them to North Canton.

PROGRESSIVE AMERICAN COMPANIES

During their stay the Kodak and Hoover children became a lively part of their local communities, enjoying American food and sports and customs and music and radio. They soon learned about American ways, like Halloween and Thanksgiving, which, for instance, in North Canton became a huge annual celebration hosted by Mr. Hoover in the company cafeteria. To the children of Hoover he was soon known as "Uncle Hoover." One evacuee, eighty-two-year-old Vina Williams, told me that she has never forgotten 'the absence of class differences' and the way she had lunch with Mr. Hoover who took his lunch in the staff canteen "different from in England."

Dorothy Mathewson (née Warren) who was evacuated with four siblings wrote later, "Before we endured the nightmare that was drawing ever closer and witnessed the devastation of our beloved England, fate intervened for my brother and sisters and me. We were spared the true reality of war through the generosity of Mr. H.W. Hoover, Sr., a remarkable American gentleman who would touch our lives in a most unforgettable way, and through a courageous decision made by our parents."

Kodak social workers had their hands full with the innumerable small crises and problems of 156 youngsters in almost as many foster homes. There were changes, mostly out of practical necessity and a few because of personality or psychological problems. Sometimes, living arrangements changed during the children's sojourn in Rochester, as the expected six-month stay stretched to five years. David Bateman, for instance, stayed with three different families and attended five schools. Some adults and children proved incompatible; for some sponsors, the novelty wore off after a few months and replacements were necessary. Kodak maintained active concern for the children's welfare while they were in Rochester and paid for health and dental care, including surgeries and Hoover did the same in North Canton. Edna Brown needed hospitalization twice and told me that "the Hoover people made sure I had the very best." Other than the expense of passage, parents of both groups and of all evacuees were unable to contribute to their children's upkeep due to a British government regulation that forbade citizens from sending currency from England.

The emphasis throughout the five years was on maintaining the youngsters' ties with their homes and homeland. Don McMaster, Harrow manager, went over to meet the children and the "parents" and to arm himself with information to take back to parents in England. Dr. W.A. Sawyer, head of Eastman Kodak's Medical department, made a special trip to England to keep the British parents informed and to relieve any anxiety.

Robert Soundy, a Hoover evacuee, says: "With the hospitality, generosity and enthusiasm for which American are justly famous, we were quickly adopted into our new families. Most of us lost our English accents within a few weeks and reveled in our new found quality of life. Through sheer love and kindness we became totally Americanized." Fred Tinsley recalls: "The novelty of being English wore off and we were just foster children." Helen Manfull, one of the American children who have never forgotten the British visitors describes how they "integrated themselves into a culture so completely that we forgot they were British."

Christmas, particularly in 1940 — their first Christmas in a new country — is remembered with special gratitude as it was a time when American families pulled out all the stops to care for the children without their parents. A big occasion for the Kodakids was the 1943 visit of Lord Halifax. He had succeeded Lord Lothian as British Ambassador. His remarks to the children emphasized the responsibilities placed on them by their homeland: "You are all British ambassadors. Your good friends here have been judging England by your good conduct; therefore you are very important people. After this war you will be part of a generation working for a better world, a world in which there must be no more war. When you go back home you will tell your parents what nice people the American are... and perhaps you will teach mother and father the American customs and expressions you have learned.'

In a letter commenting on Halifax's forthcoming visit, McMaster also describes the work in Harrow: "Life goes on here in much the same way. We are intensively busy. The factory departments are working night and day 7 days a week. Some of the employees are putting in 7 12-hour shifts a week. Girls are working up to 60 hours a week on nights and the employment of part-time women is the order of the day." Employees also served as air raid wardens and in the Home Guard.

Depending on their age, evacuees followed the progress of the war and became like Americans in their reactions to events and of course the 1941 entry of the United States into the war after Pearl Harbor. They helped collect scrap metal and raise money for war bonds. Some won badges and prizes whether for academic work or for scouting. For instance Winifred Farmborough, who was evacuated with her two brothers, Eric and William, was in June 1945 the salutatorian of the Marion High School senior class.

As early as 1943 some of the children began to leave for home. Because of their different ages they did not all return together. Some had finished their schooling and went home for military service and in some cases to work with Kodak in the UK while others got permission from English and American parents to stay and finish their education in the United States.

But transport was still in short supply as ships were full with both the food that sustained Britain and with troops and equipment in the build up for the Normandy invasion. A few boys traveled, as my brother and I did, on Royal Navy ships. Robert Soundy went on HMS *Sheffield* and still has a model lifebuoy made for him by one of the crew as a prize. A party of eighty-six returned on the *Rangitiki*. By mid-June 1945 almost all were home, and as Helen Manfull writes, "A period began that proved more troubling than their departure five years earlier. Perhaps because they were more mature, perhaps because the England they returned to was so damaged and its people exhausted, perhaps because their lives in America had been opulent by comparison, perhaps because their parents were strangers — homecoming was bittersweet."

A Kodakery report described the thirty-eight Kodakids who returned on the SS *Nieuw Amsterdam*: "It is with mixed emotions that the remainder of the youngsters bid adieu to their American parents and friends — and the American way of life. They were eager to see their own families again and to renew acquaintances with English friends, but they regretted leaving their hosts or associates here."

For many evacuees the journey home after five years was perhaps more of an upheaval than the initial separation. Hardest for many evacuees this time was the departure from families who, particularly for the younger ones, were more real to them than their own families. But they also came back with a broader view of the world. Ruthe Davis wrote in a letter to the 1990 reunion: "I am left with an overwhelming memory of the generosity of the American people and that will always be with me. From that I believe I brought back to England with me an openness and sociability in how I conducted my life."

Several evacuees returned to live in America following the 1945 repatriation. Others soon visited their wartime families or hosted them in Britain. Some attended high school reunions or enrolled in higher education in the United States. William Farmborough returned in 1947 to study at Rochester Institute of Technology where he graduated with honors; Bryan Mumford decided after his mother died to become an American citizen and served in the U.S. Army and his brother Derek taught school in Little Rock; Albert Palmer attended Kent State University and became an Episcopal minister.

Two Kodak social workers who had looked after the Kodakids, Sarah Nichols and Helen Cederquist, made a five-month, post-war visit to England. They reported that the Kodakids would always have a warm spot

Children of British Kodak employees had the card letters all ready for the cameraman as they spelled out 'Kodak' from their upside-down positions on an overhead bar at Hillside Home playground.

1985 – 45th reunion at Hoover in Perivale, England.

in their hearts for America but as one Kodakery headline on July 2, 1946 put it: "Kodakids Seen Changing Back to Englishmen" and commented, "The children miss their American foster parents, their many friends, their schools, and their activities a lot, they reported. The transition from Rochester to England has meant getting used to a different speech, customs, coinage and ways of thought, but the youngsters are taking it in their stride and are becoming reoriented."

Sarah and Helen found the English parents very interested in the country which had sheltered their children so well and of which their children talked so enthusiastically. They wholeheartedly fell in with the plans of many of the children to return to Rochester for a visit to meet their wartime "moms and dads" and see the part of America they learned to love. "A number of the children have started special savings funds for these trips. Some of the parents are reading American history and novels to better understand their youngsters' 'other country.' Many voiced the feeling that because of their unique experience the children would have in future a much broader understanding of the world in which they live. 'We can never adequately express our gratitude for the kindness and care given our children during those long war years' was the constantly recurring theme."

In the some seventy years since the evacuation many of the relationships established during the Kodakids and Hoover stay in America have grown in meaning and richness. Parents and foster parents have met, the evacuees have married, and wartime "brothers and sisters" are still exchanging latest photos of their progeny, and in some cases now of grandchildren. Hoover, like Kodak, has kept the connections until today. I talked and corresponded in 2011 with octogenarians from both groups who remain enthusiastic. Robert Soundy's foster mother was guest of honor at his daughter's wedding.

Violet Crane (Warren) wrote me that the five years with her American hosts "were some of the special times of my life." She too is still in touch with foster brother and sisters and school friends. Five of the Warren children were evacuated. They have made many visits to each others' homes and in 2011 were still exchanging letters and cards. Violet's sister, Dorothy Mathewson married an American and lives in Canton, Ohio. She has written a book about that time entitled *Sweet Memories*. She told me, "The evacuation experience was a very positive one for me. It was very difficult coming to terms with being separated from my family. Yet with the kindness and love that surrounded me here in America I eventually adjusted to life without those who were so dear to me."

Because the Hoover and Kodak children were in groups who lived in proximity to each other in Canton and Rochester, and had a corporate identity, they more than other evacuees had larger and more organized reunions over the passing decades. Hoover arranged reunions in 1980, 1990 and 2000. The 1990 reunion marked the 50th anniversary of their arrival and was attended by seventy-nine. The North Canton Heritage Society received a grant to help bring the Hoover families to America. Honorary citizenship to North Canton was provided to each of the British attendees.

Barry Soundy, nine when he arrived during the war, said in a speech, "I'm getting sentimental as I get older and I don't like the word 'foster' any more. I prefer to say Dad, Mom, brother, sister, cousin, because that is what you are." Vina Wales' father, a metal finisher, had worked in Canada with Hoover before the war and was sent to the Perivale factory when it opened. So when the opportunity came he was more confident because he had met the people. Vina, who was ten when she went to America, tells me: "We were among the lucky children of the war. We never saw the bombing, the severe rationing and restrictions that war brought to Britain, but we did know the agony of separation from our parents. That is when the folk of North Canton stepped in with a warmth and compassion unequalled." She has been back five times.

Helen Cederquist Sawyer, the social worker, and Ray Feasey, a Kodakid who had stayed with Harry Patterson, the superintendent of Kodak's printing division and was by then a supervisor at Kodak Park, had volunteered to set up the 1990 reunion. Ray had always known he would return to America, so two years after the war when the Patterson's invited him back he came and began majoring in mechanical engineering at his host parents' alma mater University of Maine. He sometimes wonders what he'd be doing today if he hadn't been a Kodakid. He is a great advocate of teenage exchange programs and acknowledges the tremendous impact Kodak and the Pattersons have had on his life.

On August 28, 2011 the Canton Repository carried a feature article "Hoover a haven for kids during World War II." It was written by Helen Manfull, then seventy-nine, a professor emeriti of Penn State University. She went to school with Hoover evacuees and one was her next-door neighbor. She told me she loved those English children and all her life had remembered them. Their years in North Canton are remembered in the Hoover Historical Center.

Beneath a tree outside The Hoover Company a plaque was placed that is dedicated to the people of North Canton by the British evacuee children who in 1940 were "brought there by The Hoover Company under the special direction of Mr. H W Hoover, Sr. and taken into your homes for safe haven during the war in Europe. It is our profound wish that this tree might convey our heartfelt appreciation for the love and kindness you have offered us."

After the war an illuminated scroll was sent by the Chairman of the Harrow Urban District Council, W. A. Harrison, to the mayor of Rochester, New York: "The Township of Harrow transmits to the City of Rochester both thanks and greetings. It does so in glad and appreciative remembrance of the shelter, hospitality and affectionate care given in the homes of the citizens of Rochester to boys and girls to the number of over one hundred and fifty, a little community in itself, who from this part of England crossed the Atlantic when the Battle of Britain was growing in intensity and bombs were falling and destructive fires beginning. The young guests returning recently to Harrow brought with them memories of kindness and courtesies which are not only a delight to hear but are also bonds of human knowledge and understanding, tender and yet most strong, uniting families to families, hearts to hearts, across the expanse of water."

As was often the way at those times parents and children rarely talked afterwards about the wartime separation; my parents didn't and sadly, I never asked them about it. I knew why our parents sent us — my mother wanted us to be away from the kind of horror she had experienced as a young girl in Ireland during the 1920s. When I first wrote about evacuation in *See You After the Duration* I did not do justice to the fears parents would have had and the regret of five years separation at a crucial growing up period.

In September and October 2015, in recognition of the 75th anniversary of the 1940 arrival of the eighty-four British children brought to North Canton by The Hoover Company, Walsh University and the Hoover Historical Center, hosted, along with other local bodies, a month-long series of commemorative events. Exhibits in the Hoover Memorial Center, North Canton Public Library and the North Canton Heritage Society and many features in local newspapers and the "Cleveland Plain Dealer" brought home to today's generation those wartime years, why evacuation was considered and why there was such gratitude to Americans. Highlight was a Conversation of Memories conducted in the Hoover Hall. This was between a life-long North Cantonian, Neva Shocksnider, and three evacuees in their eighties, Eileen Cooper and Vina Wales, who had come specially from England, and Dorothy Mathewson, who had after the war emigrated back to Ohio, and an audience of 200 whose first few rows consisted of members of the Hoover family and several generations of foster families. As Vina told me afterwards, quoting from words from a host which drew loud applause

TO THE MAYOR OF ROCHESTER, N.Y.

The Township of Harrow within whose borders nearly 200,000 people dwell, transmits to the city of Rochester both thanks and greetings.

It does so in glad and appreciative remembrance of the shelter, hospitality and affectionate care given in the homes of the citizens of Rochester to boys and girls to the number of over one hundred and fifty, a little community in itself, who from this part of England crossed the Atlantic when the Battle of Britain was growing in intensity and bombs were falling and destructive fires beginning. The young guests returning recently to Harrow brought with them memories of kindnesses and courtesies which are not only a delight to hear but are also bonds of human knowledge and understanding, tender and yet most strong, uniting families to families, hearts to hearts, across the expanse of waters.

Perhaps it may be of interest to your citizens to recall that each year during his Premiership, Mr. Winston Churchill visited Harrow to listen afresh to the songs he learned as a boy on the Hill. In the darkest and most anxious hours of the War he came, and he came when, rejoicing in the united strength and prowess of your Country and of ours, he felt daybreak to be at hand. The present Prime Minister, Mr. Clement Attlee, lived in Harrow for some years before taking up residence at No. 10 Downing Street. His wife and he loved our township, and love it still, and took full share in Civil Defence Services. Mrs. Attlee was devoted to her duties in the Red Cross and was a familiar and ministering figure in a Rest Centre in Harrow where sanctuary and succour were given to those made homeless by the action of the enemy.

Rochester and Harrow have also in common the presence in their midst of the works of the Kodak Company and it is my hope and trust that the goodwill between the City over which you preside and the township of which I am the Chairman may extend and develop as the years come and go.

May, 1946.

W. Harrison

J.P., Chairman of Harrow Urban District Council.

Chairman during the year:
1940-1941, F.T. Pennington.	1943-1944, J.W. Beaumont.
1941-1942, C. Brown.	1944-1945, A.T. Daniels.
1942-1943, C.E. Brady.	1945-1946, F.A. Coles.

Drawn: F. Beckett, Westminster, Harrow.

HARROW'S COAT OF ARMS is rich in historical symbolism comprehensive of the whole district. The torch of knowledge and the quill tell of scholarship and the expression thereof. In the centre a "pile" stands for the Gore, where meetings of the Saxon moot were held. The organ rest alludes to Handel's association with what is now Harrow.

from the audience when read out at the Conversation: "The bridge formed in 1940 still exists and lives."

Dorothy Mathewson responded to the event as both an evacuee and as a member of the local community. As mentioned earlier in the chapter, back in England after the war she met an American soldier on leave, and they became engaged and she returned to live in the United States and they have now celebrated sixty-one years together.

Not every family has such a happy story to tell, as she has, of five children evacuated safely together. One only has to think of the deaths of the five Grimmond children in the sinking of the *City of Benares*. In her book *Sweet Memories* Dorothy provides a moving perspective on her family's evacuation decision. She once asked her parents if they had any regret in making their decision to send her and her siblings to America: "They replied that although they missed them more than words could express as the months stretched into years, any lingering doubts about their evacuation were dispelled one day when her father witnessed the tragic loss of life while on duty in the First Aid. He was assisting in the rescue of victims after an air raid, and there were young children among those who were trapped in the rubble of a bomb site. A critically injured child, whom her father tried to comfort while attending to his wounds, died in his arms. "As he looked down at the child my father thought but for the concern of Mr. Hoover, and the added blessings of the generous act of the United States in welcoming the children to her shores and those who opened their heart to them, the lifeless child in his arms might have been one of his own. As he grieved for the one who would never grow up, he felt at peace with the decision to allow his children to be evacuated, and he offered up a prayer of thanks that they were safe from the unspeakable acts of war."

CHAPTER FOUR

AN
OREGONIAN
EDUCATION

DR. JOHN CHALMERS IS A RETIRED ORTHOPEDIC SURGEON FROM
EDINBURGH, SCOTLAND. AFTER COMPLETING HIS MEDICAL EDUCATION
IN EDINBURGH, LONDON AND CHICAGO, WHERE HE DID RESEARCH ON
THE IMMUNOLOGY OF BONE TRANSPLANTATION — HE SPENT MOST OF HIS
PROFESSIONAL CAREER IN EDINBURGH UNTIL HIS RETIREMENT IN 1990.
DR. CHALMERS HAS SPENT MUCH OF HIS RETIREMENT RESEARCHING
AUDUBON'S ACTIVITIES IN EDINBURGH AND HE ENJOYED WRITING
AUDUBON IN EDINBURGH, A BOOK THAT HAS PUT HIM IN TOUCH WITH
MANY KINDRED SPIRITS. HE FIRST BECAME INTERESTED IN AUDUBON
IN 1940, WHEN AS A SCHOOLBOY ON A BIRD WALK NEAR OREGON
HE SAW THE AUDUBON WARBLER (AS IT WAS THEN CALLED) AND THE
MACGILLIVRAY WARBLER ON THE SAME DAY.

—Audubon in Edinburgh

British evacuees landed all over the United States, from Juneau, Alaska
to Palm Beach, Florida, from Santa Fe, New Mexico, Dallas, Texas, and
Pasadena, California, to Dayton, Ohio and Richmond, Virginia, with
probably the largest number in the northeast. Some were in communities
where as far as they knew they were the only ones, whereas some like my
brother and I, can see in our 1942–43 Milton Academy class lists seventeen
British in the upper and nine in the lower school. Some had traveled out
together like the 240 children of Hoover employees who went to Rochester,
New York, the 120 children of Kodak who were in North Canton, Ohio,
and the fifty-four children from the Actors' Orphanage who were expecting
to go to Hollywood but ended up in New York City. Most went to complete

strangers, a few were accompanied by their mothers and an unknown number went to relatives.

In that latter category were five cousins who were evacuated to Oregon. Their parents had accepted an invitation from their cousins in America. To John Chalmers, twelve, the decision to evacuate him, "seems to have been made very suddenly for I was recalled home from a camp without any warning to sail a week later."

John and his sister Sheila, fourteen, his cousins Yselle, fourteen, and Joyce MacNab, age eleven, and his second cousin Ronald Curtis, also fourteen travelled, as I did, in a convoy on the *Duchess of York*. Their American hosts were the Gerald Beebe, and Robert Livingston families in Englewood and the Colin Livingstone family on Lake Oswego, both near Portland. They rotated in various groupings around the different families, all of whom, John remembers, were unbelievably kind and made us feel thoroughly at home: "It was certainly the most interesting and educational period of my life and thanks to the kindness of our relations a very happy time despite the separation from home."

John was obviously a good correspondent, describing in detail each week in his letters home, his many new adventures. They have all been kept — more than 30,000 words. Regular letters back and forth across the Atlantic sustained many evacuees. They were often numbered, as ships carrying the letters were sometimes sunk. Letters from England were also censored and bits cut or blacked out that were deemed to give information helpful to the enemy.

Today John's regular comments would be called a blog. His parents must have been grateful for the insight into their children's lives. His variety of activities as a young Scotsman in his formative years in Oregon echoes but were also dramatically different from what many of us experienced. His outdoor life was to have an effect not only on his life's work but also on his retirement.

John's letters home began on the day the ship sailed: "My pen is working very well and the nib is very good. There are a lot of government evacuees on board and each party has a grown up in charge of them. We are supposed to keep our life jackets with us all the time and each deck has its muster station where they go to in emergency. I get lovely meals because my waiter doesn't know that tourist class are not allowed cream and so I got a lovely jug of it with my apple tart for dinner. A lot of the tables in the dining room are becoming deserted at meal times now because nearly everyone is sick, the boat is swaying terribly to-day."

A HARVEST OF FRIENDSHIPS

My brother and I were two who were absent from meals. Being younger than him, we were not given the free rein he obviously enjoyed: "This morning a sailor asked if I would like to go up to the crow's nest with him during his watch. I of course said yes so I went inside a doorway at the bottom of the mast and climbed up a terribly long iron ladder inside the mast till we came to a small round hut fixed onto the side of the mast with a window in front. I stood up there for 2 hours which is the length of the watches, it was great fun."

One constant factor in most of his letters over the next years, as befits a future writer about Audubon, was a description of the birds he saw on sea and land: "This morning we notice some birds flying alongside us, they have white undersides and dark upper parts with one or two white bars, the tail and the head seem to be completely black, one of the men told me they were "stormy petrels" it's a kind of long distance seagull."

From Halifax, Nova Scotia, the children travelled by train across Canada and down to Portland where John reported: "We went to register as aliens and after we had filled in a huge, big form, Ronald had to have his finger prints taken, I was too young to have them done you have to be 14. In the afternoon we went on a picnic it was great fun. There were 15 of us Uncles Bob, Gerald and Colin, Aunts Mary and Ester, cousins Mable, Ernie, Robbie, Betty, Tim, Yselle, Joyce, Sheila and I and Ronald."

He was enrolled at Lincoln High School: "Now I'll tell you what we do each day. At 8.30 you have to go up to your reg. room where the attendance is taken. Then at my first period I get gym and health alternately. 2nd period I get Algebra and 3rd period I get prep. 4th period English. 5th Latin 6th lunch 7th Guidance and prep alternately 8th Science and then at 2.40 you get out, then we either catch the 3.45 bus or get picked up by Uncle Bob at 5 o'clock. I think the bus is better because we have 4 or 5 hours homework each night and the sooner you get home the better. I find that most of the work is a year behind what I would be having at home and some subjects I have to drop altogether so I'll need lots of coaching when I get home.... School is grand fun and I'm having lots of fun out here and I'm trying to be happy and to enjoy the fun as much as I can and I hope you are trying to be happy too."

He also met an English boy, John Neame, who had arrived a few months earlier and like him would go on to become a surgeon.

"On Monday as Wendell Wilkie (presidential candidate opposed to Roosevelt) had come to Portland for a few hours and was to pass by the school at a certain time. They arranged it so that they would have a fire drill just as he was passing so everyone should have a chance of seeing him. First

Host relations and evacuees in Oregon.   John on the rake at the Keystone ranch.

of all their came a lot of police on motor bikes then a car or two and a lorry containing press men and 'tecs and things then Wilkie standing in it. I got a lovely view of him. Then a whole string of cars followed with lots of people in them and Official printed on them…I've started a new hobby collecting buttons. You see every candidate has his set of buttons that you pin to your clothes such as "we want Wilkie" written in various colours."

He describes his introduction to American sport: "We went to the Multnomah Stadium where the schools were to have the opening football night. There were thousands and thousands of people from all of Portland High Schools and lots of parents. First of all the band of each high school entered the stadium (there were some wonderful bands). I forgot to say that the whole stadium was as bright as day even though it was late at night because very powerful light shone on it. After the bands the football teams came in. Then the teams drew numbers to see who would play who. The games were fifteen minutes long and they were very rough. American football is very different from our football and people have to be carried off the field every few minutes."

They visited 'Uncle Gerald's country place': "He has about 160 acres near a town called Estacada and I've never seen such beautiful country before. He has some apple trees. Thousands of pounds of apples must be wasted here. Every orchard is covered with apples just rotting. If you told people to come and eat as much as they wanted they wouldn't bother to do it."

He was soon being fully included: "I was voted for class representative for the Junior Red Cross so I had to make an announcement in front of the whole class of strange people and I stuttered and mumbled and grew redder and redder and the class laughed and laughed and I wished the earth would swallow me up and I was elected by one of my classes as chairman of people in that class who eat lunch the 6th period. You see this class is supposed to keep the neighbourhood of the school tidy, so now that I'm chairman I suppose I'll have to do all the work."

In letters he thanked his parents for presents received. They seemed quite often not to take into account his growth: "We found a huge big parcel waiting and when we opened it we found my suit of clothes and these lovely pyjamas for me. In the letter that was inside the parcel you said that you were sending me another suit. If you haven't already got the suit could you please get long trousers instead of shorts and could they please be just a little bigger in size. But thank you a terrific lot for sending on these clothes it was awfully good of you dear Mum and Dad and the stamps on the parcel were just lovely."

As the months went by he had the chance to swim in the Pacific and go clamming at Gearhart, to walk on a frozen lake and to go riding, to fish in the Metolious River, to ski on Mount Hood and to visit the Bonneville Dam and Central Oregon. Also to learn to do many things which he probably didn't do at home: "I skinned a mole which Uncle Gerald had trapped… I tacked it out on a board and scraped it down with a piece of cinder. Then I put salt on it to cure it then over all I sprinkled some sand." His letters over the months listed many animals he had learned to skin and in some cases dissect including hens, fish, a squirrel and a bullfrog.

There are two references to the British consul, James McDonald (whom I knew forty years later as Sir James when he was still in office, and I think the oldest British consul in service). The first was an invitation to a Boxing Day party where he met most of the twenty British evacuees and the second slightly different: "A lot of British children in Portland received letters last week asking them to come for a meeting at the Consul's office to-day. I went to the meeting which apparently had been called mainly to warn us against saying things against America. Evidently the Consul had received some complaints to that effect. When I came home I listened to President Roosevelt's speech, didn't you think it was encouraging? It seems to be warning Hitler not to come any further west or USA might declare war…. On Wednesday we had a Memorial Day assembly to commemorate USA's entry into the last war…."

Other new holidays feature in his accounts — Thanksgiving, Halloween, Lincoln's birthday, Independence Day. For the evacuees the war was never far away.

"From now on I am making a carbon copy of each letter so that if one is sunk, all you need to do is to tell me the number of the letter and I will send you a copy." In another: "Daddy you have been having an exciting time with snow at Tomatin, though the most exciting part of your letter was cut out by the censors — I know it must be exciting or they would not cut it out…. They attended a concert where all profits went to the bombed children's fund…."

One day when he was eating his lunch with John Neame: "Mr. Gunn, the head of the school, sat down beside us and asked us if we would talk at one of the big clubs in Portland to the American Legion, whatever it may be on the subject of 'What has America worth defending' and what is the best way to defend it. Then he asked us to talk on the same thing at the town of Milwaukie next month. He also asked us to make a speech in front of the whole school on 'What scholarship means to me', what that means I don't know."

On John's invitation he was invited to the holiday home of the Corbetts, John's host family, which led to opportunities to work at the ranch. He also spent Easter there in 1941: "Instead of going to church on Sunday we listened to Churchill's wonderful speech."

On Lincoln's birthday a wreath was laid in front of his statue at the school. It was also the day he was to talk to the American Legion: "As John Neame had to talk with us as well, Mr. Corbett asked me to dinner with John and some other people at a very posh club near where we were to speak. There I had my 2nd coke and my 3rd ice cream of the day. After a lovely dinner John and I walked to the club room of the American Legion. The audience consisted of about 50 old men who smoked like chimneys. The whole thing came off pretty well, I said that the most important thing that the United States should defend was her freedom, and then I elaborated on that. Then I said the best way to defend it was to send aid to Britain and then I chortled on about that and I think most of them agreed with me." He added in the same letter: "On Friday I got three valentines the first ones I have got in my life."

He did a radio program with John: "After the programme we went back to school where we found that some classes had procured wirelesses and had listened to us talk. If I had known it beforehand I would have had a fit."

On one occasion they joined twenty others on a "bird walk": "We saw many birds and I have a list here of the ones which I saw or were pointed out to me.

1 Brewer blackbird, 2 Redwing blackbird, 3 Western bluebird 4 Mourning dove 5 Purple finch 6 Flicker 7 flocks of Canadian geese, 8 Redtail hawk, 9 Sparrow hawk 10 Blue Jay, 11 Junco, 12 Killdeer, 13 Ruby crowned kinglet, 14 Slender-billed nuthatch, 15 Wood duck, 16 American pipit 17 Robin, 18 Pine siskin, 19 Chipping sparrow, 20 English sparrow,

21 Rusty song sparrow, 22 White crowned sparrow, 23 Cliff swallows, 24 Violet-green swallows, 25 Towhee, 26 Audubon warbler. 27 Lutiscant warbler, 28 Macgillivray warbler." In the same letter he adds: "On Monday we elected what we thought was the most beautiful girl in the school to be queen in what they call the Rose Festival, It is a huge city fete."

This, John tells me, was probably the first time he heard of Audubon and Macgillivray, who were to become such a preoccupation later in life.

He joined the scouts and describes an inter-troop contest at Camp Millard: "There was about 425 scouts at this camp. We put up our tents and made our camps ready as soon as we arrived because every few minutes people came round and inspected us. My duty was to make all the gadgets around the camp so I made during odd minutes some very professional pot hooks, a table and a shoe rack. As I was cutting a piece of wood an inspector came around and evidently saw something wrong with my chopping and took 5 precious points off our patrol I was very ashamed. Our patrol entered every contest... I was the patient for our patrol's first aid and by the time they had finished bandaging me hardly any of my blood was circulating. The weather during the camp was just terrible, raining off and on the whole time. Fortunately our tent was watertight... Out of the 74 patrols at the camp 10 got rated proficient which was the highest rating and ours was one of the ten. Don't you think that that is pretty good.

Now I have a piece of wonderful news. John Neame and I have very kindly been asked to go to a cattle ranch in Eastern Oregon. Every summer this rancher takes up several boys and pays them a little to do odd jobs around the ranch... Won't it be fun... My final grade for the term was a '1' in every subject."

The evacuees were invited to take part in a fundraising tea at the Corbett's home: "I gave Mr. Gunn a complimentary ticket to the 'benefit tea' and he bought two others." Each had to make a contribution: "Peter Kirwan was talking on British clothing, Ernest Kirwan was talking on food. John Neame was on boarding school, Ron on day school, Ivison Wheatly on certain habits and mannerisms and I on war life. At four o'clock people began to come in until there were several hundred there. I knew a lot of the people which made the talking all the more difficult. Sheila and the girls started the programme by playing very nicely the 'Star Spangled Banner' and two pieces. After tea we gave our talks. I thought that I made a terrible mess of mine... After the talks we sang 'God Save the King' and then they had more tea while the girls played their pieces again... We made more than $400 — almost £100 — to be sent for children's relief....

British evacuees at British consul's Portland office in 1943. John's sister and three cousins are in the photo, he was already at the ranch.

Evacuees at a fund-raising tea for "Bundles for Britain."

On Sunday the same group of people were having a bird walk around this district with Robbie Livingstone leading...We saw many birds including long-tailed chat, mourning dove, great blue heron, killdeer, meadow lark, band-tailed pigeons, chipping sparrow and several other varieties of sparrows, cassin vireo, several warblers. I showed them my flickers nest and they were very interested in it. I returned before the end of the walk so as to be ready for the benefit tea, and as I was walking through the woods a sooty grouse suddenly flashed past me."

June 1941: "I am now at the Keystone ranch near Prineville in Eastern Oregon where I am to work ... for 6 weeks this summer.... On Thursday they bought 6 new cows — 5 of them are very good milk cows and it takes a long time to milk them... There have been several new calfs in the last week and we're having a terrible time trying to get them to drink out of a bucket. There also has been a litter of pigs. I was given a $30 check — a dollar a day — that is pretty good isn't it...."

October: "Do you remember the radio program I was in last term, well we have been told that they want a record made so I'll have to be looking over my script. The record was very clear but it didn't sound one bit like any of our voices.... Sheila and I got a very interesting letter from a little boy in a Glasgow Hospital thanking us for some wool that we had sent him and saying that he was making a scarf for his father in the army. We couldn't think what it was until it dawned upon us that with the money we made from our benefit tea, they must have bought wool and distributed it to the various hospitals giving our names. We were deeply touched ...At biology last week we have been studying cells under the microscope.... I find biology by far the most interesting subject I have ever had, perhaps because

I have such a good teacher. Apart from biology and English I have the worst teachers. I nearly go to sleep every Latin period and maths almost drives me nuts. For instance for maths within the next three weeks we have to write an essay on the reasoning of the chief characters in any detective novel. If that's maths I'll eat my hat! I have just finished reading 'A Tale of Two Cities' and am going to start on 'Captain Blood' by Rafael Sabatini...."

November: "In the evening the whole of Portland has a practice blackout during which they were to have an imitation bombing and an air battle. However the weather conditions were so bad that no aeroplanes could take off. The anti aircraft guns and searchlights went on despite the loss of aeroplanes.... I am reading the 'North West Passage' just now, it's pretty good but its awfully long... At biology we dissected worms ...It was very interesting and I could find everything from the bilateral ganglion to the dorsal blood vessel! ...They have some lovely big snakes at school and I can sit for a whole period with a lovely smooth three foot bull snake wrapped around my neck. Do you know that bull snakes are about the cleanest pet you can have?"

Pearl Harbor: "On Monday at school we heard Roosevelt's declaration of war against the Japs. I was interested in the way the people heard the news. When Britain declared war against Germany the people were very worried and downcast, but here the people shouted and clapped and cheered for a long time.... At school we had a practice air raid alarm.... That was terrible news about the *Prince of Wales* and the *Repulse* being sunk though it was somewhat compensated by the loss of several Jap ships the next day."

February 1942: "Don't you think that now America is in the war that we might as well be at home as out here. If I'm making a mistake in saying this please don't worry because I'm just a stupid little boy still and often make 'foe pahs' (excuse spelling but it's the nearest I could get.) We are perfectly safe over here and nothing particularly has prompted me to say this...I long terribly to see you once more although we are extremely happy over here .... On Friday I started reading the *Citadel* by Cronin. I have almost finished it already. It is about the life of a doctor and it has almost decided me that I'm going to be a doctor, my civil service ambition has weakened considerably.... Doesn't the news seem terrible just now — Singapore fallen, Libyan defeats — escape of German ships and all the rest — and though victory must be inevitable I wish signs of it would show. Russia certainly is doing her part well! ...On Saturday we left for the beach. It was a wonderful day and certainly made it hard to think of fighting and chaos.... In biology we have just finished studying the human skeleton and I know everything from the metatarsels to the parietal bones via the sacro-illiac joint except the spelling."

John was invited to join the International Club, which discusses world affairs: "During the two-week pledging period I have to wear white glove and tie, have my shoes always polished, call the regular members Mr. and give them a stick of chewing gum whenever they ask for it.... I attended my club meeting where the pledges were told to provide entertainment for the members. I was ordered to quote from Caesar in Latin which was to my liking.... Next week I am going to be initiated along with two other boys. The three of us have to carry on a conversation in front of the club. One has to be Mussolini another Hitler and I am Stalin." Having been on the honor roll the previous term there was a special assembly: "Four of us had to give a speech. I was the first and though I was terribly frightened talking to over 1000 people I think I did pretty well."

By June he was back at the ranch, promoted to head dairyman instead of chore boy and hoping for a corresponding rise in pay: "I started right in milking — slow at first because I have not milked for a year but gradually getting faster.... While going to get the cows I found and killed a bull snake about 4 ft. long — a real giant. In his stomach I found ten undigested mice...."

In August he wrote: "I have now been promoted to driving a team. I have for the past week been driving a rake and I enjoy it very much, it's easy work with good pay ($3 a day). Last Sunday I went for a ride on Macks, Mr. Dickson's own horse. I saw another Bullocks's oriole this morning.... After work in the evening we often go down the creek and have a swim. The weather has been very hot recently and one gets awfully thirsty out in the fields. I get awfully sick if I drink too much water. On Saturday nights we go to town and see a picture.... Now they have mowed all the hay that is ripe and the raking is caught up so I am now working on the baler. It is very hard work but quite interesting. Every day almost I see a coyote. After dinner I have to help Mr. Dickson milk the cows. Usually I get a little reward in way of a peach or a melon.... I am having a wonderful time and am having quite a bit of riding after cattle and horses...."

One day John was asked to herd a flock of cattle, which had broken into a hay field, to the furthest boundary of the ranch. He had a great day riding his horse "Pinto" who had a natural instinct to heard cattle — anticipating breakaways and nibbling the tails of animals that were going too slowly. He returned to the ranch feeling very satisfied with his day's work: "The next morning, guess what, the cattle were back in the field."

In September he wrote: "I regret that this letter is a bit late, but my last few days at the ranch were very busy as the crew was becoming rather shorthanded.... The whole crew was called out to fight a forest fire several miles away. The first day the fire was very hot and there were over 100 people there. My duty was to squirt water on burning logs and stumps with what is called a 'back pack pump,' which holds five gallons. Our crew was one of the few that had to stay for the next day. We had to sleep in the forest services sleeping bags over night and really got quite good meals. The second day I used a pump and a shovel in the morning and a fire hose in the afternoon. It was a lot of fun with that powerful hose and I certainly doused lots of fire. For a while at the ranch I was driving the second fastest team on a mower. It was lovely white team. For the rest I drove an old team on the rake and pitched hay into the baling machine. It's hard work but it builds up your muscle. After dinner I would milk the cows and do chores, and because of that I was the highest paid boy on the ranch next to the foreman.... Including a check of $12.65 for fighting fire I made over $180 which is between £30 and £40, isn't that pretty good? ...I killed three rattlesnakes and saw many coyotes and porcupines this summer.... When I arrived home I learnt a wonderful piece of news. I went over to see John Neame who had left the ranch several weeks previously. By pulling a lot of strings the Corbetts have arranged a passage home for him very soon, and they are trying to arrange one for me.... I can just hope and pray that I may get home, as I long so much to see you once more.... School starts Tuesday so I'm just counting the days until the dreadful event."

Later in September: "I am at school once more and find it a very unpleasant change from work. There was an assembly at school where a British airman presented the school with a belt that he had taken off a nazi that he had killed.... Petrol rationing starts soon when we will get 16 galls a month so we are wondering how we are to get to town with the buses as irregular as they are. Stalingrad seems to be holding out awfully well doesn't it?"

In October: "A lot of people here think that it was a bad mistake to put Gandhi in prison.... This week there was a tremendous scrap drive, and also a prize for the school that got the most.... Our club rented a truck and five of us got excused. We went to old junk yards and loaded up with old car bodies, old stoves and metal barrels. At a bank we got a load of old cabinets...At another place the five of us had to get a huge metal hotel sign weighing many hundred pounds... All this junk we dumped on

John on board escort aircraft carrier.

Leaving the Portland docks.

the street in front of the school until that was filled...anyway we won the drive, and will all see a free picture next week.... "

November: "At long last I got my long delayed exit permit, so expect me home any day now."

February 1943: "News has this very minute arrived that we have received an "A" priority and will probably be going home soon...."

March: "You were asking me if I was thinking what I would like to be Daddy, and I have been thinking quite a bit. I would still like to be a doctor or in the Civil Service.... If it should be that they were impractical I think I would turn to the agricultural-scientific field.... I've come to the stage where I'm wondering what I shall do this summer (having given up hope of getting home until the war's over) ...I might work on one of Uncle Spen's many farms and ranches, but what I would like to do most would be to work in the shipyards.... However Aunt Mary feels that there is such a shortage on farms that I should go there and I think perhaps she is right."

There was a gap in the correspondence from March 21 to May 9. During this time arrangements were made for him to come home on HMS *Searcher,* an escort aircraft carrier, built in Seattle but finished in the Kaiser shipyard on the Willamette River, a few miles from Portland. These shipyards during the war produced Liberty Ships — 10,000-ton vessels made in two to three weeks from prefabricated sections welded together. Several hundred were produced in Portland. The escort carriers were adapted from the hulls of Liberty Ships. HMS *Searcher* was made for the Royal Navy and manned by a skeleton British crew as it was being taken back to Britain for commissioning. He and two other boys were accommodated in the officers' ward room. He kept a diary on the trip.

April: "Completed my affairs at school and said good-bye to my teachers, got a letter and transcript from Mr. York. (The Headmaster) Spent the day buying stuff that I forgot yesterday and saying goodbye to everyone. Got a letter from the Dicksons asking me up to the ranch this summer to which I scribbbled an answer.... Sad partings with all the kind relatives... My cabin is a comfortable, two bunks, two chest of drawers including writing cabinet and closet.... Spent the evening getting acquainted with some of the officers...."

"Slept well, had breakfast of grapefruit, ham and eggs and coffee. Spent morning watching tugs pull ship down river... Kept my eye on the shore and saw and waved to Uncle Gerald. In afternoon electric cables were wound around the ship to degauss it or render it safe from magnetic mines. Very nice engineer showed and explained to me the catapult mechanism and let me operate it and fire it. Went down to the engine room and met an engineer from Glasgow who showed me around and explained some of the workings."

April 30, 1943: "Came down the Columbia River... Mr. McDonald came on board. Felt first waves toward evening, did some typing for Sub Lt Gunn. Found that my typing came back to me quite easily."

May 1: "Awoke to find the engines broken down and accordingly no electricity. When I went on deck I found that we were in the Jean da Fuca Straits. After some time the engines were repaired and we got under weigh. Very beautiful scenery all day coming down the Puget Sound. Spent two hours in the afternoon testing the degaussing on a range within sight of Seattle. Saw the barrage balloons over Bremerton. Docked in Seattle in the evening."

May 2: "Worked all day on one of the lifeboat motors but we could not get it to work. Got a pass to go on shore in the evening."

May 3: "Worked all day on the evaporators with Mr. Pratt. My job was to regulate the water levels entering and leaving, to take brine tests, to find out when it was dense? Enough to turn the brine out. After some difficulty with one of the six pumps we got the machine working fine and produced 100 gals of fresh water in 25 mins. After dinner we were shown the picture 'Charlie's Aunt'."

May 5: "Moved to a larger 6 bunk cabin so as to be with the other boys when they come.... The Governor General of Canada (Earl of Athlone) came on board and inspected the ship but I did not see him."

May 6: "Copied a chart of the chief engineer and did some typing....

Simon and Christopher Creswell came on board." These were two younger boys whom he was supposed to look after.

May 7: "During the morning action stations were sounded and we were 'dive bombed' by a lot of planes. In the afternoon the guns were all fired to test them. Did some work for the chief engineer."

May 8: "The morning was spent doing speed tests. I spent all morning taking temperature and pressure readings in the engine room…. I then copied down the figures on the chart that I had made several days before. In the evening I went ashore and bought some things that I needed. I also saw the picture Casablanca which was very good."

May 10: "Tested the fire extinguisher and water came up into the "Foamite" container and spilt it all over the engine room floor…. In the afternoon I did some typing and filing for the Captain's secretary. Then watched the guns shoot at a sleeve drawn by an aeroplane. The first aeroplane dropped the sleeve very skilfully on the deck, but no hits had been made. In the evening the four inchers were fired at a target."

May 13: "Left Seattle for the last time. Spent the morning drawing graphs…."

On May 18, he wrote his parents: "I am fine except that the heat is rather uncomfortable at times and makes sleeping almost impossible. I am not able to go on deck much during the day, because I have no hat, but in the early mornings and evenings I take a breather. It is very interesting watching the flying fish, they are such a beautiful blue colour and the phosphorescence is also very interesting. We get up at 5 every morning to attend our battle stations. My station is at the battle dressing station (where the wounded receive preliminary attention). I don't know what I'm supposed to do, though I will probably be a stretcher bearer, which I don't think will be too difficult as there are four to each stretcher…. Many of the officers are giving me typing jobs to do. My real 'boss' is the chief engineer, for whom I copy out in ink each day, the 'engineer's log' which is quite an extensive affair. I have bought two pairs of white shorts from the ships store, and they are very comfortable during this weather. My typing is now reasonably good, and I can manage about 35 or more words a minute…. The other day the officer, with whom I was working in the 130 degrees of very humid heat, fainted, and many others in cooler temperatures have done the same thing. I do quite a bit of work in the engine room, sometimes on the evaporators and sometimes repairing various things."

May 29: "I suppose you know by now how I am coming and that accordingly you will not worry about my safety. I have been seeing some very interesting things lately which I am longing to tell you about. We had quite a bad storm which lasted for two days a short time ago, and for the first day I felt pretty miserable and occasionally fed the fishes, but on the second I felt like a real sailor."

This was a real hurricane in the Caribbean with waves breaking over the flight deck. The welded seams of the ship started to come apart in places and John reported that they had to put into the naval dockyard in Norfolk Virginia for a month for repairs: "I have very little to do and time hangs rather heavily on my hands although quite often the chief engineer gives me work to do…. I have seen several pelicans and what I think are frigate birds…was very flattered the other day because the chief engineer invited me to accompany him for a walk on the deck. He is a very nice elderly man, and worked for several years on the *Duchess of York* before the war."

June 22: "Three days ago I got a big thrill for I at last thought we were on our way home, but engine trouble has brought us back here for goodness knows how long. I miss your letters more than I can say. It's funny but I never realised how much I look forward to news from home. I suppose that it is just one of the many things we take for granted and don't really notice until it is taken away from us."

That was John's last letter. From Norfolk, the ship went to New York for a few days to await a convoy to cross the Atlantic. He wrote in his diary that he got permission to go ashore: "I cashed a War Bond which I had bought which I think yielded $25 and with that large sum I went into Manhattan and went up the Empire State Building and went to a cinema where in the interval Cab Calloway's band played. When the time came to return to the ship I realised with horror that I had no idea where it was. It had never occurred to me to take note of the dock number and Brooklyn docks cover a vast area. I decided to make enquiry at a police station where I was treated with great suspicion and almost arrested as a spy and they would not help — security in war time was very tight. I wandered about getting more and more desperate as I knew that we were to sail that night and eventually I went to another police station where they were more sympathetic and phoned around to find where the ship was although I had great difficulty in understanding their Irish/Brooklynese accent when they did eventually gave me the location and I managed to get lost once more. I managed to get back to the ship after midnight just minutes before we sailed and got a severe rocket for being late. I think it was one of the worst experiences of my life."

In his diary, John noted that they had joined a convoy of about sixty ships which made a very slow crossing. They were not equipped to do escort duties and were not part of the convoy's defense although they had many 'action stations' and exercises: "I recall dropping a 'casualty' whom we were trying to extricate from a gun turret! We had no incidents during the crossing but I think that one or two of the ships in the convoy were sunk."

They landed at Liverpool late in July and he took the train home: "A bill was sent after I got home for my expenses during the three months aboard ship which I recall came to about £5 — surely the bargain of all time."

CHAPTER FIVE

RHODE ISLAND'S FORGOTTEN SCHOOL

ONE DAY KAS GAVE ME SOME CLIPPERS AND ASKED ME TO CUT FLOWERS FOR THE DINING ROOM TABLE. THAT SOUNDED LIKE FUN. THE GARDEN WAS VERY BRIGHT IN THE FALL WITH LOTS TO CHOOSE FROM. I THOUGHT THE ARRANGEMENT WAS QUITE BEAUTIFUL WITH VARIOUS COLORS AND BRIGHT GREEN SHINY IVY LEAVES WHICH I HAD NEVER SEEN BEFORE ALL AROUND THE EDGE. THAT WAS MY INTRODUCTION TO POISON IVY — OBVIOUSLY THERE WAS A LOT TO LEARN ABOUT THIS NEW COUNTRY!

—Vicki de Kleer (née Scaramanga)

A Rhode Island couple, Chris and Mary Beth Kreger, decided to set up a B&B in an old historic landmark, The Tower House, in Narragansett. When they moved in with their five children in May 2002 there were only two objects on the walls, an old framed postcard from 1905 depicting the water tower out in front of their house and a letter signed Elizabeth R. thanking the owners for sharing their home with children from the United Kingdom during World War II.

Mary Beth wanted to "restore the Tower House to its perfection" and was surprised to find symmetrical holes in the living room floor. She asked her realtor what they were. He said that several children from the United Kingdom had studied in the house during the war and that was where desks had been bolted to the floor for their "school." She also discovered a little trap door in the floor that led to a dirt cellar under the foundation, and on the underside of the floor boards was painted "SHHH School in Session." "My young son," she says, "was convinced there was pirate treasure buried there!"

The letter from The Queen and the discovery under the trap door has always intrigued her. She often wondered who had been there and where they were living now and whether it was a happy time for them. "This" she says, "is the beautiful language of the manuscript on my wall:"

> *I wish to mark, by this personal message, my gratitude for the help and kindness which you have shown to the children who crossed the sea from the United Kingdom many months ago.*
>
> *Since the early days of the war, you have opened your doors to strangers and offered to share your home with them.*
>
> *In this kindness of your heart, you have accepted them as members of your own family, and I know that to this unselfish task you and all your household have made many great sacrifices.*
>
> *By your generous sympathy you have earned the true and lasting gratitude of those to whom you have given this hospitality, and by your understanding you have shown how strong is the bond uniting all those who cherish the same ideals.*
>
> *For all this goodwill towards the children of Great Britain, I send you my warmest and most grateful thanks.*
>
> *—Elizabeth R*

I came into the story because over Memorial Day at the end of May 2010 Diana Holdsworth, a guest from Amherst, Massachusetts, was staying at the B&B and heard from Mary Beth this piece of wartime history. When she got home she searched the internet for possible references and then emailed me: "I read with great interest the June 2009 *Patriot Ledger* article online regarding your experience as an evacuee to America during WWII and the pivotal role it played in your adult life. If I may, I would ask your advice on a matter having to do with British refugee children." She had recently stayed; she told me, at a B&B in Narragansett and described what the present owners had found there. 'They are interested in the history of the children. If you have any suggestions as to how they might uncover the story and perhaps contact the now grownup children, I would be most grateful."

I said that I would do my best and got in touch with Mary Beth who repeated the story and also told me, "I feel an obligation to these children from England and will extend my hospitality to them at no cost, should they want to return." I assured her I would do what I could to track them down

The search proved difficult and took more than three years, longer than I expected, as I contacted many people I had been in touch with who were evacuated to Rhode Island or New England in general as I had been. None, however, could shed light on this group. Nor did a mention in *The Evacuee*, the magazine of the Evacuees Reunion Association (now known as the British Evacuees Association), produce any responses. I had earlier helped another American, Melanie McMillan, in Brandon, Mississippi, to link up with a wartime family who were evacuated to a friend of her mother. She had letters from their father that she wanted to return to them and was shortly visiting Britain. I was able to locate the English wartime visitors and she met up with them in London. She had emailed me, using similar words to Diana's: "I just read an article online from the *Patriot Ledger* about your evacuation to the U.S. during the war. I was led to this article in my search for information about two evacuees — siblings — that I have been trying to locate."

I caught Melanie up on my latest search for information. The *Patriot Ledger* article had reported on my own recent visit to Milton MA the town where I had spent five years.

I told Melanie about the Narragansett B&B and the fact that after many hours of pulling volumes of land documents from the dusty shelves at the Town Clerk's office Mary Beth had at last discovered the name of the owners of the property from 1939 to 1956 — Isaac Peace Hazard and Katherine M. B. Hazard. On her own initiative Melanie went back to the internet and produced for me the name of the Hazard's granddaughter, Lucy Hodgson Robinson, and added, "It looks like she lives in New York State." I then managed to find a possible postal address and sent the granddaughter a letter about the B&B.

Lucy responded enthusiastically, "I was a small child in Narragansett during WWII and I remember our English children well since they were really the first children I had ever known. Even if it was a time of great turmoil, for a small child it was very exciting and the solidarity between my family and the English was very apparent. As the youngest child in the household I probably benefited the most from having such an extended family." Lucy, who is a sculptor, said that her grandmother was a good painter though with her responsibilities she didn't have much time to acquire a large body of work and a reputation. "The girls were all devoted to my grandmother who certainly reciprocated and they maintained contact with her long after the war."

She also wrote, "Since your B&B owner mentions a classroom, I suspect that the house was one that was used as a schoolhouse for the English children we knew. These were the children of friends that my family met and knew in Davos in the 1930s. Having a rather large house in

Lucy Hodgson remembers her grandmother making this woodcut of their home.

Vicki in 1940.

Vicki meets Mary Beth Kreger, the B&B owner.

NARRAGANSETT TIMES

"The Castle" 1942.

Narragansett, my grandparents thought it natural to open it up to 'evacuees' who they treated like family." Lucy gave me the names and addresses of some of the children she found in her aged mother's faded address book in her shaky hand. She had died in 2011 at 97. "You've reminded me that I haven't seen these people for ages, and you've prompted me to write them. Thanks very much."

In June 2013 I wrote to these children in Canada, South Africa and the United Kingdom. One of them, Vicki DeKleer who lives in Ontario, was equally responsive as "those five years were undoubtedly the most important of my life and certainly the happiest." She very swiftly phoned Mary Beth who found her "delightful" and encouraged her to come for a visit.

Already a few weeks later Vicki wrote me that she and Lucy had been "busy with emails, making plans to meet when my daughter and I go back to Narragansett in September." It was clear that the Tower House B&B was indeed the school she attended and The Castle, a fifteen-minute walk away through the woods, was the Hazard home where she lived and was Lucy's grandparent's home and is now the Middlebridge School.

In September 2013 I had an email and then a postcard from Vicki: "Just a note to say hello from Narragansett. Mary Beth says hello. B&B is superb! Quite wonderful. We go over to The Castle after lunch. Good to be back here — home!" She and her daughter had driven from Ontario to Narragansett and met Lucy and spent the afternoon at the Castle/Middlebridge School. "I had of course looked forward to seeing it again. What I had not even thought about was that as soon as I walked through the door all of a sudden I was home again. And the school is incredible." I also had an email from Lucy: "Vicki and I had a wonderful two days reminiscing over events at The Castle, and our tour through the building brought forth a whole lot more memories. We were even interviewed by some of the students — on camera! The more I think about it, the more I realize how much this period during the war and the English visitation meant to me even though I was quite small at the time."

Mary Beth also heard full stories of her wartime time in Narragansett "of the harrowing journey from England" when she was ten, aboard the *Duchess of Richmond* in August 1940, having exchanged her constant possession, a gas mask, for her lifejacket. While docked in Liverpool, the ship caught a hawser round in her propeller, delaying sailing for two days, which meant missing the convoy with its naval escorts. They eventually set off unescorted across the Atlantic arriving in Halifax safely. But what impressed Mary Beth most was "the gracious hospitality that Vicki spoke of shown her by the family that took her and other children in for those years." ...Also that they were treated as a family with no distinction between the two. "Peace Hazard and his beautiful wife, Katherine, showed her such kindness she remained friends with her long after her time was over in Narragansett."

Vicki also had a interview with a reporter from the *Narragansett Times* arranged by Mary Beth. She heard what lay behind her first discoveries in the building, the origin of the school and why the Queen of England had written her thanks. In June 1940 Lucy's grandparents, the Hazards, had written to Vicki's parents inviting them to send Vicki to them "for the duration." They had also added, "And, by the way do you know of any other youngsters we could also take?" Vicki still has a letter written by her grandmother to her father in which she writes, "We have talked over the wonderfully kind offer your American friends have made and I have tried to put myself in your place. The heartbreak Vicki's going would mean needs no discussion. It is obvious, but it is of the child you must think. The risk is the passage across. The advantage is that she will be spared now at her impressionable age the horrors which will certainly descend upon us here. She will be with friends on whom you can rely and when this is over she will return to you with the same love she has always given you. Weigh well in your mind before you say no and consider how far the advantages outweigh the risks."

So besides Vicki, ten, they travelled out on the *Duchess of Richmond* with Maud Wenham, a nanny, a girl of seven and a boy of two, also Tina Travers, fourteen and her brother, eight. Arrival in Narragansett "opened up a whole new world — a house full of people, large grounds, trees to climb, a small pond, a rocky ocean to explore, etc. House rules and routine but also much freedom. Katherine Hazard (known to us as Kas) was the most wonderful person I have ever met — compassionate, kind, no nonsense, reliable, all this while running a household of about a dozen, over half of whom were completely unrelated and I was the only one she had ever seen before."

Soon another girl, Clare Thomson, arrived — her family of four young children and their mother, staying in Peacedale with the Leonard Bacon family. Then Clare's mother died and Clare moved over to the Hazards, sharing a room with Vicki. "So now there were eight." Clare was the same age and became like a sister, more a sister than her own who was back in England doing war work in London and later in Ceylon. They both joined the local scout troop, earning badges particularly related to marine life and twice went to summer scout camp. Anne, one of the Hazard's cousin's daughters, made up the third of a trio who spent a great deal of time together.

The school was started by the Hazards for them and several other local students, ten or twelve of them together in one room, grades three through eight, and one teacher, Mr. Turner, who was addressed as "Sir." For Vicki there were music lessons on Saturdays and she remembers that: "this involved bicycling to class in Wakefield with my music, violin — and a dozen eggs for the rector of the church that we went to." The girls went swimming and riding together, and climbing trees, and she even learned to drive a tractor. "All the time we had wonderful care — taken to the dentist to get our teeth straightened, bought new clothes as we grew — and generally grew up as free as American teenagers."

One day they discovered in the barn an old Penny Farthing bicycle. "Somehow we got it all cleaned up and in working order. That was not difficult because there are very few parts that move. The difficulty was learning how to actually ride it, having climbed on from the back porch. This consisted of much trial and error. Having mastered that, Clare and I took to riding into Narragansett, one on a proper bicycle, the other on the Penny, switching over on the way back. The local policeman took rather a dim view of this maneuver as it involved stepping down on the roof of the nearest parked car to get off it."

The *Narragansett Times* reporter heard another of Vicki's memorable traffic experiences. "One day I was late going home on my bike, watching the speedometer, trying to go faster. And that was when I hit the bus that had stopped in the middle of the road. Then I remember sitting in the front seat of a car between two men who asked my name, and where I lived. I assumed that I was being kidnapped and wouldn't answer. They were driving very fast, even through a red light. Later I found myself in the local hospital — with a fractured skull — and Kas was there. The Narragansett police had picked me up off the road."

Occasionally on a Sunday afternoon friends and relations would arrive to play classical music for a few hours. They sometimes went to the movies and once they all attended a performance in Kingston by the von Trapp family, the original *Sound of Music*. Baron von Trapp was there himself with all the children. "That was exciting and their history was not lost on us."

After Pearl Harbor there were ways they could contribute to the war effort and an unexpected opportunity presented itself. "The USA was aware of the fact that German submarines might be off-shore and their planes could make an appearance. And therefore the Aircraft Warning Service was set up. This consisted of a chain of observation posts along the Eastern seaboard. They were to be manned by civilians trained to Navy standards. This included teenagers! Why not, good eyesight and many with a built-in interest in this sort of thing. Clare and I got involved; this meant evening courses at the Quonset Naval Air Base, the largest one on the coast. We had the same instruction, exam and standards as those in the forces." They were given a formal certificate and then, always with an adult, they were permitted to stand four-hour watches, once a week, taking time off from school. On her recent visit to Narragansett she was able to present to the Quonset base, which is no longer operational, but has a museum, books, exam papers, and a couple of model airplanes she had saved from that time.

Every evening they would all gather as a family in the living room to listen to the 6 o'clock the news on the radio "to be brought up to date for better or for worse on what was happening to — or in — England. I know there were times when it looked quite probable that there would be no England to return to as we had known it. Apart from the bombing of cities, perhaps places we knew, the shipping casualties were still awful. They never wanted us to think that just because we were safe that it was like that everywhere, because it wasn't. There was a war going on and they wanted us to know the facts instead of hiding it from us, and I'm very thankful for that. We did get letters from England but by the time they arrived the news was out of date." Often they had been censored. Sunday afternoons the children all wrote letters to family back in England. "Looking back it seemed a bit bizarre. We might have walked along the rocks by the ocean looking for crabs one morning, while the other side of that same ocean the beaches were blocked by barbed wire and the search was for periscopes."

Being by the sea had always meant a lot to Vicki, first very young in the Isle of Wight, then in a transatlantic crossing and with a sail boat in Narragansett. Then her return and later crewing on the *Lord Nelson*, one of tall ships, across the Atlantic and even in her eighties, she told the Narragansett paper, back in Ontario she "enjoys kayaking every morning."

By 1944 most of the evacuees had returned to England. "When Clare's father wanted her to go home Kas took her and Anne and me to New York to see her off by ship. We went shopping and Kas brought each of us similar friendship rings, which we still have and wear." Years later when she was living lived in Ontario Vicki drove down to Peacedale

Outside the Peace Hazard home (front row l to r) Lindsay Travers, Clare Thompson, Vicki Scaramanga, Tuppy (Ingrid) Wenham and Charles Wenham and (back row l to r) Tina Travers, Maud Wenham (mother of Tuppy and Charles), Kas Hazard, Ollie (nurse to the Wenhams) and Benjamin Hazard, son of Kas.

Clare and Ann.

Kas.

"in a secondhand army jeep with no doors" to Anne's wedding to Eliot Richardson who became the U.S. Attorney General.

With many having gone home and Peace Hazard having to go to the hospital, Kas closed the house and Vicki went to Holmquist School, a boarding school in Pennsylvania. Then it was time for Vicki to return home. She had a long talk with Kas about this but it was "non-negotiable," a lot had changed and she did not really want to go.

Vicki returned on H.M.T. *Aquitania*, arriving in Southampton on September third, six years to the day that Great Britain declared war on Germany. One of the ship's officers, H.L., wrote that day: "The fact is the more poignant because many of the passengers aboard are returning to their homeland to see for the first time the honourable scars of battle. On this day let us remind ourselves:

"On September third· 1939 the British people set out on a great pilgrimage. They can never set out on any journey more reluctantly but they were resolved to make it, for in their hearts — sad, foreboding, but utterly determined they knew it was to be. It has proved the greatest journey in the history of these islands. The fact that this voyage of ours is now complete, that the passage has been made under pleasant and peaceful conditions, makes our gratitude for all the fortitude and gallantry of our people the more sincere. Looking back on it now in the light of the United Nation's strength, it seems inconceivable that success has become a fact; yet freedom and decency would have would have perished from this world had it been otherwise.'

"Our roads need repair, our undamaged buildings need painting, our wealth of possessions have been seriously reduced, casualties have been many. There are inconceivable difficulties head for everyone, but we may all share in the proudest of all possessions; the spirit to overcome all difficulties in the past and in the future. When things appear strange and meagre, sometimes lacking the normality of simple comfort, let us never forget."

Back home Vicki finished her Oxford School Certificate and then did a year at a Home Economics school in Devon and, as she says, was probably one of their poorest students on record as she had no interest in the curriculum. She had a chance to go to Canada where she caught up on subjects needed to qualify for the Ontario Veterinary College. After five years she graduated and got a job at a veterinary hospital in New York State, married another veterinarian, and set up a mixed practice in Ontario. He died very suddenly and very young. Vicki had stayed in touch with Kas and spent time with her at Christmas the first year of their marriage "so when he died the only person I wanted to turn to was Kas." Vicki kept the practice for a year, looking after her two-year-old daughter whom she had named after her. On a year's sabbatical she returned to England to live in Arundel in a cottage next to her father and to teach at the Royal Veterinary College in London. She was on the faculty of the University of Guelph all her working life.

During the war Vicki had lived, as she puts it, in the very middle of unassuming generosity and love, with a house, stability and security year round. From the Hazards she had learned about the give and take of life, about how to develop your own individuality. "Kas lived with enormous common sense and there was a feeling that how you live your life, use your skills and choose your work is infinitely more important than what you possess. What you own does not matter nearly as much as what you do with it."

She sums up her years at Narragansett: "Probably the most formative and happiest days of my life were in Rhode Island and there I came to meet some of the people who were dearest to me. There was never the slightest indication from Kas that she and her family were doing anything more but looking after me on behalf of my own family and that I should return once again to them. This was their contribution to the war effort."

Lucy Hodgson wrote me, "I am grateful to you for bringing this all back. Vicki says they were the happiest years of her life and frankly they may have been the happiest of mine. War creates some great alliances."

Mary Beth sums up her part: "My search to find a life that was touched by the human kindness and goodwill of the family here in Narragansett so many years ago was successful. Vicki Scaramanga DeKleer DVM is a bright, brilliant jewel. Her story is inspiring to me and to those I share it with often here at my little Tower House Bed and Breakfast."

CHAPTER SIX

TUXEDO PARK CHILDREN'S HOUSE

IT WAS A RELIEF TO BE AT LAST FREE OF THE BOTHERSOME GAS MASK, BUMPING UNCOMFORTABLY ON ONE'S BACK AS WE CLIMBED INTO THE SLEEPER TRAIN FOR NEW YORK. SNUG BEHIND DARK GREEN CURTAINS WE SLEPT IN TIERS LOOKED AFTER BY A SMILING BLACK ATTENDANT.
—Fiona Ross Buchanan

Just as the discovery of a message from the Queen of England on the wall of a B&B in Narragansett, Rhode Island (see previous chapter) opened up a completely forgotten story of British evacuees and the school set up for them in World War II, so the clearing out of an attic in Oxford, England provided hitherto unknown documentation on a most imaginative American initiative to provide sanctuary and schooling for other young British evacuees in the New York village of Tuxedo Park. Both discoveries led to a greater understanding of the importance to the children and their hosts of the transatlantic effort.

Christian R. Sonne in Tuxedo Park had for a long time wanted to write the story of "the extraordinary outreach of the community in housing, feeding and educating more than a dozen English children for more than 3-1/2 years from October 1940 until May 1944." His parents had been very involved at the time and he still retains memories of the children, particularly at Thanksgiving lunches in his parents' home. But the only documentation he could find was two articles in the *New Yorker* in 1940 and 1944 and a *New York Times* article about a reunion of the British children at Tuxedo Park in 1998.

TUXEDO PARK CHILDREN'S HOUSE

Chris's mother had died in 1970 and his sister, who was married to an Englishman, had taken their mother's papers to England. The attic discovery by his niece in 2011 included a seventeen-page typewritten report written by his mother about this community outreach. His mother had been chair of the group of residents who organized and financed the so-called Children's House Project. What more could Chris, who is now the retired Town Historian of Tuxedo Park, wish for! The report now resides at the Tuxedo Historical Society and I am grateful for his assistance in telling this story.

In 1980, in recognition of its historical and architectural significance, the entire village of Tuxedo Park was listed on the National Register of Historic Places.

Tuxedo has an unusual history. Situated in the Ramapo Mountains, it had in the colonial era undeveloped iron deposits and an English company and later American-owned companies built furnaces and mines there. In 1813 an iron-making furnace located on the Ramapo River very near the present entrance to Tuxedo Park was acquired by Pierre Lorillard II, together with several thousand acres of land. Lorillard closed the furnace and he, and later his son, Pierre Lorillard III, lumbered the property and occasionally hunted in the forests and fished in the Tuxedo Lake. What is now the village and the areas around it were developed as a private hunting-and-fishing reserve by Pierre Lorillard IV of tobacco fame in 1885. It was named Tuxedo Park after the Native American name of the lake which is part of it. Three trainloads of fashionable visitors came for the gala opening celebration. It became so popular that he organized the Tuxedo Club and the Tuxedo Park Association and surrounded the property with a high game fence which no longer exists. However Tuxedo Park is still a gated community of 2050 acres which includes three lakes, two created by dams, and is restricted to the use of the residents who in the 2010 census numbered 623 as well as members of the Tuxedo Club, the majority of whom do not reside in Tuxedo Park.

Tuxedo Park enjoyed many prosperous years from 1885 until the 1920s. *The Blue Book of Etiquette* was written by Emily Post whose family lived there. She wrote the book based on what she observed inside the great stone gates. For it was an early gated community. We have it to blame for that dress form, the tuxedo, which in other places is called a dinner jacket or 'black tie.' Tuxedo Park was the first place in America where the dinner jacket was adopted for gentlemen dining by themselves or informally in mixed company, and when they did so publicly in New York City others called the strange new garment "a tuxedo."

A HARVEST OF FRIENDSHIPS

At the start of World War II, historian Chris Sonne told me, it was still in the top echelons of New York society even though many families had lost all their money in the crash. "All the houses of men who were members of The Club had servants and were quite large and had business and banking connections with London and certainly had their suits tailored there. At that time there were approximately 200 houses of which fifty to sixty were outbuildings in many cases having servants' quarters. There is also a hamlet outside the gates, many of whose present homeowners are descended from the gardeners, chauffeurs and other staff of the families "inside the gates." Most of the work force came originally from Italy and Slovakia although many of the maids were Irish and the butlers of course English."

In her book *Tuxedo Park,* Jennet Conant focuses on a different aspect of Tuxedo Park's life and fame, the extraordinary achievements of a brilliant and wealthy scientist, Alfred Lee Loomis, who had moved there in 1913. She writes that Lorillard, after selling his grand Newport mansion "the Breakers" to the Vanderbilts, had wanted 'to simplify his life and commune with nature' but over the next two decades Tuxedo Park 'had become a greenbelt of extravagant mansions, the bigger the better. Many of them were monuments to vanity — and folly — and Loomis had his choice of architectural extravagances, ranging from Tudor, gothic revival, Spanish mission, Georgian, Jacobean and Queen Anne.'

Loomis transformed one of these large mansions into a laboratory which became a meeting place for the great names nationally and internationally in science and finance. In the late 1930s it attracted men like Einstein, Heisenberg, Bohr, and Fermi. Early in World War II senior British scientists who came over to brief President Roosevelt and his scientific advisors on what they were doing went straight from the White House to Loomis' lab at Tuxedo Park. With growing recognition of the significance of his work to the Allied war effort his laboratory was moved to MIT in Boston and Loomis personally bankrolled pioneering research into new, high-powered radar detection systems that helped defeat the German Air Force and U-Boats. With Ernest Lawrence, the Nobel Prize-winning physicist, he pushed Roosevelt to fund research in nuclear fission, which led to the development of the atomic bomb. His Tuxedo Park home is now divided into nine apartments.

This then was the unusual community where eighteen young British children grew up in World War II.

"The Story of Children's House," as Chris Sonne's mother entitled her report, began in June 1940 soon after the evacuation of the British and

T.P. Mitchell home which became The Children's House.

The evacuees outside The Children's House in October 1940. *Front row:* Philip Robinson, Tony Robinson, Peggy Robinson, Margaret Ross, Susan Carnegie and Nicky Roles. *Back row:* Tania Savitski, Fay Robinson, Penelope Roles, Fiona Ross.

French soldiers from Dunkirk and the growing doubts whether Britain could withstand a German invasion. His mother had been asking French war relief societies whether the Tuxedo community could help with French refugee children but had been told that all communication with France had been cut off. She thought that perhaps the Mitchell House with nineteen bedrooms, which her husband had recently bought, might be used as a clearing house where refugee children could stay while appropriate foster homes were found for them.

Chris Sonne describes what happened next: "On the evening of June 22, 1940 my mother sat between Mr. George Grant Mason and Mr. Alexander Tomes at a dinner at the Tuxedo Club to benefit French and Belgian war charities. Mr. Tomes told her that his nephew-in-law, Windham Baldwin, who was the son of the former Prime Minister of Great Britain Stanley Baldwin, soon intended to send his young son with his nurse to stay with them. My mother mentioned the empty Mitchell House and asked if it would be possible for the nurse to chaperone other children across the Atlantic. Mr. Tomes agreed to cable his relative. My mother then turned to Mr. Mason, who is one of the figures in the Tuxedo Historical Society's mural of Tuxedo's most important people, and asked him if he thought the necessary funds could be raised to set up the Mitchell property to house English refugee children. In a gesture typical of his generosity Mr. Mason hastily approved of the plan and offered to pay 10 percent of the cost.

"The next day Mr. Tomes and my mother sent a cable to Windham Baldwin outlining the Tuxedo Park proposal and soon had an answer stating that Tuxedo had to produce 50 guarantees from Americans who would be personally responsible for the children. My mother immediately approached Mrs. Ernest Adee who in five minutes signed the first pledge which involved a down payment of $475 (the estimated cost for a child in the clearing house for several months). Within the incredibly short time of a few weeks, states my mother, she and her colleagues had collected the requisite guarantees either to take a child into their homes or to donate $475."

Responding to the offer to house British children, Windham Baldwin wrote to Alexander Tomes: "Please take this letter as meaning all the heartfelt gratitude that a human being can feel. The time is getting short, and the German plans are ripening, and though the invasion that we expect will be greeted with all of the force and determination we are capable of, I shall be surprised if it will be easy to get children out of the cauldron once it gets really boiling.... Without the children we shall fight better, knowing what hands are stretched out to receive them. Don't have any doubt of our being able to cope with the Germans and Italians with your generous American support… Remember when we get to the Finals we will be playing on our Homeground! — God bless you and the good people of Tuxedo and keep your own children from such a situation as that on the continent of Europe. You have our everlasting and loving thanks."

"As my mother puts it," adds Chris Sonne, "the plight of the English children had a terrific appeal and at the same time everyone in America was burning with indignation at the Germans and longing to be able to do something tangible to help the British, whose courage aroused our admiration to a fever pitch. Moreover, many of us realized that they were fighting our battle as well as theirs."

Just two weeks after Chris' mother's conversation with Mr. Tomes the first meeting was held of the Tuxedo Committee for Refugee Children. Mrs. Sonne was elected Chair and Mr. Tomes Treasurer. A United States Committee for Overseas Children had been set up under the leadership of Mr. Marshall Field to coordinate operations. As the national committee would take in all types of children, the Tuxedo Committee decided to rely on Baldwin to select children who could most easily feel at home in the Tuxedo community. The Tuxedo Committee was set up as an independent branch of the Children's Aid Society in New York. The Society gave them advice and assistance and was a help in raising funds which were tax exempt. The Committee offered to take in forty children into their various homes.

Back in England the Baldwins wrote to their friends or to people recommended to them. Windham's wife, Elspeth, in a letter of July 4th to Mrs. Ross at Astley Hall, Stourport on Severn, wrote that she had heard from Rita Cowen-Douglas that she was interested in some plans for sending children to America. "A scheme was originally raised by me, having a brother living on a private estate, just outside of New York; and my husband and I are going to send one small boy and Nanny there. The place is an enormous park with about 150 private houses, lakes, woods, children's school, hospital, swimming, riding, etc. These people have formed a committee guaranteeing to take 50 children and 5 adults, so our friends and friend's friends who would like to send their children there, ages 5–15 years old, apply to me where I can furnish particulars of British passports, Permits, American visas and finally sailings. If friends are not guaranteed from the American side they are not allowed into the country and that is why my husband and I are doing it for children here." She added that she did not yet have the full complement of children as she could handle all the details and spare several visits to London. "It is difficult to advise, I only know that Tuxedo Park is an ideal place for children, wonderful care and a happy and best life for them. So if you really intend to make use of this offer I'll attend to it at once."

The Ross's daughter, Fiona Buchanan, still has the letter, and one that followed on July 20 about the shipping: "As far as we have been able to discover, no passenger ships have a convoy, nor are they likely to have one in the near future as you have probably read in the newspapers. The government can't afford the convoys at present, and no one can say if, or when, America may send over to fetch children. So the risk is there, though it may be a small one.... My husband has had personal conversation and correspondence with shipping people, which seems to result in each family of our Tuxedo group having to make up their own minds whether to face the risk or not. I can only tell you some are willing to do so, and some are not!"

Most of the children were too young to appreciate the significance or danger and parents helped awake in them a sense. Eighty-three-year-old Fiona Buchanan told me when I was researching this book that her parents had told her, "This is going to be a great adventure, you know, the States, an ocean crossing. They told us of ocean liners, Red Indians, automobiles, skating and skyscrapers. My father remembered as a small boy skating in Central Park. Our exercise books were filled with drawings of all these new experiences. We left home without a backward glance."

The ten children boarded the SS *Empress of* Australia in Glasgow in mid-September the only ones of Windham Baldwin's plan for fifty youngsters. But they did not sail for more than a week as mine detectors needed to be installed, and so their ship just missed a west-bound convoy. The convoy they missed included the ill-fated *City of Benares*. Also traveling on their ship were other evacuees from Britain's Actors Orphanage and Fiona remembers the children putting on a performance of *Sweeney Todd* , "...in an effort to distract 100s of bored and rampaging children." The wait for news that the children had arrived safely in Canada was for parents "agonizing." It was some three weeks before the parents heard the news after a voyage that normally took five days.

Fiona was then nine years old but still has distinct memories: "The ship was in some ways a terrifying place. Every corridor filled with boys fighting and shouting. The indoor swimming pool was stacked with furniture, all covered with dust sheets. Here, in the dark under the tarpaulins were alarming games of hide and seek which drove us back to the tranquillity of Miss Willson's (our escort) cabin, the only place one felt safe. The dining saloon seemed to me like a vast gilded ballroom — and perhaps it was, for this liner had taken the king and queen on their 1939 visit to Canada. For us lots of ice cream, jellies, balloons, cake and streamers. Other memories, sleeping in our clothes until past Ireland where we left the convoy behind. Hateful life jacket, large lumps of cork sewn into a dingy cotton bodice — the occasional U-Boat alarm, and standing at the stern rail watching the wake of the ship's zigzag course."

Meanwhile in the United States in July and August the Committee had been busy cleaning and equipping the house as well as sending to hosts the plans for the children after they arrived. This was the period when overseas evacuation, both private and company- or government-sponsored, was at its highest numbers. In September enemy bombardment in ports and submarine activity as well as difficulty of securing places on ships and the necessary paperwork and the assembling of convoys, was making departure dates difficult to know. In the second week of September the Tuxedo Committee was informed that no children would sail until the end of September and even that was doubtful. But on September 25th when they were only half ready, Mrs. Sonne was informed that the children would arrive in a week. However, they didn't arrive even then and the Committee learned of the sinking of the *City of Benares*. They were told first that their expected children were in the same convoy and still at sea and later that their ship had returned to port for repairs. On board the same ship they sailed again and on October 4 word arrived that the children had arrived safely in Canada.

The *Empress of Australia* docked in Halifax and the children spent several nights in Montreal. Fiona wrote me that as they boarded the train to New York: "The good ladies of Montreal presented each of us with a small bag of necessities, soap, wash cloth, pad and pencil, toothbrush, candy, comb, small toy, etc. I remember feeling guilty in accepting such kindness, for we hadn't crawled out from under mountains of rubble, our home in ruins, but were from Cumberland and had never heard an air raid siren. We each had a large trunk of pretty clothes and everything we could possibly want. Our only war experience was 'helping' our parents dig a hole in the woods for an Anderson shelter. A good place for playing houses except it did fill up with water." It was not until they reached the great marble hall of Grand Central station that they met the other children who would be their family the next three and a half years. They had medical examinations at the Edwin Gould Foundation where the Actor's Orphanage (see next chapter) were to spend the war years. Cars were then organized to take the children to Tuxedo Park. Wedged in the back of Mrs. Sonne's car Fiona fell asleep but forty miles later the cars slowed. The nine-year-old awoke, she says, as the Park police waved Mr. Sonne through the great stone gates. She recalls the roads twisting off through the trees with glimpses of the occasional house in the distance. Skirting the lake and up through the woods they arrived at a large mock Cotswold Manor House. Two huge flags hung in the lower hall — the Stars and Stripes, the Union Jack and some polo sticks, also a stuffed tortoise. Dashing through the drawing room French windows the children all clambered onto a huge granite boulder at the end of the lawn from which they could see for miles in all directions.

Mrs. Sonne thought that the children looked tired and thin but showed truly remarkable composure and few signs of homesickness and had ravenous appetites.

Over the war years "the English children," as they became known, did everything the Tuxedo Park children did, with swimming and sailing in summer and skating and sledding in winter. "We spent long days exploring and playing in the woods — with no boundaries — we could go as far as we liked." They did what most of us evacuees did, learned American history and how to play American games like baseball, broadcast to their parents or were broadcast to, adjusted to American schools, and adopted with varying degrees American accents. They were taken to the circus at Madison Square Garden and even learned for air defense purposes how to identify silhouettes of German planes. They also wrote weekly letters home and some learned a poem a week. Jill Sieveking, who now lives in Ireland, says, 'The Children's House committee and other Tuxedo Park residents were unbelievably generous.'

The children were fitted into the private school in the Park run by Mr. and Mrs. Arthur Eneboe. The Eneboes took over the school in 1914. It had been founded in 1900 to provide the best elementary education for the children of the Park. According to Mrs. Sonne: "They took a great deal of personal trouble to bring the children's scholarship up to the highest level of their school." Once they caught up they did very well and were awarded many prizes.

The children walked about two miles to school every day. "On arrival at school we would visit each classroom, curtsy and wish the teacher good morning. In fact, we always curtsied when shaking hands with grown ups and I felt rather awkward not doing so on our return to England." Fiona and her sister were both in the same grade. They had never been to school but had lessons with a governess at home. "The most surprising things happened during our first lesson Miss Van Vlack, the teacher, asked the children a question but nobody answered. They sat quite silently but some put their arms in the air. I could not understand it. What were they doing?"

Fiona Ross, nine, and Margaret Ross, eight.

Carol and Hans Sonne with their children, Sheila, Sophia (Fifi), Carol and Christian.

The children inside the house.

A HARVEST OF FRIENDSHIPS

Every Christmas their little school in the Park put on a musical nativity play. Heading the cast was Jill Sieveking as Joseph and Fifi Sonne as Mary.

Outside the Park gates by the railway station was a drug store and a post office and shops. Local stores gave large discounts of 15 to 20 percent all the years the children were there and doctors and dentists all donated their services. The children also enjoyed visiting the library for which "Mrs Alfred Lee Loomis worked tirelessly and enthusiastically, serving on a board of trustees from 1919–1940 and raising a large endowment fund. She was fluent in classical Greek which she read for pleasure."

From Children's House the woods stretched for miles in all directions. In winter they sledded and also skated on the little lake where a section of the ice was always smooth and prepared and changed in a log cabin on the shore where if you had enough pocket money hot chocolate could be bought. The Skater's Waltz and other suitable music played from a wooden tower. Brightly painted kitchen chairs on runners were there for propping yourself up or giving a friend a ride. They spent happy days prospecting fast tracks for their own flexi-flier sleds and banking up the corners with ice where necessary. They explored in all directions searching for caves with traces of Indians' fires or bears. "In all our three and a half years at Children's House I never once remember anyone saying 'Don't go there'." In summer they swam every day in the Club pool. There were no private pools in the Park and no swimming in the lake as it was a reservoir, which was why the Sonnes had an electric launch. Built in 1907, it was a rare survival from Tuxedo's Edwardian beginnings. The children sat in basket chairs under striped awning, cruising silently round the lake; the Stars and Stripes fluttering at the stern.

Most evenings after supper they sang their way through the *Oxford Songbook* with the addition of some patriotic numbers (There's always be an England, The King is still in London, the Road to Mandalay, Gilbert and Sullivan etc., etc.)

On the radio they heard the young Frank Sinatra interrupted by "Lucky Strike means fine tobacco; so round, so firm, so fully packed; so free and easy on the draw." The children went occasionally to the theatre and Fiona calls 'Life with Father' the best, and also visited the New York World's Fair where apparently Gregory Peck was selling balloons at the gate, but they missed him "One movie we were not allowed to see was *Mrs. Miniver*, for fear it would make us homesick. I think that no one's mother looked like Greer Garson."

The Sonne's gardener was a Scotsman called Macdonald. "When Maggie and I had outgrown our 'Ross' kilts, I remember feeling a twinge of clan loyalty when they were given to the gardener's daughters." Between Children's House and the Sonnes was "The Farm," a picturesque range of half-timbered stables and stores with a gardener's cottage, all painted pale blue and white. A duck pond and an overgrown garden with Mulberry trees and box hedges was where they grew vegetables and squashed Colorado beetles. Not far away were Mrs. Wagstaff's kennels. "She bred chows and we were fascinated to find that the dogs had a maid, a kitchen and a fridge full of delicious mince." A frequent visitor to Children's House was old Mrs. Spedden. She would tell the children's age by looking at their teeth — "just like a horse." She and her husband with their small son had been on the *Titanic*. All survived but shortly afterwards the boy was killed riding a tricycle in New York.

Early on it was clear to the committee that Children's House should not be seen as a clearing house but as a home. The arrangement was working well for the eleven children there but the committee was aware that there had been unhappiness in some foster homes who had not thought through fully all that was entailed. The financial support for Children's House had remained firm and those who had pledged money were happy with this suggestion and there were generous gifts of money to cover costs of schooling.

My first interchange with one of these "English Children" was in 2004 when I was completing *See You After the Duration*. While gathering information I heard from Tony Robinson. He told me that he and his wife celebrated their fortieth wedding anniversary in 1998 by a trip to the United States to visit each other other's childhood homes. He wrote to the school which he attended — I did not know then it was at Tuxedo Park — and with their help organized a reunion. After fifty-five years he was able to recall seventeen children who had been at that time in the "Children's House" and to track down nine of them; seven came to the reunion, including one from Italy and two from Australia. The school, he told me, also did their part and had traced and collected about a dozen of their old schoolmates from all over the United States. "We had a wonderful weekend and the *New York Times* gave us almost two full pages including two or three pictures, with the headline, 'Revisiting a World War II refuge — seven sent from Britain as Children return to their Haven.'" Reporter Charles Strum wrote, (October 11, 1998): "If there are soul-deep scars from being sent away by their families to cross the submarine-infested North Atlantic on their own, they do not show. In Tuxedo Park, they say, life was safe and good, and perhaps most important, normal."

A HARVEST OF FRIENDSHIPS

Peggy Gibson, Tony Robinson's sister, wrote me to say that "apart from an understandable amount of homesickness," they had settled in well into their new environment. "We were really like a big extended family. We attended the local school, and a couple of the older children went away to boarding school. We were cared for by some really dedicated 'house mothers.'" She remembers extracurricular activities such as nature club, geology club and listing birds, and participating in the *Time* magazine current affairs competition. It was "an enriching experience" and "a beautiful place to live."

To Jill Sieveking her schooldays at Tuxedo Park School were "the happiest of my school life" and "my years in 'Children's House' were also very happy."

In an interview in the *New Yorker* in February 1944 Mrs. Sonne said that by that time the Committee had cared for thirty children. Despite rising costs the people who pledged money had fulfilled their pledges 100 percent. Though the cost of feeding the children had grown they had been able to keep costs steady at just under a thousand dollars a year per child. "The neighborhood stores have given us a large discount on everything we buy, and doctors and dentists have contributed their services free of charge."

She was able to report that throughout the stay of more than three and-a-half years, and even the first winter "there were no epidemics or children's diseases such as measles and mumps. Only one tonsillectomy and one appendectomy required hospitalization, as well as a few days for minor illnesses." This was, she said, "truly a remarkable record."

By that time some of the children had gone home, particularly a few older boys who had joined the forces and travelled on a Royal Navy escort carriers as my brother and I did the following year.

Nearly seventy years later the evacuees are very conscious of the care given by their hosts and by those who helped run "Children's House."

"What selfless good women they were with never an ounce of favoritism shown to any of us, just lots of love. And they didn't fuss. We spent long days exploring and playing in the woods — with no boundaries — we could go as far as we liked." Jill Sieveking says, "Our housemothers were always impartial, they never tried to supplant our parents in our affections." In general the Children's House and staff tried to prepare the children for the post-war situation in England. "The children made their beds, set and waited on tables, worked in the kitchen and garden and walked to school." Indeed one mother mentioned that after the war when her daughters discovered a shortage of staff at a hotel at which they were temporarily staying, "they volunteered to make their beds and clean their room."

"It was a difficult situation for them," said Tony Robinson. "They didn't want to take the place of our parents and it wasn't a boarding school. They made sure we maintained a relationship with our parents, we wrote to them, we talked about them." Even so, in 1944 when most of them learned they would be returning to England on the Cunard ship *Mauretania,* some wept at the prospect of departure. This was an experience shared by many of the younger evacuees in other places as their host parents had become more real to them than their own.

In 2013 Peggy Gibson wrote me from Australia, "We were shown extraordinary kindness, for which I shall always be grateful." Mrs. Sonne records in her report that when the children returned home their parents remarked on their poise and independence which helped them readjust to their life in England.

Children's House adds yet another aspect to Tuxedo Park's unusual history.

CHAPTER SEVEN

JUST A LITTLE DETOUR

THIS IS THE ONLY HOME MANY OF THEM CAN REALLY REMEMBER. THEIR FRIENDS ARE HERE, THEIR SCHOOL LIFE AND THEIR GAMES ARE HERE. NEW YORK THEY KNOW NOW, EVERY NOOK AND CRANNY OF IT. BUT LONDON IS ONLY A NAME.

—*Evening Standard,* London

One group of evacuees who set off to live on one side of the United States found themselves instead living on the other. They were the boys and girls from the Actors' Orphanage at Silverlands in Chertsey, Surrey, who went together to the United States. Granville Bantock was one of them.

In the twenties his father, Leedham Bantock was a popular actor and comedian and later general manager of the Lyceum Theatre, and his uncle Granville, after whom he was named, was a well-known composer. Leedham Bantock died in 1928.

In his memoir, *Lucky Orphan,* Granville pictures the situation in 1940 after Dunkirk with classes as usual and Spitfires flying overhead, with signposts removed and pill boxes springing up all around. No air-raid shelters were built but mattresses were put down in the cellars and all the children were ushered down when planes could be heard: "We would be glued to the wireless set but it was all terrible news.... We were in despair but at least we had saved our army; the miracle of small boats and their crews braving the English Channel, Great Britain was now alone. My brother had joined the RAF but there was just a tiny pleasure — I heard my uncle Granville on the wireless, presenting a program of the national anthems of all the Allies."

Into this already alarming milieu came a startling announcement. In July the Silverlands School was gathered in the assembly room to be addressed by members of the Actors' Orphanage Committee. Peter Jackson, the secretary, announced, "Noel Coward and the committee consider it advisable that all the children under the age of fifteen be evacuated to Hollywood in California. We have written to all your parents and guardians to seek their consent. Noel Coward is on his way to Hollywood to make all the arrangements." Coward was president of the Actors' Orphanage.

A London newspaper published a big photograph of the excited children. Granville was as excited as the others and cycled home to his mother and learned that she and her uncle had decided that he should go. Parents of ten children declined the opportunity and ten were too old to go, leaving fifty-four to travel. By early August they were told that the evacuation was definitely on and that they were going to Hollywood as soon as travel arrangements could be made. "In the meantime a farewell dinner was organized for parents and guardians to which came his mother, brother and many others. It was the largest gathering ever at Silverlands. Many committee members came to mingle with parents, to give assurances that the California sunshine was just what we needed. After the fond farewells, the parents left. Now it was just a case of waiting."

On September 10, packed and ready, issued with passports, name labels and gas masks, the children were assembled and told they would be leaving for Liverpool the next day. But then the departure was postponed. Five days later they left in coaches (buses) for Euston station, this time their destination would be Greenock on the Clyde. As they left they could hear guns and bombs and planes overhead. It was, as they discovered later, the last day of the Battle of Britain. The boy sitting next to Granville remarked, "We'll never get to Euston, let alone Hollywood."

The next day they and other evacuee children boarded the liner, the *Empress of Australia*. Most of the other passengers were sick and wounded Canadian soldiers returning home. The ship had been underway for about an hour but suddenly stopped and proceeded back to her berth. An antimagnetic mine cable was not working and needed repair. It took several days by which time the news had broken that the *City of Benares* had been sunk with many evacuees killed. It had left from Liverpool. Glanville writes, "Had we left Silverlands on the scheduled date we might have been on board this liner. Our parents were, at the time, very worried indeed having no means of knowing that we were not on board." They left on September 26 and because it was a private evacuation the ship could travel unescorted.

The children are excited to be going to Hollywood.

HMT Aquitania arrives arriving back in Southampton in September 1945 on the sixth anniversary of the start of the war.

From Halifax the party took the train to Montreal where a surprise awaited them. Bantock recalls: "We were all very excited about the long train journey to California, but then the bombshell dropped: Peter Jackson announced after breakfast that there was to be a change of plan. We would be going to New York instead of Hollywood. There were sighs and moans of disappointment. I think this had been arranged before we left England, but not divulged in case parents withdrew their children from evacuation."

When they arrived at the Edwin Gould Foundation in the New York Bronx, with visions of sunny California, the Foundation buildings were a disappointment and there seemed at first to be little play area. "But soon realizing we were away from the food rationing, blackout and bombs of the war, we quickly settled in, grateful for now being guests of the United States. Going from a blacked out England to a New York ablaze with light was an incredible experience, as were the generous, kind people all round who helped us. We were, of course, very worried about our families back home facing the mighty German army poised across the Channel."

Philanthropist Edwin Gould had established the Foundation to care for American children but during the war it hosted various groups of English children, sometimes as a staging post and in the case of the Actors' Orphanage as their permanent home. They had been allocated one large building, divided into three "cottages," one for boys, one for girls and the other for the very young boys and girls. The Foundation was well equipped with medical and dental facilities, including a sanatorium and within days of arrival they had to undergo thorough medical and dental examinations.

It came time to go to school. Twenty or so of the older boys and girls, like Granville, some just under fifteen and some a little older, were to attend a nearby high school. The Foundation bus driver made sure they were all comfortable before they set off "on the wrong side of the road." They drew up at a huge building and all remained seated thinking they would be moving on. The driver in his best Bronx accent said, "'Youse kids, this is Columbus High School — they teach thousands of stoodents in there." It was a shock. They had just come from an English country house surrounded by green fields, woods and only seventy pupils, and were now facing a factory-like building surrounded by suburbia and containing thousands of pupils. They had been used to classes of twelve or so but here were classes of thirty-five, each with a considerable ethnic mix.

The school principal gave them a warm welcome and told them the staff and students knew of their arrival and would help in any way they could. First they had to go to a "home class" to sort out curriculum — which took all day.

Compulsory subjects were now maths, English, another language, American history and civic studies, but necessary points for graduation could be made up by taking other subjects. Granville chose music, craft arts and geography. "The geography was okay but the arts crafts and music later proved to be a bad decision." (Apparently after two years he still couldn't sing and he made just three rabbits from his lump of clay). They learned that teachers remained in their classroom all day and students came for their lessons. "It was incredible; a bell would ring and thousands of students had just four minutes to get to their next lessons. There were one-way corridors, up stairways, down stairways and plenty of toilets. It all worked like clockwork." The day would start with a visit to the home class before assembly which took place in a huge concert type all complete with stage. He remembers vividly his first full school day. "It was traumatic: outnumbered by thousands, England at war, America at peace, and totally lost in the huge crowd of students, there were twenty English children." They marched in to their first homeroom to Land of Hope and Glory. Granville thought at first it was a gesture to the English kids. Not so, he quickly learned from the boy sitting next to him who exclaimed; "It's the finest American patriotic song ever written." After the Pledge of Allegiance they went on to sing God Bless America and listen to readings from the Gettysburg address. "With such a broad mix of ethnic students, engendering patriotic enthusiasms was essential."

They only had to say two words to be immediately recognized as "Limeys." Several of the English boys were still in short trousers which was even worse: "Where's the other half of yer pants?" the American children would exclaim. At Granville's first history class he was introduced to the teacher. She was of Irish extraction. For what seemed to him an age she delivered a tirade of abuse about Britain and the British. When Granville didn't answer back a girl next to him stood up and told the teacher to shut up or she would take the matter up with the principal. The teacher then apologized.

His first English class was entirely different. Again he introduced himself to the teacher. After a while she said, "Class, we are extremely fortunate to have one of the English boys join us — please stand up Granville." There was a chorus of "Hi, Granville." Then she said, "I'm going to ask him to read a page from this book, please come up here Granville." He was acutely shy; he had never done this at Silverlands. There were thirty-five strange faces staring at him. He read out the whole page and when he had finished she asked him to sit down, saying, "Thank you, we all enjoyed that. Now class," she continued, "before Christmas I want every single one of you to speak just like that, with no slurring — just good, solid English." A boy at the back immediately stood up. "Please, teacher," he said, "I didn't understand a single word." It became a weekly event for the students really did like to hear him speak.

Granville sat next to a Japanese boy and they became close friends, only to have him suddenly disappear from the school a year later just before the Pearl Harbor attack by the Japanese when America entered the war. He had a difficult name so he became Mick to Granville.

Not long after arriving at the Foundation Granville received a letter from Hollywood. It was from actress Dame May Whitty introducing herself as his sponsor but saying it would be impossible for her to travel to New York to see him. Instead she asked her daughter, Margaret Webster, a theatrical producer involved with the Shakespeare Foundation in New York, to act for her. The list of Hollywood sponsors for the children included most of the British actors and actresses living in California and they would visit the children at the Foundation whenever they were in New York. Charlie Chaplin came several times and so did Cary Grant and Douglas Fairbanks. "When Joan Fontaine visited I fell madly in love in spite of her husband Brian Aherne coming with her," says Granville.

Brenda Lorden, another of the students, kept an autograph book containing many of the visitors like Charlie Chaplin, Ronald Colman and Boris Karloff. Gertrude Lawrence wrote in the book that it was wonderful to have the children safe in America with these generous and helpful people, and ended: "There'll always be an England so 'thumbs up'." Brenda was quoted in the *New York Journal American*: "Brenda Lorden, eleven-year-old refugee, likes toys, too, but the one gift she asks for is *Peace*! 'That would be the very best present,' says Brenda. 'Next would be *going home!*'"

Boris Karloff arranged for all the boys and girls to see *Arsenic and Old Lace* in which he was starring and when Chaplin came to New York he had them bussed to a huge cinema to see his latest film *The Great Dictator*. "We were asked to sing 'There'll always be an England'" remembers Granville. "I was a little embarrassed by this but thoroughly enjoyed the film."

Many Americans likewise did what they could to make the evacuees feel at home. A presidential election was underway and the New York World's Fair was in full swing. They were taken to the Fair. "It was fantastic," remembers Granville. "Our hosts showed us the British pavilion — it was heart-warming to see the Union Jack flying and a Spitfire as the main exhibit outsides.... We sat down nearby to listen to Irving Berlin play God Bless America and hand out autographed copies of sheet music. There was popcorn, Coke and ice-cream."

The evacuees enjoyed their first Halloween party and Thanksgiving Day celebration. Granville's sponsor Margaret Webster came to see him before Christmas and asked what present he would like. Without any idea what it would cost he asked for either a camera or a small radio set. She had come to the Foundation with Maurice Evans who was a leading Shakespearean actor on the New York stage. "I was to see one of their productions in the New Year. Whenever actors or actresses sponsoring a child were appearing on the New York stage they would come and see us." He had enjoyed seeing the glamorous ladies who had visited the Orphanage in England and now, at the Foundation, there were even more.

Under the Christmas tree there were three presents for him — a wallet from his mother, a camera from Margaret Webster and a radio set from Dame May Witty. "The Gould Foundation did everything possible to make our Christmas a happy one and I am sure we all appreciated the generosity we were shown."

In his memoirs Granville recalls his first American girl friend. Though I think with his musical family background it was not Mary Ann but the matinee classical concert at Carnegie Hall to which she took him that made the bigger impression. 'Toscanini was conducting the NBC Symphony Orchestra and the main work was Beethoven's Fifth Symphony. At the end I had goose pimples all over and was inwardly shaking and my heart racing. This was it — I was hooked forever. We went to a diner but I couldn't eat; the music would not go away. Mary Ann was quiet too. I was taken back to the Foundation where I rushed to the radio in my room and twiddled the knob hoping to find more Beethoven, but there was only Glenn Miller."

Church attendance was also far more cheerful for him than "the dreary ones at the Silverlands local parish and when we finished, we would all sit down to a sumptuous breakfast." The young ladies in the choir would take some of them on sightseeing trips in the afternoon. Affiliated to the church was a scout group so all the English boys formed into a special "patrol," with the church providing uniforms and other necessary equipment. There were also special scout camps in the summer. "I must have enjoyed it because I still have my Siwanoy camp certificate showing that I passed all the tests."

The Orphanage boys even formed a baseball team, which held its own in the area and though there were usually a couple of Americans playing they called themselves the British Lions.

In the new year Margaret Webster arranged for Granville to spend a day with her, first at the theatre where she was directing, and then at her apartment, returning again to the theatre for a performance followed by a quiet meal with some of the cast.

Mr. Griffin, principal of the Foundation, had heard that a British warship was under repair in Brooklyn naval dockyard and contacted the ship's captain who immediately invited all fifty-four children on board his ship — the cruiser *Phoebe* — for a real English tea. "It was a welcome taste of home to hear the English voices of the crew as they told their stories, entertaining us and making us feel welcome," says Granville.

Another time Griffin came into the playground and asked if anyone would like to ride in his big Buick. Ten pupils squeezed inside and he drove them to Pelham Sound and there, anchored a short way off, was a large merchant ship flying the Red Ensign. "I thought you'd like to see the flag," he said.

On one occasion his older brother, Paul, who was training with the RAF in Canada was able to pay a visit.

In May 1940 the children staged a musical revue called "Gratefully Yours" at New York's Imperial Theatre as "an expression of thanks for American hospitality." A large part of the enthusiastic audience were local children. The *New York Herald Tribune* reported that the "intimate revue" in eleven scenes received the ultimate American acclaim from 500 tenement children. "Their performance was greeted by a double-barrelled, royal Delancey Street salute, better known as the two-finger whistle.... From the opening chorus: 'California Here I Come' to the final singing of 'God Save the King' and 'My Country 'Tis of Thee' the show was a success." Proceeds went to the American Theatre Wing War Service and the British and American Ambulance Corps. The review was directed by Constance Collier, an English actress in New York at the time, Mrs. Cahan, daughter of Gertrude Lawrence, and Mrs. Chase of the Gould Foundation.

Another evacuee who was in the show was Hugo Bergström whose parents had been opera singers with Sadler's Wells. His mother had died when he was two and, with his father on tour, he entered the Actor's Orphanage when he was six and a half. He and Pete Gifford performed a Pearly King number: "The show was our way of thanking the American actors and actresses for all their help in enabling our orphanage to come to America." He was officially sponsored by Lynn Fontanne and it was due to this show that he was also able to get to know two people who treated him with great kindness, Gertrude Lawrence and Paul Robeson." Gertrude Lawrence was "a real sweet lady." There was one time when he had the best seat in the house on Broadway when she was playing the lead role in *Lady in the Dark*. "After the show she took me out to dinner with some of her friends

Chaplin and other actors signed Brenda's autograph book.

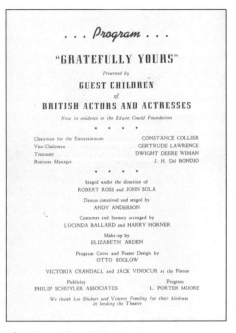

Theater announcement.

27 Young British Blitz "Exiles" Returning with Revolutionary Ideas

BRINGING AMERICAN OUTLOOK TO LONDON

From F. G. A. COOK, *Evening Standard* Correspondent
NEW YORK, Wednesday.

Twenty-seven British children who came to the United States at the time of the 1940 raids, when the Silverlands School at Chertsey, Surrey, was evacuated, will be returning home shortly. And they are bringing some shocks with them for parents who probably do not realise what four years and America have done for them.

Little girls who were eleven when they said "Good-bye" with sticky fingers and their hair in pigtails are completely self-assured young misses to-day, with fashionable "hairdos" and well out clothes. ... nine or so when they left home, man... ...young footballers at the 40 club. I must admit I felt quite important sitting next to her

In an unpublished memoir Hugo writes of Paul Robeson, "Now there was a big man in every sense of the word, and for that matter so was his chauffeur Joe who on several occasions collected me in a huge limousine to take me to Mr. Robeson's house. I guess Joe was pretty highly regarded because besides driving Mr. Robeson around, he was also his friend and bodyguard. Once he took me to a baseball game between the New York Yankees and the Brooklyn Dodgers. Cripes! Never have I seen so many raving mad people, gathered together in one place. They kept shouting and screaming, not only at the umpires and players, but also at each other. Of course all these well-informed supporters regarded the outcome of this local Derby as a matter of life and death, in which case I guess their behavior is not wholly inexcusable. The game was terrific, but crowds give me the creeps and are not my cup of tea. I can still see Mr. Paul Robeson in his flowing robes, starring as Othello with Gertrude Lawrence as the leading lady. Yessiree, they were two might good people."

Granville says, "We were so very fortunate, with kind and generous Americans everywhere and New York appearing to be so safe. We were allowed to go anywhere, and we could, for just a nickel ride on the elevated railway."

In 1942 he heard that his brother Paul who was in the RAF had been killed on special fight operations and he fell into a black depression "which seemed to last forever." It began to lift when heard that his cousin, Leslie, who was serving in the Royal Navy on the cruiser HMS *Manchester* which had put into Philadelphia for repairs and was able to visit him.

Mr. Griffin, knowing that Granville was depressed, arranged for him to spend the Easter weekend in Washington, D.C. with Colonel Henry Breckinridge, a senior politician and friend of President Roosevelt who was involved with the committee responsible for the care of evacuated European children. He was also a close friend of and later married Miss Smith, who was a "housemother" to the girls at the Foundation. They were also going to stay with his friends, the Vances. Granville was thrilled with the sights of Washington, D.C. which he photographed and they had lunch in the city: "Just after leaving the restaurant, whilst walking back to the car, Colonel Breckinridge spotted someone walking towards us, a lady he said I should meet. He introduced the lady as Eleanor and me as Granville from England. We shook hands and she spoke to me for a while. I could hardly believe that I had just shaken hands with Eleanor Roosevelt. It was to be an incredible day." At dinner he sat next to Mrs. Vance who asked him if he would like to spend the summer holiday on a farm near Washington.

With arrangements made Colonel Breckinridge arrived at The Foundation to pick him up and after getting him outfitted in farm clothes, jeans and a multi-colored shirt, took him to the Canby Farm and said goodbye. "He was a truly great America who had shown me kindness and generosity never to be forgotten."

Granville enjoyed every minute at the farm, the food, helping with the jobs in hand, either pulling corn or haymaking or gathering tomatoes and other vegetables. Their son Tom and he would collect wild grapes from vines near the river, taking them to the Washington market whenever Mr. Canby set up a stall. "In addition to providing my keep, Mr. Canby gave me a small allowance which was most generous considering how much I ate." Mrs. Canby was "delightful," making him cups of tea throughout the day believing that the English would not survive without gallons of it. "The weather was always hot and whenever the family took a break they guzzled ice cold Coke whilst I sipped hot tea. After a while I convinced Mrs. Canby that I really did like Coke and that I could survive perfectly well without tea."

August 1942 was nearly over and he was hoping the holiday would never end. "I would like to have stayed on the farm for ever as they were such a pleasant family."

The older boys, like him, started to go home to England the following year. They had to return for military service which in his case was to last four years. His first sight of the ship on which he was to return was not reassuring: "I walked up a gangway and thought we were boarding the tug which was to take us to the liner, but this was not so. This was the MV *Thorstrand*, 2350 tons which was to take us to Liverpool. I was shaken; I would have thought twice before crossing from Portsmouth to the Isle of Wight on this boat."

Granville concludes his American memoirs, 'The ship slipped her moorings and proceeded down river to the sea. Slowly the New York skyline disappeared and I fought back the tears. It was October 4 1942, two years to the day since the Actor's Orphanage children landed in Canada and now, once again, 3000 miles of very hostile Atlantic Ocean lay ahead. I loved America. Thank you, Uncle Sam."

Private Bantock was soon into army basic training and was posted to an infantry battalion preparing for D-day and then to The Highland Fieldcraft Training Centre in. Scotland and then went on to serve in Calcutta and Singapore and, as a captain in the Queen's Royal Regiment, to take part in the Victory Parade in Bangkok with Lord Louis Mountbatten and King

Ananda of Siam taking the salute. It was there while supervising Japanese prisoners he met Mick from the Christopher Columbus High School who had been serving in the Japanese signal corps. He became Granville's interpreter.

With the latest Box Brownie camera presented to Granville in New York by Margaret Webster and then with a Univex 35 mm camera which had been issued to his brother in the RAF, he was able to record much of his war. "The Battle of Britain and the bombs, two wartime Atlantic crossings and four years in the army. I had got away with it and had been especially fortunate to have secured a commission and the privilege that went with it. My brother David had served in the army fighting the Germans and I had served four years not fighting. I just had to be a LUCKY ORPHAN — in spite of going down with Malaria at the very end." Captain Bantock was demobbed in early 1947.

He wrote in 1993, "For me, the American experience will always be remembered with considerable affection…. the New York High School with six thousand students. Theatrical people visiting us at our 'residential home' in The Bronx and generous Americans with invitations to their homes… I will always remember the two summer holidays, the first at a camp on Long Island, unpolluted sea and sand, it was taken for granted that it would stay the same for ever…and the second holiday on a farm in Maryland with the loveable Canby family with whom I have kept in touch these fifty years."

In early 1945, F.G.A. Cook, the correspondent of the London *Evening Standard*, visited the remaining children at the Foundation. By then nearly half of the original evacuees had already returned home. His article appeared under the headlines "Bringing American Outlook to Britain" and "27 Young British Blitz 'Exiles' Returning with Revolutionary Ideas." Reporting that they would be home shortly, he wrote, "They are bringing shocks with them for parents who probably do not realize what four years and America have done for them." He also said that he would not be a truthful reporter if he did not straight away warn their parents that not all of them are in the least enthusiastic about the idea of going home. "It is not that they have forgotten mummy and daddy. But this is the only home many of them can really remember. Their friends are here, their school life and their games are here. New York they know now, every nook and cranny of it. But London is only a name." Brenda Lorden, quoted earlier, was one of those interviewed by Cook. She was certain she wanted to stay in America. "I want to go through college here," she said decisively. "Then I want to study fashion design and make my career here. I think there is a bigger future for

Granville and Brenda were married at the end of the war.

HMS Sheffield.

me here in New York. And some day I would like to marry an American. If my husband was a business man and making a lot of money, perhaps we could." At that point her sense of humor got the better of fourteen-year-old Ursula Weait. She interrupted her friend, 'Oh, Brenda, aren't you going kind of fast.'" Apparently she was, as five years later she married Granville Bantock and they have celebrated their diamond wedding.

Hugo Bergström, being younger than Granville, was one of the group who returned later to Britain. It was in the last days of the war in Europe. He was three days out from Boston on HMS *Sheffield* which had been refitted there and was desperately seasick. "I was the most miserable boy on earth. Lying back in my hammock, I tried to forget the revolting stench that exuded from the engines and galley and the never-ceasing sway of every damn thing. I remember shutting my eyes tightly and forced to myself to think of people I would never see again." He thought of an Italian-American boy who befriended him in his first days at school. "He was the guy that educated me in how to survive alone in the Bronx, and also to travel with reasonable safety on the New York subway." He thought of two American boys he would surely miss and only one English boy he would. There was "dear old Monty," Miss Montgomery, one "sure dedicated teacher" for whom he had great respect. "Probably for the first time in my life I really contemplated and thought of all the actors and actresses who had visited the Gould Foundation over the years. My mind flitted over most of them, because like a ship that passes by in the night, the fleeting moments of my personal involvement meant very little. Lying down in my swaying hammock I began to realize that all these people were important and helped us in our hour of need. Fame and fortune in the theatrical world had never meant much to me, but it's a good thing that there are those who succeed in these two respects. They are the people who are in a position to be able to help the offspring of the more unfortunate sons and daughters from the world of entertainment."

CHAPTER EIGHT

TEA AT THE
WHITE HOUSE

MY FATHER TOOK ON AN ENTIRE NURSERY OF FIFTEEN CHILDREN
AND THEIR TEACHERS, RENTED A LARGE COUNTRY HOUSE NEAR
WARRENTON, VIRGINIA, FURNISHED IT HASTILY, AND LODGED THEM
FOR THE DURATION OF THE WAR.

—Katharine Graham

A further group of evacuees who found themselves transported to another
world, albeit for a shorter time and most of them much younger than we were,
travelled out in August 1940 on the same ship we did, the *Duchess of York.*

Their story was told by Angela Pelham in a book *The Young Ambassadors*
and later became a BBC Radio 4 play. Many years later the author's niece,
Hermione Ravenscroft, wrote up the story in the *Times Educational Supplement*
commenting that "despite their relatively well-heeled backgrounds, the
children were overwhelmed by their opulent new surroundings: refrigerators,
big car, no rationing. Their experience was not that of the typical refugee
child." Her online article which first caught my eye is headed: "The cook, the
laundress, the maid and the aunts (plus twelve refugees)."

In *See You After the Duration*, I quoted from *The Young Ambassadors* not
realizing that Angela Pelham was a pseudonym for Barbara Ravenscroft and
the book a fictionalized story. I liked it as I found it acute in its observations
and reflected my own reactions and those of many evacuees I have talked
with. I particularly enjoyed Angela's quote from a letter home: "The radio
in this country is strange to us, each program is advertising something and
a man will suddenly interrupt a lovely piece of music and gabble off about
soap or cigarettes, but on Sunday the Ford Symphony Orchestra plays some

really good stuff which we all enjoy listening to, and I am sure you will never believe it but Carter's Little Liver Pills do a most exciting mystery play, real blood and thunder, and then at the end a man says, 'Are you sluggish or constipated, do you need two-way relief, etc.'" My memories are not that precise but I can still quote, with the appropriate accent, "This is Jack Armstrong, the all-American boy brought to you by the makers of Wheaties, breakfast of champions."

The true story is that a group of young children whose parents were mostly stationed overseas were boarding in 1939 with their respective thirty-year-old aunts on a farm in Sussex. It was obviously not the ideal place to be and so they moved to Devon, just in time, three weeks later, to be bombed out. The U.S. military attaché, whose daughter spent summers at the farm, had been looking for ways to get them to America and persuaded Eugene Meyer, a banker and owner of the *The Washington Post*, to be their sponsor. Hermione's Auntie Bee, and Aunt Amanda, Christopher Leaver, his older sister Gillian, his cousin Bob Hicks, and nine other children aged between twenty months and twelve years "swapped their gasmasks for lifejackets" and sailed for Halifax. This was the port of destination for almost all ships with children, before they went on to the United States, Australia, New Zealand as well as all parts of Canada.

As Katharine Graham, Eugene Meyer's daughter wrote in her *Personal History*, "By this time, as the war in Europe went on escalating, English children were pouring into the United States to seek refuge from the falling bombs. My father took on an entire nursery of fifteen children and their teachers, rented a large country house near Warrenton, Virginia, furnished it hastily, and lodged them for the duration of the war. It was called Clover Croft School."

Hermione Ravenscroft writes, "The Clover Croft children, a self-contained group of twelve 'little refugees' with a high profile sponsor, became instant celebrities. Meyer had furnished the rented house in the Blue Ridge Mountain town down to the last doll and tricycle and hired a cook, laundress and maid."

Being so close to Washington, D.C. and a focus of interest as well as being so well connected, they were taken on occasions to the capital. Gillian Leaver (later Kelly) recalls, "We had a wonderful Easter tea at the White House, with Eleanor Roosevelt as our hostess. We were each given a magnificent sugar egg with a different picture inside. I have a clear memory of my father, who was a naval doctor, coming in on his ship to Washington and Christopher and I were brought up to Washington to meet him and there was much press coverage.

We were even on the *Pathé News* in England and my mother, who was an ambulance driver, went to watch us at the cinema."

Virginian Richard Gookin filled me in on the house "a country place that has been in my wife's family for several generations." In 1940 it belonged to his wife's uncle, the late Baldwin Day Spilman, Jr., who lent it "for the purpose of sheltering English children."

"We live on the adjoining property, again a family house, known as The Oaks, built by my wife's uncle and aunt, the Rev. and Mrs. Paul Bowden who lived here until her death in 1994. The Bowdens took a great interest in the children next door and were kind to them while here and on their return to England."

Warrenton was visited by many personalities including the British ambassador, Lord Lothian, who was the children's legal guardian, as all of us British evacuees were, and the Duke and Duchess of Windsor. Lothian came several times before he died unexpectedly in December 1940. A December 13 tribute in *The Washington Post* was headed "Lord Lothian as America knew him." It was above a huge photograph of him sitting on the grass with the English children captioned: "In September just before the leaves of fall came tumbling down, Lord Lothian sat on the lawn at Clover Croft, an estate in the Virginia Hills not far from Warrenton, and talked about America to these young subjects of the King of England. Safe from the Battle of Britain and happy in their new surroundings, the children were glad, too, because their visitor was a Briton." The aunt remembers the ambassador saying how fine it was to have a little colony of young English children in Virginia and they were all as much ambassadors as he was. This was the source of the idea for the book title, *The Young Ambassadors*. In the book one of the children comments, "A very funny thing happened at tea which we are going to tease the aunts about because you know how fussy they are about our manners. Well! When Lord Lothian sat down he pulled up another chair and put his feet up and had his tea like that, so this afternoon we are all going to put our feet up and say it must be all right as the British Ambassador does it."

When the Duke and Duchess of Windsor came to Washington in October 1941, just before America entered the war, she wanted to see old friends in Warrenton, for that was where she had lived in 1925–6 when she was getting her divorce from her first husband, Win Spencer. This had required a year's residence in the United States. "My first year at Warrenton," she wrote, "was the most tranquil I have ever known. I simply rusticated and when I wasn't rusticating I vegetated with equal satisfaction." She finally got the divorce in 1927 in Warrenton's Fauquier County District Court.

WASHINGTON POST

British ambassador Lord Lothian meets the evacuee children.

Bland (Greene) from a Warrenton family that was also hospitable to the English children, takes tea with Jeremy, Willow, Betty and Christopher.

MRS. RICHARD GOOKIN

MRS. RICHARD GOOKIN

The Duke and Duchess of Windsor visit Clover Croft in 1941.

A HARVEST OF FRIENDSHIPS

The newsletter editor of the Fauquier Historical Society, John Toler, wrote in 2000, "Wallis loved Warrington and Warrington loved Wallis, for a more personable girl never lived. She was universally popular with both sexes and certainly 'the last word' in smartness of attire and neatness."

Gillian remembers the royal visit as there was 'such a to-do and they all had to look their best' and Bob Hicks because "I remember the practice in bowing and curtseying we all went through."

Meyer insisted on the school-age children attending the local school. He believed that at that stage that the children's "parents would be down to rock bottom by the end of the war, and they must get those swell ideas out of their heads now."

The Japanese attack on December 7, 1941 and its aftermath contributed to one of Bob Hicks' clearest images of Clover Croft. He had been one of the children and emailed me from the Olympic Peninsula where he now lives, "Having experienced air raids in Somerset before leaving, I remember going outside, looking up and wondering where the Japanese planes were. Of course, I had no idea where Hawaii was."

The Gookins still have some of "the charming letters written to the Bowdens from the children and their governesses in 1943 and 1944 when they had returned to England and have the original photos taken with the Duke and Duchess and clippings about their visit." His wife's aunt, Mrs. Harry Pool, is pictured with the Duchess, a long-time friend from the time when they were at school together in Baltimore.

In 1942, soon after the United States entered the war, Gillian and Christopher's mother took them to join their father in the West Indies; six children came back to England with the aunts who wanted them to share their peers' experiences of rationing and blackouts. The Meyers gave up the house as with gas rationing, and the local doctor called up, hospitals in Washington would be impossible to get into in an emergency and they felt it was too great a responsibility to keep the children there. So the rest of the children were sent to join the Gould Foundation in New York which was already hosting fifty-four children from Britain's Actors' Orphanage (See chapter 7). The Foundation could house 160 children in a number of residential buildings and three of them were occupied by evacuees. Bob remembers learning to swim in their pool.

After five years in the United States, Bob returned to England, as my brother and I did, on a Royal Naval ship, his the cruiser HMS *Sheffield* and ours the escort carrier HMS *Patroller*. In a way, he told me, he was glad that he had not been with an American family: "as I can only imagine how wrenching it would have been to live with them and how strange 'home' would have been."

The returning evacuees, whether they came in 1942 or 1945 had to contend with challenges, the older ones with an interrupted education. Bob was very behind in some subjects and had to be tutored for a year. But his war years had affected later life and attitudes to the extent that it resulted in being sent to the United States in 1957 for an English company that had a thriving export business to North America and meeting and marrying his wife in Chicago. In 1961 he joined an American company, working for them in four states, and retired thirty-seven years later to Washington State near Port Angeles.

Christopher Leaver had the same experience as I did of failing the school common entrance exam for school when he came home. But he did well, becoming a wine merchant and in 1981 Lord Mayor of London and was knighted. Being only two and a half when he set sail for America he does not have clear memories of those war years. When he returned to Clover Croft in 1982 Katharine Graham lent her car and chauffeur and "we were accompanied by a lady reporter — never missing a chance for an article in her *Washington Post.*" He was greeted by the present and past owners whose two families had married and found his way straight to his old room. The yellow wall paper had not changed in forty years. His sister Gillian Kelly, two years older, trained as a nurse. Auntie Amanda, when she was ninety-one, remembers: "We missed the American way of life, we had been spoiled," but added that her clearest memory was "how thoroughly glad we were to be home."

The Clovercroft family benefited from a well-connected American host in Katharine Graham's father. Evacuees who faced most difficulties were women who came with their children but without that kind of strong support. For at that point no money could be transferred from Britain.

One London family, Morris and Anne Benjamin and their two children, Pamela, nine, and Valerie, three, were Jewish, and had of course particular concerns as invasion threatened. The Benjamins described themselves as being very left wing. In the late nineteen thirties they had worked to get aid to the Republicans in the Spanish Civil War and then on the eve of World War II were both active in getting Jews out of Austria, Germany and Poland to Britain.

Morris Benjamin was a manufacturing jeweler in Hatton Garden (incidentally his partner was the father of Sir Martin Gilbert whose words appear in the Appendix). When war began his company was converted by the Ministry of Defence to making navigational aids and bombsights. He

Bob Hicks, businessman in Britain and the U.S., and retired to the Olympic Peninsula of Washington State. He is with the Spitfire he assembled.

Sir Christopher Leaver GBE, JP, a wine merchant, as Lord Mayor of London in 1981.

also became an air-raid warden. Anne meanwhile owned two hair dressing salons. Because of his wife's work to rescue Jews Morris said he never knew when he came home how many people would be staying in the house.

After Dunkirk they heard about the possibility of evacuation to the United States. Daughter Pamela had already been evacuated from London to Oxford and the parents looked into what was possible. Anne learned at Grosvenor House that if she wanted to go to the United States and work there she would have to go as an immigrant. The only people she knew in the United States were German refugees but they couldn't sponsor her, and be sponsored. So she was in touch with German refugees she had helped to get away from Germany and whom were now in New York City. Armed with just the refugees' address in New York City they boldly left from Glasgow at the end of July on the RMS *Cameronia*. Theirs was a ship that was not only carrying children and escorts but also Scottish seamen who were going to crew other "Liberty ships" being promised from America. Pamela remembers the sailors entertaining them in the evenings out on deck playing accordions and harmonicas. "Of course in total darkness they could not even have a cigarette because of danger from the enemy."

Pamela Fisher, now eighty-four, described to me how, arriving in New York, her mother hired a taxi and gave the driver the address. When they arrived they knocked on the door and there was no reply. There was no one home. Having no American money on them they could not even pay the taxi. A neighbor came out and asked if they were the expected English family and told them that their friends had gone to "South Bend Indiana." Mrs. Benjamin asked the driver if he would take them to South Bend. "Lady," he said, "That is as far as you have just come from England." He said that he had a friend who had a hotel on the docks and he would take them there and she could give him the money for the fare. "My mother had only been allowed to take £30 from England. The arrival in America was horrible, my courageous mother, what a nightmare!"

They stayed a few days at the hotel and as there was no support available in New York they took a Greyhound bus, which was all they could afford, to Indiana where they knew accommodation was waiting for them. "America was experiencing their worst polio epidemic in history. All public places where people and particularly children could gather were closed." Her mother soon found that finding work was no easy task: "Not because she was Jewish but because there were still many unemployed local people due to the depression." She was informed that she had to have a thousand hours of study to qualify and be a hairdresser in Indiana. The local Jewish Refugee

Aid Committee recommended that this study was necessary, and then gave her a subsistence allowance so that she could do so. "It was hard for my mother but she had no choice. I did not know it at the time but when I went to Sunday school every week I was given an envelope, the money to live on." Anne became a manicurist in a successful salon which allowed her to work sitting down because of the intense heat and humidity in South Bend.

Pamela was enrolled in the local school and Valerie went to a lovely Catholic nursery. "I went to the nursery after school to wait for my mother to collect us when her day's work was finished. I was happy at school, made lots of friends and was quite advanced educationally as the American children start school much later." Because of her English accent she soon found herself being cast in plays.

A newspaper cutting from the *South Bend Tribune* featured the children at Christmas time 1940 under a headline: "Sisters Await Santa Safe from Bombs." Over the years they had to stay in various homes but what they remember most is all the generosity, "When America entered the war in 1941, we became involved in a great many activities to aid the war effort" Pamela also stressed to me, "Neither my mother or I were aware of any anti-Semitism in South Bend."

A photo of the sisters published in the South Bend Tribune, Christmas 1940.

In 1944 when the heavy bombing had more or less ceased in England Pamela's mother thought it was time to return home, particularly as her father was seriously ill. "My mother was also afraid that I would become Americanized." They returned that year on a neutral Portuguese ship the *Serpa Pinto*. From Lisbon they flew home to England arriving back on the 13th of May, her thirteenth birthday. Anne's father died shortly afterwards.

They returned to resume their education in London in time, however, to be threatened by the German V-1 rockets. But by 19th June both their schools had been blasted by V-1 bombs and good friends had been killed. They were taken to the country once again only to learn that the back of their house had been destroyed by another flying bomb. After the war their mother continued voluntary social work with children, in this case inviting the children of the French and Dutch resistance to her home, to help with their rehabilitation.

"Our family was grateful for the way we had survived. My mother's brother was in the Kings Royal Rifle Corps in the 8th Army — and my father's two brothers were also in the army with the youngest serving in flail tanks for the Royal Engineers in the Normandy invasion on D-day Plus 2. And they are grateful to the Americans in South Bend: "They were such wonderful generous people. And now after more than seventy years we are still friends with every generation of their extended families who now live all over the United States. My mother lived to a great age and often recounted her World War II experiences to me."

Pamela Fisher went on to qualify as a speech therapist and later did voluntary work with the League of Jewish Women and, subsequently, the Association of Jewish Friendship Clubs becoming their Senior Vice-President.

CHAPTER NINE

WHAT'S IN
A NAME?

YOU ARE GOING, FOR A LITTLE WHILE, TO A COUNTRY WHERE
EVERY CHILD LEARNS BY HEART AT LEAST ONE OF THE THINGS IN THIS
BOOK: THE WORDS OF *LINCOLN* AT GETTYSBURG. THEY ARE GROWN-
UP WORDS ABOUT A GROWN-UP IDEA. BUT THEY ARE A TOKEN THAT
WE AMERICANS, LIKE YOU, HAVE BEEN *DEDICATED TO THE GREAT TASK*
REMAINING BEFORE US: THAT WE TOO SAY THAT THE THINGS YOUR
FATHERS FOUGHT FOR *SHALL NOT PERISH FROM THE EARTH.*
    —*The Token of Freedom*, compiled by Bruce L. Richmond

Many families drew on their family or business links with Americans
to find homes in the United States for their children. One of the most
unusual initiatives, built on family history, was taken by Kathleen Vassar in
Mitcham, Surrey. After the evacuation of British and French troops from
Dunkirk brought home the danger of invasion she was anxious to send her
daughter Christine to safety.

The family was distantly related to Mathew Vassar, who founded the
well-known Vassar College in Poughkeepsie. They knew that Mathew had
immigrated as a child of four from Norfolk, England, to Poughkeepsie
and had later visited his cousin William in Norfolk in a house in which
Christine's family later lived. He was at that point investigating what to do
with his wealth, which had been founded on the brewing of beer in the
town. They also knew that he offered financial aid to Jessie Vassar, a young
cousin from Norfolk, if she was able to attend college. They even had a book
entitled *Uncle John Vassar: or The Fight of Faith*, by Thomas Edwin Vassar,
about a relation who had been an itinerant preacher in the county where the

college is located. Indeed, Mathew was a cousin of their great grandfather. So, they felt comfortable in contacting the college.

On June 24, 1940, building on this historic link and with her husband already serving in the army, Kathleen Vassar dispatched an anonymous telegram to the Head Warden of Vassar College:

> WOULD YOU OFFER SANCTUARY DURATION WAR CHRISTINE MARY VASSAR AGE THIRTEEN ENGLISH PUBLIC SCHOOL GIRL FATHER ARMY MOTHER BUSINESS UNIMPEACHABLE REFERENCES URGENT NEED

Two days later a telegram came back:

> REFERENCES DESIRED MACCRACKEN PRESIDENT VASSAR COLLEGE

Following these exchanges the Vassar family sent three names to the president who then sent them telegrams requesting references. In her reply to MacCracken, Miss Winters, Headmistress of the City of London School for Girls, described Christine as a "very nice hardworking girl" whom she would "heartily recommend." This produced a firm offer from the president:
REFERENCE SATISFACTORY OFFER SANCTUARY ONE YEAR WILL MEET HER NEW YORK CABLE PASSPORT NATURE
It was only seven weeks after that first telegram that Christine was parted from her parents. Her father had left his army unit in the Midlands to say goodbye to his thirteen-year-old daughter. "Little did we know then," she says, "that I would not see my family for seven years." Later, when she learned that more than three quarters of the housing stock in the area where her family lived had been damaged, her family's decisions "became more understandable." Later, too, she could say, "When I left for the United States Mother said the war would be over in two years and I would be home." I was amazed at the naiveté, or denial, but maybe that is how the family coped."

So, on August 16 she found herself, along with several hundred other British children, on the *Duchess of Atholl* sailing for Canada. She was part of a large group who were responding to an invitation from the *Boston Transcript* newspaper.

After disembarking in Halifax they went by train to Boston and were housed temporarily at Wellesley College. Christine wrote home on September 2 describing the college's beautiful buildings, grounds and a lake: "Our counselors are college girls who have graduated and are very kind to us. They think we are much better behaved than American children. It is altogether like England as America can be. We have excellent food here." She was given there a copy of *The Token of Freedom* (see last chapter), a collection of writings which was given to all of us evacuees and they were joined by a second group of *Boston Transcript* evacuees. They enjoyed a picnic where they cooked their own food and for the first time tasted corn on the cob and hot dogs, drank punch and roasted marshmallows. "Tomorrow we go to the pictures and you would think we were prize scarecrows the way people stared at us."

A roommate at Wellesley was one of the girls who went to the Frick home (Chapter 2). In another letter home Christine wrote, "She has gone to live with a millionaire but says that it is not the kind of home she would have chosen. They are going to have two cocker spaniels and they have marvellous rooms but they are left to a fussy old dame in the winter."

Eventually Christine's foster father came to pick her up, "but not before his friend Mildred McAffee Horton, President of Wellesley, had told me that he was a very important man and I must not keep him waiting. He took me to the family summer home in Connecticut. All the family were sitting around the living room waiting for the newest member of the family."

The next day she was taken to the president's house, which to her eyes was "a very grand place." She was enrolled in Arlington High School as a ninth grader, though she was placed in an eighth-grade history class. She was soon coming back to tell the family about the "Abominable Acts" of the British Parliament, which helped give rise to the colonists' rebellion. "In my English school we were hardly out of the Middle Ages and I knew nothing about the American Revolution." Dr. MacCracken decided, in cooperation with the High School, that she did not need this at the time and she was placed in an American Civics class with a fine teacher, Miss O'Connell. "To this day when I go to vote I am grateful for her."

Chris describes mealtimes with the MacCrackens: 'As a family we met together for all three meals and were expected to be on time. Table conversations were by today's standards formal; no gossip or talk of health problems or food being served but discussion of local and world events and a platform for Prexy's stories. The youngest child at the table was often sent off to get the *Encyclopedia Britannica* or the *Oxford English Dictionary* for him to look up a word or subject he wanted to know more about. He would then expound upon the matter to lock it in his memory."

She was soon introduced to another "faculty brat," Carol Howson, who lived opposite the campus and who immediately invited her to her birthday party. "It was a close knit group and, in retrospect, our life and escapades together roaming the campus, playing games, and visiting back and forth, seems idyllic." Seventy-five years later she says, "We still get together as a group yearly. The MacCracken family very much became my family. They were very good to me and I am still in close touch with my foster-sister and foster-brother."

Like many evacuees she participated in a transatlantic broadcast arranged by the BBC. This was a time when transatlantic broadcasts were much less common. The *New York Mirror* (January 20) carried a story including a picture of Chris. It began, "Modern magic yesterday transmitted a big ecstatic kiss from a 13-year-old girl, 2500 miles away, to her mother in England. It brought to other parents first-hand reports of little boys that are 'studying hard' and that they like American ice cream. It told others that their offspring are drinking their milk. Millions listened in on these 'private conversations,' and exchanges of words of affection. It was the second of the British, Canadian and Mutual Broadcasting Companies' 'Children's hours,' the get-togethers of English child refugees and their parents. There were eight kids in NBC's studios here, and nine in six Canadian broadcasting stations, the mothers and fathers and a grandmother crowded into the BBC in London. ...Christine Vassar is the little girl who sent the great big kiss to Mamma. She is being cared for in the home of Dr. Henry MacCracken, Vassar College president, because she is a descendant of the president of the college."

The radio broadcast was also described enthusiastically in the *New York Times* the next day with the headline: "17 Child Evacuees Greet Parents in Two-way Broadcast to Britain: Humor and Pathos Mixed in Talk of Youngsters, Safe in U.S. and Canada — Plenty of Milk in 'the States.'" The paper reported that Christine Vassar told her mother that she had to practice the piano "one single solid hour of daylight every day."

"Oh, I say," Mrs. Vassar replied. "You wouldn't practice at home, and neither would you drink milk. But you do drink milk, plenty of milk, in the States?"

Christine replied that everybody drinks milk here; then there was silence in the studio as Mrs. Vassar said that sometimes she forgot Christine was away and "I put your plate at the table."

"Oh, mummy," Christine said.

After Pearl Harbor the evacuees found themselves involved in the American war effort and one Michigan newspaper reported in the summer of 1942 fifteen-year-old Christine's participation with other Girl Scouts in farm work: "When manpower began to trickle off the farms towards

A HARVEST OF FRIENDSHIPS

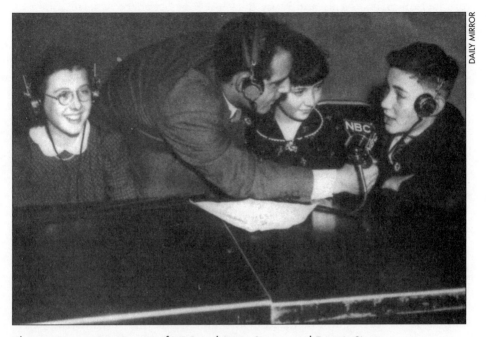

Christine Vassar, Ben Grauer of NBC and Jessie Simons and Francis Simons.

Christine (right) with Maisry MacCracken, daughter of the Vassar President and a lifelong friend, in 2006.

17 Child Evacuees Greet Parents In Two-Way Broadcast to Britain

Humor and Pathos Mixed in Talk of Young-sters, Safe in U. S. and Canada—Plenty of Milk in 'the States,' They Say

N.Y.Times Jan. 20, 1941

Seventeen young English evac-uees, now safe in the United States and Canada, spoke in voices unmis-takably British, though traces of American slang already showed in some vocabularies, to their parents in embattled England yesterday in another two-way transatlantic scendant of the founder of Vassar College, told her mother she had to practice the piano "one single solid hour of daylight every day."

"Oh, I say," Mrs. Vassar replied, "You wouldn't practice at home and neither would you drink milk. But you do drink milk, plenty of milk, in the States?"

production plants, Army and Navy duty, the Girl Scouts of America came forward with their version of what to do about it. As a part of the farm-aid program instituted this summer as a special wartime project, Detroit Girl Scouts summering at Camp Metamora, near Oxford, MI, have included regular farmerette duty in their vacation schedule. That is, they have scattered daily in twenty-four-girl units to help on farms within a radius of a few miles where crops were dwindling and the farms running down for lack of customary labor.

"Now the weed-choked truck gardens and wilting corn rows are getting back on a producing basis. Trained to thrifty habits under the Scout's peacetime program which strives first of all to develop in its girls the ideals of sound citizenship, these youngsters have proved they are acceptable farm hands. They have proved they can work with energy, initiative and skill for no reward greater than the knowledge they have put in a good day's work helps their country dodge the disaster that a widespread waste of national resources could invite.

"In the front rank of camp and farm enthusiasts this year is fifteen-year-old Christine Vassar, an evacuated British girl." Christine was at Metamora because the college student who was also living with the MacCrackens was like an older sister to her and had been a counsellor there before college."

After graduating from high school in 1944 Christine had wanted to return to England but her parents decided that she should stay on in America to attend Vassar College. Her parents were able to be at her graduation from Vassar in 1947. "I had very much wanted to go back after high school in 1944 and was very hurt that my family decided that I should stay and go to Vassar. I am pretty sure it was because I was doing so well at Vassar and could go to college on a full scholarship as a relative to Matthew. My family sent me pocket money on a monthly basis when they were allowed to. The MacCrackens were not paid in any way. They were very generous folk. After a year at Columbia University I went back London to live with them but decided that my life was really in the United States."

Christine had kept the telegrams which were going to change her life in a way that could not have been imagined at the time, and also some six hundred pages of wartime family letters to her. She decided to place them all in the Vassar College Library. "Before I did that I photocopied and cut and pasted them to make a more coherent narrative for children, grandchildren and English cousins. I was led to any group who would care to listen to the story of one family's life living through the Blitz, and about the war in Europe generally." She recorded her story for the Vassar Encyclopedia, an

CROSWELL BOWEN

Metamora Camp: Girl Scouts help with a wartime farm project. "In the front rank of camp and farm enthusiasts is 15-year-old Christine Vassar, an evacuated English girl."

Liliane Vasseur (left), a descendant of the French branch of the family and a French evacuee was also at Vassar. She and Christine are beneath a painting of the college founder Mathew Vassar.

Christine, with her husband, speaks in Vassar Library in 2012.

online work in progress under the direction of Vassar College's historian, and the letters from England, edited down, became the substance of her book *London War Letters of a Separated Family 1940–1945.*

In the book there is a letter of thanks from Christine's mother to Mrs. MacCracken and to the American people. It was written on VE Day and concludes: "This joyous day is nearly over. It has been a gigantic fight and I doubt if we would have had V.E. Day for many years but for the mighty help that America has sent us. I know what your individual help and sympathy has meant to one home and one little girl!"

Also in that book Christine speaks of her gratitude to the MacCrackens and their family. The way they welcomed her "was not an unusual occurrence for them for they had other young people live with them over the years, but their commitment to me over the war years and beyond was awe-inspiring…. I was a very fortunate young person to be invited into the MacCracken home at that time in my life. I remain grateful beyond measure for the opportunity given me to share their life with them, to know them and love them."

In 2012 Christine participated in a public meeting with Vassar students, faculty members and administrators and local high school students for "Conversations across the Generations." She had been for five years her class president. "I was safe here at Vassar," she told the crowd, "I'm proud of growing up here and associating with my class…. I have had a great life here. My husband and I are both eighty-six and living in a retirement residence near our daughter and her family."

During Christine's senior year at Arlington High School 1943-44 she wrote an essay which took first place. It was entitled "United Americans":

> *I am writing this as I see America — that is, through the eyes of an English girl who has been fortunate to receive your kind hospitality during the last three and a half years. No country is perfect, and if I criticize it at all, I am sure that you will realize that is because I have been made to feel so much at home here, and because I feel that for the nations and people of the world to understand each other, we must be able to talk frankly to each other about ourselves.*
>
> *When I came to America, I decided that because I had received no American history in England I had better take a course in it. During the first six weeks of the course we went through the causes of the American Revolution step by step. We even had to learn the Intolerable Acts of the British. The Intolerable Acts were just a little more than I could take at that*

time, and I left the class, but as I look back over American History, I realize
that the revolution did something more to America than just free them from
the British. It made them united, and determined to have freedom of speech,
religion, press, and assembly for which they had come to the New World.
The colonists had to suffer for which they believed in and after the war they
were determined that the people of the United States should never have to
fight another war to preserve freedom of thought and enterprise in the country.
Today we are fighting a war because the Americans and the British have come
to love this freedom so much that we will not willingly give it up.

This freedom has become one of the symbols of the American way of life:
people going into an old New England church to worship, other people sitting
round a table and discussing, the children of the melting pot of the world going
to school together, the hundreds of papers published weekly, and everything else
that indicates that Americans are tolerant of other people's ideas, creed and race.

Yes, America is all this and sometimes a bit more too. America does have
its race riots, exclusion acts, Jim Crow laws, poll taxes, and barriers that
do separate the people of one race and creed from those of different races and
creeds. When we talk about the necessity for freeing the conquered peoples of
Europe and Asia, let us not forget that we still have work to do at home.

Yes, this is the way I see the United Americans — trying hard to be
tolerant of each other, always willing to point out the mistakes of the other
party, always full of hope for the better age which is sure to come.

CHAPTER TEN

INHERITING A PENNSYLVANIA FARM

I HAD BEEN ASLEEP FOR SOME TIME, WHEN A HAND ON MY SHOULDER SHOOK ME VIGOROUSLY. HALF ASLEEP, MY FIRST REACTION WAS TO WONDER HOW MY LATEST MISDEED HAD BEEN DISCOVERED SO QUICKLY. IT WAS A RELIEF TO HEAR THE MASTER SAY, "BARLOW, YOUR FATHER WANTS YOU ON THE MORNING TRAIN TO LONDON. YOU ARE GOING TO CANADA" THE OTHER BOYS WERE SUITABLY IMPRESSED BY MY FORTHCOMING ADVENTURE.

—Brian Bohun Barlow, from *Only One Child*

With a few exceptions all British children who were evacuated to the United States returned home either during the war or soon after. It was part of the agreement with the United States government that allowed them into the country in the first place as temporary visitors. Their visas, extended annually, were only good for the duration of the war. The first time I heard about someone who did not return was when I shared a bookstore's platform in Maine with Brian Barlow who was launching his book *Only One Child*, about their family's evacuee experiences. Their story is certainly an exceptional one.

The Barlow family's home and Brian's school, Orwell Park were on the flight path of London-destined German bombers. The students at his school had for this reason already been sent for safety to Devon. One August 1940 evening twelve-year-old Brian Barlow was woken from sleep in the new surroundings of his Devon school by a teacher telling him that he was going to Canada in the morning. As he had been used to going away to boarding school since the age of seven, travelling alone didn't bother him. On reaching home he discovered that he, his twin sister, his younger sister and his younger brother would all be going as well, and without the parents and without his older brother, because he was seventeen and liable for military service.

The decision to send the children, Brian, Malcolm, Susan and Sheila, followed a suggestion by Caldwell Johnston, an American friend of his father who had worked in the American Consulate in London. He had just been posted to Montreal and offered to have two children while the other two would stay with a friend on the same street. "My parents must have been greatly relieved to know exactly where the four children would end up in Canada," writes Brian.

After the evacuation from Dunkirk the likelihood of a German invasion was very real and overseas evacuation more urgent. Barlow life centered on equipping the children and getting the necessary permissions from the American embassy whose evacuee operations were centered at the Grosvenor House hotel. English parents had to bring with them valid passports for each child, two birth certificates, five photographs, a cable from the American friend or relative guaranteeing support of the child or children while in the United States and also one from their banker stating that in the bank's opinion the sponsor was financially able to comply with the terms of his or her undertaking. In addition, the parents were required to pay a visa fee of $10, and they had to sign a consent form in triplicate if the applicant children were proceeding to the United States unaccompanied by father and mother.

Meanwhile in Pennsylvania in response to an appeal by the United States Committee for the Care of European Children "to enable a child (or children) seeking to be safe from the dangers of war, to secure asylum and refuge in the U.S.," farm owner Henry Gibson Brock had in July signed an affidavit agreeing to support, for an indefinite period, five evacuee children. They had no children of their own and planned to house evacuee children at Muncy Farms, a property that had belonged to the Brock family since 1803. The Brocks also filled out a two-page registration form including: "if the children are unknown to you, please fill out the following: boy or girl, age range, religious affiliation, nationality and background." A deposit of $138 per child was requested to be sent with the registration form and affidavit to the U.S. Committee. On July 29, 1940 Mr. Brock received a Confirmation of Sponsor's Deposit in the amount of $690. Of that amount $375 was to be used for "reception, care and transportation," $250 went into a trust fund, and $65 was to be used for "tax, visa and investigation."

All this was unknown to the Barlows, children or parents, as they presented themselves at the American Embassy. Brian remembers his father taking his hand and telling him that he was in charge of the two sisters and younger brother. As he was leaving, his father turned to take a last look at his four children. "When he did so a sudden premonition flashed into my mind: I thought I would never see him again. As I looked at his retreating figure I had a hollow feeling in the pit of my stomach. There were tears in Sue's eyes; Malcolm started to cry and I took father's departure more stoically."

On September 16 the four Barlow children set sail from Liverpool on the SS *Antonia*. The chief escort of their group of fifteen children was tennis professional Nancy Tresawna. It was on the very next day that the *City of Benares*, which had sailed three days earlier from Liverpool, was sunk.

The young Barlows, leaving mid-September rather than early August, had experienced bombing at their London home and on their way to Liverpool and this continued the first days at sea. Their escorts did their best to keep them from getting homesick including focusing their attention on icebergs and whales. On September 28 they and 112 other evacuees docked at Montreal and the *Montreal Gazette* called them "Little heroes."

"The reason we docked in Montreal instead of New York was due to the convoy encountering a U-Boat attack of the convoy," Malcolm told me. "The Captain of the *Antonia* decided we were sitting ducks staying with the convoy at 8 knots while being a passenger liner capable of more than 20 knots. By heading for Montreal the Antonio would be protected in the St. Lawrence River from U-Boats by the Canadian Navy. Interestingly, the British Navy did not realize the U-Boats now could range out 1000 miles from Brest because of the fall of France rather than the 500 miles from Hamburg. The British Naval escorts left the convoy at 500 miles leaving convoys vulnerable."

The children were met by Consul Johnston and his wife who arranged to pick them up the next day. However, arrangements had been made without their knowledge to send the four to New York City. "It seems that because we had American visas, the Canadian government would not permit us to remain in Canada. The fact that we were under the auspices of the U.S. Committee for the Care of European Children probably also entered into the decision to send us all to New York."

As with all of us there were many first impressions. On the train to New York City one of the children told a reporter, "When they gave us our lunches on the train we were all very surprised. The lunches were in little boxes just like those used for gas masks home, and we wondered why we should be getting gas masks in America." Likewise, like many evacuees, they were enchanted as they arrived in the evening to see so many bright lights, a startling contrast to the "blacked out" London and Liverpool they had left behind.

INHERITING A PENNSYLVANIA FARM

Arriving in the Bronx, they found the massive brick building of the Gould Foundation "rather cold and forbidding." The Foundation was one of several facilities used by the U.S. Committee for housing evacuees in transit. For Brian it was his "first bout of homesickness since leaving England." Up to this time he had been too involved in looking after his younger brother and two sisters to give much thought to home. The only consolation was that "the four of us were still together." He soon cheered up at the thought of new worlds to explore.

At the Foundation they were visited by celebrities like Douglas Fairbanks Jr. and Charlie Chaplin (see chapter 7 on Actors' Orphanage) and they were taken out on visits to the city and to the New York World's Fair. They still had no idea where they would eventually end up.

Unbeknownst to them, Mr. Brock, who had signed the affidavit, had died suddenly while the Barlow children were at sea and his widow, who was not in good health, hesitated to follow up on the offer. Her husband's aunt, however, persuaded her to at least look them over so she got in touch with the U.S. Committee. Near the end of October the evacuees were visited by two women unknown to them, Mrs. Brock and her late husband's aunt, May Gibson. Brian was startled by their appearance as they were dressed in black and thought they must be nuns. Malcolm tugged on his older sister Sheila's sleeve and whispered, "They're witches." His eyes grew round as he gazed at the two women. Sheila said later that Mrs. Brock had fallen in love with him on the spot, that younger brother Malcolm was one reason she agreed to take all four as "she just couldn't leave that big-eyed little boy behind." Next day Brian was asked if he was willing to live with Mrs. Brock for the duration of the war. She could take a large family but if they didn't accept they might have to be separated as American families were applying for no more than two children. He said he would go with Mrs. Brock providing they could return to the Gould Foundation if they were unhappy with her. "Our parents knew nothing of my decision, made at the age of 12."

So on November 3 Brian and Malcolm, Sheila and Susan moved into the large historic farmhouse with its some 500 acres of fields and woodlands. "It was a working farm. We could eat all the smoked ham, sausage, eggs and chicken we wanted, and could drink as much milk as we liked. After the rationing we had experienced in England, this seemed too good to be true." Near the house were a tennis court and a large swimming pool. They had no idea it would become a permanent home.

Up until mid-November the only communication the children had received from their parents was a telegram acknowledging letters received.

Malcolm and Sheila with
Mrs. Brock.

Entrance to Muncy Farms.

The children at
their new home
with their Irish
terrier Circus.

"Finally on Nov. 15 I received a letter from my father addressed to the Gould Foundation in New York. It said, "We had a cable from a Mrs. Brock, Muncy, Pennsylvania. We cannot write as we do not know her address." Two days later he wrote to Sue, "Now remember, all of you, keep smiling, laugh, be bright and pleasant. Learn to like your new parents. Be good."

Father had heard by that time that they were not living in Montreal with the Johnstons. "However, he was obviously not aware that Mr. Brock had died before we arrived at Muncy farms. All he knew was that they had been given shelter somewhere in Pennsylvania and were together."

Mother's first letter to "My dear Mrs. Brock" was dated January 8, 1941 describing the children's sporting abilities, their nature, what pocket money they had been given, what their bedtimes had been. She concluded, "My husband is always saying when this war is over, if we have anything left, we shall come and live in America or Canada. I am sure the children will never want to come back to England."

"Thus was forged the first link between two women who had not known of the existence of each other before the war brought their lives together."

Like many other English parents who had sent their children to safety overseas, they were worried that their children might misbehave. Father wrote of the Brocks, "You must learn to respect them and treat them as if they were your father and mother." He did not yet know Mrs. Brock was a widow. She soon became known to the children as Aunt Peggy.

"Like other English parents of evacuated children, our father felt it necessary to justify his decision." He wrote me, 'Always remember the reason why we allowed you all to go to America was this part of the world has gone mad and a mad dog, Hitler, has been let loose in our civilization and his brain works for destruction.'"

His parents shared the concern of other English parents that their overseas children would forget their English heritage and no longer speak or act in the English manner. On November 17 his father wrote, "Always be proud of your name, Bohun Barlow." All four children had Bohun as their middle name, this dating back to 1066 when their ancestors arrived from France.

By the summer of 1941 their mother wrote that she and their father were quite determined to come out to them when the war was over: "We are saving every penny we can, so as to be able to make a home out there. You would all find it very dull in England after the outdoor life you have in America…. So, darlings, learn all you can, so that you can all become really useful in the world and make a name for your selves."

A HARVEST OF FRIENDSHIPS

It came as a surprise to the four children whenever their parents' letters mentioned that they were seriously considering emigrating to the United States after the war, "if we have any money left by then."

"Such talk did not please," writes Brian, "because I looked forward to the day the war would be over and I could return to England. The King had no more loyal subject in the Colonies than me."

I will not describe all the adventures of the family in America during the war, as these are covered admirably in Brian's book. He describes their growing up like all of us evacuees in wartime America, including a stay in Arizona because of the need for a warmer climate due to Aunt Peggy's ill health. Brian attended Episcopal Academy as a day student. Like many private schools it offered reduced fees for evacuees though that became difficult for the schools as the years went by. The headmaster wrote, "We have a dozen of these English boys at The Academy; some of them have been over here for two years. We took the stand at the outset that we would give them all half rates and have tried to collect some funds toward this purpose. Of course, we had contemplated that the war would not last indefinitely when the arrangements were made. People have been very good in helping us."

Letters from home kept the children up to date on the progress of their older brother, Derrick, from the Home Guard to being a glider pilot in the Normandy invasion and then serving in Palestine. Apart from gaps which the children did not at the time understand and a few excisions by the censors, they heard all about the challenges and dangers and upheavals of life in wartime Britain and about their mother's service in the Red Cross. For that story, I recommend *Only One Child,* which I have drawn on for this chapter. I will concentrate here on the circumstances that made them American citizens.

 Brian writes that the "Americanization" of the children began in 1941. "It was not intentional on Mrs. Brock's part. Her goal was to return us to our parents as little changed as possible." She did not encourage them to lose their English accents and manners or diminish their love of King and country. "However the erosion of our Englishness was swift and unstoppable."

Letters had come steadily through 1941 but then for a time ceased. "Whereas 1941 was an exciting year for the four of us in America, for our parents it was to end up as a disaster." The children were unaware that their parents were in divorce proceedings but there was a brief reconciliation in 1942. That year their father wrote to his old American friend, Consul Caldwell Johnston: "Keep your eye on the children. I doubt whether they will ever see England again."

Malcolm at the Russell Ranch School in Tucson, Arizona with his roan horse Strawberry.

Derrick who was a glider pilot in the Normandy and Arnhem invasions.

Father's early 1943 letters revealed obliquely his concerns and, viewed with hindsight, they sounded to Brian "like a farewell." A letter on Jan 17 was eight legal size pages in length with a great deal of personal and business advice. "Do not do anything you are likely to be ashamed of — keep the name BARLOW clean, and do not break the laws of any country, whatever the inducement offered. Your name and liberty are worth more than a mountain of gold. At school you will be taught about legal contract laws, but lessons in school do not impress upon your mind the serious part they will play in your life in the future. Coming from your father, who is trying to give you the benefit of his 35 years of experience, so that you can avoid the traps and pitfalls that exist for the unwary and uneducated, may make more of an impression....

"This letter is written also for another purpose, to impress on you the necessity to really work hard at school — make it your number one objective. Then your school and masters will be proud of you, and if they see you are trying hard, it will give them encouragement to help you. Play and sport may seem important, but the future is very uncertain for everybody in every country owing to the war, because the whole business structure and fabric has been destroyed, broken up, disorganized. When the war stops there may be chaos. Only those with learning and education will be able to reconstruct and rebuild the business of the world. Your future job in life entirely depends on yourself and what you learn at school. Plan your life ahead; safeguard your future by saving every penny. Strive to get one thousand pounds in your bank. When you have succeeded, it will bring you confidence and stability and happiness — freedom from worry. Always think of rainy days ahead. Nobody goes through the world without trouble and adversity. Keep your temper; refuse to quarrel. Only fools quarrel and make enemies. Laugh and the world will laugh with you. Remember, keep your troubles in your own circle. Other people have their own."

The letter concluded: "Nothing else, except remember the BARLOW TEAM, which means unity and strength."

A few months later in June 1943 came the news that their father had died. Aunt Peggy wrote a friend, "I have seldom faced a harder task than that of telling the children. How awful to face one's first tragedy so far away from home." Brian writes, "After Aunt Peggy told us our father had died, I remember that the four of us cried out on the lawn in front of the big house."

His father's death made Brian homesick for England for the first time since his arrival in America in 1940. "Whereas in the past I had been uncritical of everybody and everything American, I now tended to be critical of both. Perhaps the fact that I had turned fifteen over the summer had something to do with my becoming a critic. The fun had gone out of the summer vacation as far as I was concerned."

It was a whole year later, in 1944, before Aunt Peggy and the children heard the circumstances of their father's death — he had committed suicide.

1944 was a particularly difficult year for their mother after her husband's death, also financially. She had been sending Aunt Peggy each month the sum allowed by the British government to be exported — $144.36 in American money for all four of them — and she put the money into war bonds. Mother was not only short of money but had found it hard to get a job.

The children had by then begun to wonder what would happen to them and to ask questions whether they were going to stay on or to return and would she come over. Unknown to them Aunt Peggy had been corresponding for some time on the possibility that she might adopt the children. She was aware that it would be difficult for the children's mother to make a home for them in England and that their continuing education was a big issue. She felt that they would then be able to continue their education in the United States and whether the war ended or not they would be given a sense of permanence rather than just living from day to day. She wrote to their mother, "You speak of the worry you have had should they have been sent home (as others have been). Of course I should not have even considered this without consulting you and only then if circumstances had changed drastically.... As to our personal relations with the children, I do not see that they have altered in the least, simply because the matter of finances becomes legal and binding on me. As I told you, my intention would be to bring the children to England as quickly as visitors are allowed passage."

Over the next three years, from the second half of 1943 to 1946, there were innumerable roadblocks to be overcome as they battled through bureaucracy over adoption and visas, many of the actual details only becoming known to the children some fifty years later. The British consulate in New York informed Aunt Peggy that the adoption of British children abroad was prohibited by law. Lord Halifax, the British Ambassador, said he could not help as it would require a vote in Parliament to change the law but he was encouraging about their being allowed to stay in America to complete their education. The British visa quota was full up for two years after the war but their American consul friend, Caldwell Johnson, advised that the British Foreign Office might accept having the four of them re-enter the United States from Canada on immigrant visas.

On July 5, 1945 they all flew from Burlington, Vermont, to Montreal, were given non-quota immigrant visas and readmitted through St Albans, Vermont. This was a little more than a month before their visas would have expired.

What was remarkable, younger brother Malcolm underlines, was that their mother only knew their would-be guardian through correspondence and the entire process was carried out by their mother's solicitor in the UK and their guardian's lawyer in Williamsport, Pennsylvania. "During times of war," he wrote me, "many decisions must be made that later seem strange out of context." He also notes, "Our reaction was complete acceptance since Muncy Farms had become our home after five years and seemed natural."

The one exception was their oldest sister Susan who had been only twelve when they left the UK and was upset they were not returning there: "She had a close relationship with our father and remembered the home life in England that no longer existed."

Susan, twin sister of Brian at the farm in 1946.

Sheila and husband Jim.

Muncy Farms buildings.

Brian and wife Posey in 2013.

Half brother Derrick Steedman with Sheila, Malcolm and Brian in 2001.

Brian in uniform.   Malcolm in uniform.

For many months after the war their mother had been trying to obtain a passage to the United States, which was very difficult at that period. In May 1946 she finally arrived. She never doubted that adoption was the right course, wrote Brian: "Mother's visit to America seems to have convinced her that it was not possible for us to be divided in our loyalties." She recognized that the children's adoption by Aunt Peggy confirmed what had transpired since their arrival in October 1940. "'Home' for the four of us had come to mean Aunt Peggy and Muncy farms. Aunt Peggy never intended this outcome, but too much time had elapsed after our departure from England to bring about a different result."

The meaning of the title of Brian's book *Only One Child* which eluded me until I finished the book now becomes clear — their mother still had Derrick.

When Mrs. Brock died in 1961 she left the Pennsylvania farm to the English children. Malcolm, who now lives at Muncy Farms, wrote me in 2013, "I have conferred with Brian and Sheila about our thoughts on inheriting Muncy Farms. We all agree Mrs. Brock, from the start upon our arrival at the farm in October 1940, treated us like her children.

Besides being warm and affectionate (which we were not accustomed to, coming from a very formal English household where we virtually only had parental audiences before their dinner) she also established rules on how we were expected to behave.

"As the war years went on we all, except for Susan, felt Muncy Farms was our home. Therefore upon her death we expected to be her heirs. Interestingly, upon her death in 1961 the Federal and State death duties combined were 73 percent. All our guardian's liquid assets were consumed by taxes. We were as the common phrase; 'land poor.'

"In a rational world it would make complete sense to sell the farm, divide the proceeds and move on in life. However, we all felt Muncy Farms was our home and every effort should be made to keep in the family. Also, Mrs. Brock had written an amendment to her will urging us to keep the farm as long as it was not a financial burden. Being British, she felt we needed to have an anchor in America. She was wise since Sheila returned to the farm upon her divorce in 1962 living there with her children until she remarried in 1968."

Brian also returned to the farm in 1984 for a year when health problems required him to sell his business in New Mexico. Upon his retirement in 1999 Malcolm too decided to return to the farm and has "enjoyed the experience immensely."

He told me, "We are all *patriotic Americans* having made the choice to become American citizens."

Brian was in the final days of U.S. Army Officers Training school in 1951 when the Army realized he was a British citizen. He was made an American citizen overnight and served in the United States and Austria during the Korean War. Malcolm was about to enter the U.S. Navy and discovered he too had to be a U.S. citizen. "I did it along with 8 German war brides who all took the pledge of citizenship." Sheila became a U.S. citizen in 1952. Brian Bohun Barlow writes of the BARLOW TEAM, "Like most converts we are very proud of being American."

CHAPTER ELEVEN

YOUNG AMBASSADORS

BRITAIN HAS 3,500 UNOFFICIAL AMBASSADORS. THEY CARRY NO DIPLOMATIC PASSPORTS, NOR DO THEY CLAIM ANY DIPLOMATIC PRIVILEGE. THEY WORK NOT IN THE LIMELIGHT OF OFFICIALDOM, BUT INSIDIOUSLY IN THE VERY HEART OF THE COUNTRY IN WHICH FOR THE TIME BEING THEY ARE AT HOME. THEY CARRY NO INSTRUCTIONS IN SEALED ENVELOPES, FOR THEIR INSTRUCTIONS ARE SIMPLE AND EASY, EVEN FOR THE VERY YOUNGEST OF THEM TO REMEMBER. "BE TRUTHFUL, BRAVE, KIND AND GRATEFUL" ARE THE WORDS WRITTEN IN THEIR HEARTS. SIX SIMPLE WORDS ACCEPTED WITH CHILDLIKE FAITH AS SUFFICIENT TO ENABLE THEM TO MEET ANY SITUATION THEY MIGHT HAVE TO FACE IN THE COUNTRY FAR FROM HOME WHERE THEY NOW WORK FOR BRITAIN. FOR THESE ARE THE CHILDREN OF BRITAIN WHO DURING THE MONTHS OF JULY, AUGUST AND SEPTEMBER 1940 SAILED FROM THE THREATENED SHORES OF OUR ISLAND FORTRESS TO THE KINDLY WELCOMING LANDS OF OUR GREAT DOMINIONS AND OF THE UNITED STATES OF AMERICA.
—*Pilgrim Children* by Jean Lorimer, 1942

"IT IS AN HONOUR TO PLAY FOR AND REPRESENT YOUR SCHOOL AT SOME GAMES BUT IT'S A MUCH GREATER HONOUR TO REPRESENT YOUR COUNTRY ABROAD AS YOU WILL BE DOING."
—Sir Geoffrey Shakespeare, to evacuees

It is fair to assume that my parents and probably few parents would have taken such an action if they thought that their children would be away for years. It was a temporary move occasioned by frightening events which would mean a separation of a year or at most two years. To some children it was even put forward as a summer holiday.

One father, Francis Rodd, was because of age and experience perhaps a bit more aware of what might happen. He had made his name in administration and finance and in 1940 was about to depart on a mission to set up an intelligence post in Northern Nigeria. It was also just at the moment that the government was arranging for children to be sent overseas (CORB). He describes in his diary how he and his wife Mary discussed what to do and, learning that the government wanted children of all classes to go, put their children on the list. "It was a bad moment. She and I thought it was right. I was afraid not of bombing or even of invasion but of semi-starvation. I had known too much of what happened in Europe during our blockade during the last war. I was afraid of the children being permanently impaired by malnutrition and ill-health. So we decided and that made the parting between us even more difficult. Anyway, so it was decided and I left Euston to a world of adventure again in Africa (he was recognized as a distinguished geographer because of his Saharan expeditions in 1922 and 1927) and she to loneliness in England with the children in strange hands in America or Canada. At least they would be strong and healthy and able to live as women and men in whatever world was left after the war — provided they got there. I never doubted that they would get there. The *City of Benares* had not then been struck. Poor Mary, she was brave and good."

It was on arriving in Nigeria that Francis received a telegram announcing that Mary and the children and cousins had arrived safely in the United States. "I danced for joy but only learned months afterwards what had happened. Within a day of putting the children down for the government scheme Mary had received a telegram from Morgan Grenfell, a company in America where her husband was a partner offering her and the children hospitality for the war in Long Island. "That telegram was a great relief. It meant I was free from worry and free to do what I could or go where I wanted in the certainty that Mary and the children would always have enough to eat even if they had to stay in America ten years or forever.

After his work in Nigeria Francis was appointed Chief Political Officer in East Africa and made an acting major general and in 1943 became the Chief Civilian Affairs Officer with the job of setting up an acting military administration of Southern Italy. After the war he became president of The Royal Geographic Society and served in the House of Lords.

Many people marvel at how well the evacuees coped with this separation. This is not to say that some children didn't suffer. They did. Not as large a proportion it would seem as those who were evacuated within Britain. There was homesickness, there were unhappy placements, some abuse, some exploitation, some misunderstanding. One woman told me that until she heard me speak she just thought that her mother wanted to get rid of her.

Many people nowadays, when hearing about this overseas evacuation, are appalled. How in the world could parents think of sending their children away and over the dangerous Atlantic at that, and for so long? I realized when our daughter was eight and again when our granddaughters were eight and six what a big decision that must have been and how dire the situation must have seemed for our parents even to contemplate such an act.

My experience and that of my brother and my friends was a happy one. On the whole we see the gain in our lives in terms of breadth of perspective, of experience and of lasting friendships rather than focusing on what we lost through it, with educational handicaps and family disruption. Only in the last ten years have I realized that even I have a downside I had never recognized. That is that my family never again had that closeness of family that one might have expected.

There are further elements that might help today's readers understand the very different circumstances and attitudes that prevailed in the forties. Let me note a few comments I have extracted from a book I have been reading:

> *Parents had to make painful decisions about what were the safest havens for their offspring.*
>
> *He never re-established a close relationship with his parents.*
>
> *His "floating free independence" and "detachment from close relationships" sprang from his transient childhood.*
>
> *Parents found it difficult to realize that if they let their children go for that length of time they will forge other loyalties and affections because they need surrogate parents.*
>
> *At the time he "just accepted it all."*
>
> *"Same kind of bulldog pluck."*
>
> *She apparently showed "Churchillian qualities."*

Full of excitement.

Acquired a "premature independence" as a means of coping with the pain of separation.

Children develop to varying degrees "a detached character as a defence against the fear of rejection."

Susan did not at first recognize her mother at the railway station but she settled down quite quickly.

These extracts are not, as one could think, about wartime overseas British evacuees; they are actually about peacetime British children living with their families during the last years of the British rule in India but sent home to England for schooling. They dovetail, however, with the attitudes and experiences of the former and come from Vyvyen Brendon's book *Children of the Raj*. She also notes, "It seems that the long British tradition of sending children away from their parents had helped to form the national character." Vyvyen even compares the two sets of children and writes of overseas evacuees:

They were in many ways akin to Raj children being sent to Britain in normal times:

They were despatched for their own good but without consultation;

They travelled so far that returning home was virtually impossible;

They did not know how long their exile would be;

And they were told that if things went wrong they should remember that they were British and grin and bear it.

Jessica Mann, the crime novelist, whose parents were Jewish refugees from Germany, and was an evacuee, makes the same point about evacuation: "British society had been accustomed for centuries to Empire-builders sending their children away from hot climates to foster homes or boarding schools. Our contemporary horror at the idea of parting children from their parents is a post-war development, and although it is often tempting to use that early "trauma" as the excuse for all my deficiencies, I have the impression that the majority of the evacuees survived intact and even enriched."

These glimpses of life in the late thirties may help the modern reader understand why some parents were more open to the idea of parting from their children than would be the case today and why many overseas evacuees coped so well with a separation that by today's standards seems extraordinarily harsh. 1940 was a different world. This may seem obvious, but worth being reminded of it when we transfer today's attitudes onto yesterday's practices. Hindsight is easy, as is the propensity of younger folk to pontificate with assurance on matters they were not involved in. This has been particularly irritating to those who were evacuated within Britain and who have resented the way some of them have been depicted. It was, indeed, this misrepresentation that largely led to the formation of the Evacuees Reunion Association (now known as the British Evacuees Association). This has been less the case among overseas evacuees, where it is more the fact that little is ever heard about their experiences that is irksome to some. What they share with internal evacuees is that within their respective groups you can find divided, often entirely opposite views on what happened to them.

Another big difference with today is the palpable patriotism and the fact that Britain was at war and under serious threat of invasion. Most of us who were sent overseas missed the later phases of the Blitz on the big cities and my brother and I were on the high seas when the Battle of Britain began. But even at the age of eight, evacuated from London to a school in Surrey, I remember the soldiers around us in the woods who had been rescued from Dunkirk and while we were learning to drill on the cricket field. I admired the older boys cutting up balsawood frames for model gliders and enjoyed reading the popular stories of war heroes. Our parents were both in uniform. We had already been outfitted with gasmasks and we could sing the popular songs and even parodies like "Underneath the spreading chestnut tree Mr. Chamberlain said to me, if you want to get your gasmask free join the bloomin' ARP" (Air Raid Precautions).

It is fashionable today to frown on patriotism, to repeat well-worn phrases like Samuel Johnson's "Patriotism is the last refuge of a scoundrel." I don't share that view. I believe patriotism is a great asset to a country provided it is married to an honest appreciation of a country's failings and a dedication to what you can do to remedy them. Certainly patriotism was very tangible to those of us who were British in World War II and not least to the very young at that time. Even if it is what historian John Keegan has called the "fierce patriotism of a war child." It was equally so for many young Germans even as the war was nearing an end and Germany's defeat was sure.

Some children before they left these shores would have heard Sir Geoffrey Shakespeare giving one of his pep talks at the dockside. Sir Geoffrey, who headed the government's overseas evacuation scheme, saw off many of the parties of children and usually told them that they did not represent themselves when they were sent overseas, and therefore they could not behave as they liked. They were going as the children of Britain. They were, in fact, like British ambassadors, he used to say, and consequently they must behave even better than they knew how. If they behaved badly people would say "What frightful children! Their parents in Britain can't really be worth fighting for." On the other hand, if they behaved well, people would say, "What splendid children these are. We must do everything we can to help their parents win." He said, too, to the children, "When things go wrong, as they often will, remember you are British and grin and bear it."

We had already imbibed attitudes that, even if we didn't personally hear Shakespeare's words, may seem quaint by today's standards. Soon after our arrival a local paper described a woman observing a group of English children awaiting homes. One of them fell down, and he must have hurt himself but he did not cry. "You must be a very brave boy," she said to him. His reply "It's all for England." The paper commented, "There are many of us here who are learning new lessons of self-control and courage these days."

Like writer Anthony Bailey, we genuinely saw our role as ambassadors for our country. He writes, "Whether because of wartime patriotism or the Portsmouth naval tradition, perhaps transmitted in a school history lesson, I had taken to heart Nelson's flag signal flown on *The Victory* before Trafalgar, 'England expects every man to do his duty.'" We knew we had to stand up for our country. Historian Alistair Horne says that with comments like "Why, I was doing Virgil before I left England" and "We don't wear helmets to play rugger, or gloves and masks to play cricket" he and older evacuees at his school were sometimes so arrogant that it was almost a mystery "why most of us were not massacred within a week of arrival." I remember even in my preteens studying reference books so that I could point out that such and such an invention was by an Englishman and was inwardly glad that English boys at my school came top in work and sports. Most of us were, as the late Janet Baker (Lady Young) confirmed to me, "intensely patriotic," and this helped us deal with such difficulties. Tremayne Rodd, an evacuee in kindergarten on Long Island, who later played rugby for Scotland, learned that America had beaten Britain in the War of Independence. His stout response, "It's not true. I won't have it."

Our host's son-in-law, Hoel Bowditch, who later became head of engineering at the Foxboro Company, welcomed us with a five-foot-long model of HMS *Rodney* which he had made when he heard we were coming, with two searchlights that worked and one gun turret which could fire slugs. Dry ice in the funnel would produce smoke. In the garden we had a sandpit where we would re-enact land battles or the evacuation from Dunkirk with toy soldiers and it didn't matter that some of our British soldiers were in parade uniform and were of a different size than American ones. Many American schools went out of their way to be welcoming to the influx of young British. I was proud that a painting I did of a spitfire over the Channel was hung in the assembly hall.

In our American home we had a wind-up gramophone and we used to play wartime songs from the first as well as the second World Wars. Whether it was "Tramp, tramp, tramp, the boys are marching" or "We're going to hang out the washing on the Siegfried Line, have you any dirty washing mother dear." "There'll always be an England" became almost our signature tune, being sung at many occasions when evacuees got together. When the evacuee ship the *Volendam* was torpedoed, no lives were lost but passengers had to take to the life boats and an escort said later that it was the most moving experience of her life to hear in the darkness, borne on the wind, the voices of the children singing, "Roll out the barrel" and "There'll always be an England." Sir Martin Gilbert, who was an evacuee to Canada, even chose it forty years later as his first record on the popular BBC program "Desert Island discs." He says he cried involuntarily, as he read its words in *See You After the Duration* for which he wrote the Foreword.

My reading, too, reinforced a patriotic attitude that might be hard to recognize today. Most readers may be familiar with the story of *The Lion, the Witch and the Wardrobe.* Like the Narnia evacuee children I had a magic wardrobe. Opening its doors, however, did not transport me to a make-believe land inhabited by Aslan and the other denizens of the wood. Rather I was carried into the very real world of the British lion and the trappings of empire. My wardrobe was not in the New Forest but in New England. The "wardrobe" was a huge cupboard in which my American hosts stored on its shelves back numbers of the *Illustrated London News* and *The Boy's Own Annual.* Their enthralling pages contained stories of bravery under fire, wonderful color portraits of the Royal family, vivid cross sections of Royal Naval ships and much more which fed my pride in country and no doubt helped to sustain me in five years of separation from my parents. My reading at that time also benefited from the fact that my host family still had the books of their six children. It meant that they had many of the Henty stories of Empire builders and such like in their bookshelves which I read avidly. I soon moved on as I got older from *Just William* through the Ransome books to the adventures of *Biggles* and my favorites, the stories of Dave Dawson and Freddy Farmer. Freddy was an RAF pilot and Dave an American pilot. I looked at a copy recently of *Dave Dawson with the RAF.* Its chapter headings make clear its approach, for instance "Two Junkers less!", "Nazi wings over

London" and "England must never die." The last words of the book are, "Air Vice-Marshal Saunders looked at Colonel Fraser and smiled. 'I ask you,' he murmured, 'What chance has old Adolf got when he's up against chaps like these two?'"

The Japanese attack on Pearl Harbor on December 7, 1941 brought a dramatic change. We were no longer outsiders. As President Roosevelt wrote to King George VI, "Our two nations are now full comrades-in-arms." America entering the war introduced a wider dimension as we were soon encompassed as well in the American patriotism. We collected scrap metal, dug Victory gardens and saved for war bonds. As the school chapel was used for spotting for planes and we lived next to the school grounds I was permitted to join the team of spotters. Many evacuees were, of course, already very knowledgeable when it came to aircraft recognition and made model planes or had pictures of planes covering their walls. I remember saving cereal box tops to send to an address in Chicago to get a cardboard mock-up of a bomber cockpit, also collecting militaria from German and Allied forces. We used to spend a lot of time inventing codes or experimenting with invisible ink.

Every week I had to learn stirring poetry, ranging from Tennyson's "The Charge of the Light Brigade" and Newbolt's "Drake's Drum" to American classics like Oliver Wendell Holmes' "Old Ironsides" and John Greenleaf Whittier's "Barbara Frietchie." All Americans know or did know then: "'Shoot if you must this old grey head but spare your country's flag', she said."

I went like many to summer camp and can still sing the college and patriotic and traditional songs we learned round the camp fire. Whether it was "Anchors Away" from the U.S. Navy or "Off we go into the wild blue yonder" from the Army Air Corps or "Over hill, over dale" from the Field Artillery or the now possibly politically incorrect "from the Halls of Montezuma to the Shores of Tripoli" praise of the U.S. Marines and its extravagant: "If the army and the navy ever look on heaven's scenes they will find the streets are guarded by United States Marines."

Older evacuees found themselves making speeches or christening planes. Shirley Williams, Baroness Williams, writes that "all of a sudden we, the British, were America's brave allies. So we British became the heroes of the hour, and I became the local hero because I was one of the very few British children in the Twin Cities." She became "the embodiment of the little girl ally" and was always being handed up on platforms like Bundles for Britain and even presented bouquets to Lord Halifax, the British Ambassador, and

Lady Halifax when they came to town. As an eleven year-old I was there in the crowd of thousands in Harvard Yard, mostly students in uniform, cheering when Winston Churchill emerged after being awarded an honorary degree. I was proud when my father came on a mission to Washington, D.C. in 1944 and we saw him for a couple of days. He came to visit us in uniform. We enjoyed being given the chance to polish his buttons, with a metal plate under them and *duraglit* to make them shine.

He came to see us at the second school which I was then attending, Rectory, in Connecticut and was a little taken aback when he heard me say "I will not sing 'God save the king.' We were rehearsing a play about Nathan Hale. At Rectory I was entrusted with responsibility for hoisting and lowering the Stars and Stripes, learning to fold it correctly and never letting it touch the ground. We spent time marching and drilling and practicing the manual of arms with model wooden guns and had a color guard. We also got fitter with an army obstacle course and became proficient in morse and semaphore. Gerald, by then nine, remembers feeling important sitting in the back of a truck being driven to the fields to dig vegetables as part of the war effort. At school my "war job," as it was called, was looking after the chickens. Many of the movies we watched at school were patriotic ones like *Gunga Din* with Cary Grant and Douglas Fairbanks and *Corvette K225* with Randolph Scott. The school newspaper was soon reflecting in its columns the difficulties of rationing, staff shortage and above all the fact that several hundred alumni or old boys were in the services "somewhere in England" or "somewhere in the Pacific," that some were being killed or wounded or decorated. The war was brought home to us when the father of one of my best friends at school was killed. We were encouraged to read *Time* and enter its annual current affairs quiz. As a stamp collector I was aware of the Four Freedoms enunciated by President Roosevelt – freedom of speech, freedom of worship, freedom from want and freedom from fear — and was pleased to add to my collection the new issue of flags of oppressed nations.

In all this, too, one must emphasize that it was not just the patriotism that sustained us, it was being part of a great adventure.

Shirley Williams, in her autobiography *Climbing the Bookshelves,* describes leaving her parents on the quayside and walking through the slit in a huge black tarpaulin screen "into another world." "Like my brother I was not even apprehensive. Indeed I don't think I had any sense of fear at all, only a sense of excitement." She was to experience, she said, a completely new culture in the United States. "My new life was so exciting that I can't remember feeling homesick after the first week or two."

All the time we were growing older and absorbing changes we might also have experienced at home but were new to us and in the context of new families. Indeed, one of the important, or probably most important, contributions to our adjusting came from the wisdom of many hosts in helping their "guest children" to feel at home but not too much at home that we forgot our own parents. Weekly letters home provided a link. The family we lived with had six children, the youngest of which was sixteen when we arrived. That may account for the fact that we always knew them as Mr. and Mrs. Hinchman. Gerald is sure this was deliberate not because of their age but because they didn't want to supplant our real parents. Certainly for many of the youngest evacuees the time to return home was more traumatic than the time they left, with the youngest hardly remembering parents not seen for five years.

That last Christmas, in 1944, I stayed with another English boy in New Hampshire. There I was introduced to a new board game, called Target for Tonight. It consisted of throwing dice to advance on bomber raids; that is where I first learned names like Dortmund, Essen and Hamm. On Christmas Eve I was asked to bring down from the upper house precious, breakable Christmas decorations. I imagined I was one of those Norwegian children I had just read about in a book *Snow Treasure* who used sleds to spirit gold away from the Germans.

Some of us returned to Britain on neutral or Royal Navy ships, and Gerald and I came back on a little escort carrier, HMS *Patroller*. There was a captured Japanese Zero plane in the hangar and we even had the thrill of watching a surrendered German submarine being towed back to the United States. Now we could actually see uniforms and recognize ranks we had studied in the *Illustrated London News*.

CHAPTER TWELVE

A PREMATURE FUNERAL

DEATH NOTICE:

THE SPECIAL RELATIONSHIP. DIED AT HOME AFTER A SUDDEN ILLNESS ON THURSDAY, AUGUST 29, 2013, AGED 67. BELOVED OFFSPRING OF WINSTON CHURCHILL AND FRANKLIN D. ROOSEVELT. DEARLY LOVED BY MARGARET THATCHER, RONALD REAGAN, JOHN MAJOR, GEORGE BUSH SR., BILL CLINTON, TONY BLAIR AND GEORGE W. BUSH. FUNERAL TO BE HELD AT THE FRENCH EMBASSY, 58 KNIGHTSBRIDGE, LONDON SW1X. NO FLOWERS PLEASE.

When the Coldstream Guards band play the "Star Spangled Banner" in the courtyard of Buckingham Palace after the 9/11 attack on New York's Twin Towers, or the London marathon holds a half-minute silence at its start after the bombing at the Boston marathon a few days earlier or, indeed, when President Obama, whose Kenya family suffered under British rule, and Michelle Obama, build an obviously close relationship with our Queen — the "special relationship" is evoked. At times overrated and at times undervalued, even prematurely buried as in the brilliant front page in *The Sun* (above) but it won't so easily go away. President Obama told Prime Minister David Cameron in 2011, "The United States has no closer friend than the United Kingdom. I reiterate my deep and personal commitment to the special relationship between our two countries, a bond that has endured for generations across party lines and that is essential to the security and prosperity of our two countries and the world."

Two organizations in Britain, the Pilgrims Society (along with its American counterpart) and the English–Speaking Union (ESU) can claim a significant part in helping maintain that legacy and I am glad to be a member of both. My earlier book about the evacuation, *See You After the Duration,* was launched at Dartmouth House, the ESU headquarters in London, by Sir Martin Gilbert, Churchill's biographer who contributed the Foreword for it and I was on the ESU SeaVac Committee which together with the Evacuees Reunion Association (now known as the British Evacuees Association), the Imperial War Museum and the Reading University Centre for the Study of War Children recorded the memories of several hundred evacuees. In 2010 I was on a panel at Dartmouth House arranged by the Pilgrims Society to evaluate the legacy of those war years. The two organizations have over many years maintained a close relationship.

The Pilgrims Society of Great Britain was founded in 1902 to promote "good-will, good-fellowship, abiding friendship and everlasting peace between the United States and Great Britain." The following year the Pilgrims of the United States was established. The two are independent but interlocked as U.S. members are automatically members of the British Pilgrims and vice versa. The name is not, as might be assumed, meant to hark back to the pilgrims who landed at Plymouth Rock but rather to express the idea that English and Americans could promote international friendship through their pilgrimages to and fro across the Atlantic. It became a focus for those who saw the abiding importance of an alliance of interests across the Atlantic and has always been a forum for significant speeches. A custom has been established, for instance, that the first official speech of a new American ambassador is to the Pilgrims. This has been the case for over a hundred years. Ambassador Robert Tuttle in a farewell luncheon at Dartmouth House recalled how after going through the rigors of a Senate hearing and a briefing in Washington, D.C. before he took up his appointment he was told, "Oh, and your first formal speech will be to the Pilgrims and it had better be good." He said that by the time for his speech arrived he was terrified, and paid tribute to his wife, Maria for her support and ingenuity.

World War II naturally saw both the British and American Pilgrims playing a significant role. In May 1940 Prime Minister Churchill spoke at a Pilgrims occasion in honor of Lord Halifax, ambassador-designate to the United States, who was replacing Lord Lothian who had died suddenly. In December that year the Pilgrims, according to the *Centennial History of the Pilgrims,* 'were spared the embarrassment' of deciding whether to give

PILGRIMS EXECUTIVE COMMITTEE

The Pilgrims emblem.

ENGLISH-SPEAKING UNION

Dartmouth House English Speaking Union Headquarters in London.

Sea Vac Project committee members (L-R) Michael Henderson, Roderick Suddaby, Annette Fisher, Dr Martin Parsons and Sir Brian Fall.

a farewell dinner to U.S. Ambassador Joseph Kennedy who returned to America before his resignation was announced.

It was Kennedy's defeatist view of Britain's prospects in 1939 that would have caused the embarrassment. Margaret, Duchess of Argyll, in her book *Forget Me Not* writes of a dinner she and her husband had with the Ambassador. She heard him say that the country was finished, it would be overrun by the Germans in a matter of weeks. All the roads would then be blocked with refugees, just as they were then in France. "He turned to me: 'You and your children must get out. As the wife of an American you would be crazy to stay here.'" The United States Embassy then began to send letters to all American nationals in Britain. "In large red letters we were constantly warned that a ship was being sent to evacuate us from 'this beleaguered island'; that we were STRONGLY ADVISED to take it, as it might be THE LAST CHANCE; and that if we chose to remain in Britain it would be at our own risk."

In July 1939 in a speech to The Pilgrims Lord Lothian, before he left London to take up the post of British Ambassador to the United States, said, "I am certain that in the end moral principle is more powerful than bayonets and guns and that in addition, it is backed by guns and bayonets it will inexorably and speedily prevail." His first speech in the United States as Ambassador was in October to the American Pilgrims. He believed that the future of freedom in the world would turn on the relations between the British Commonwealth and the United States. A better understanding of the two great branches of the English-speaking peoples was the cause for which he was working with all his might. His essential theme was the meaning of democracy and the deadly danger with which totalitarianism threatened it, delivered scrupulously within the limits to which, in Lord Lothian's view, a spokesman of Britain to the United States must conform.

His speeches throughout the country had a powerful effect. His view was that we could not arrive at any sane program of peace unless we talked frankly to each other. One midwestern paper wrote that "the subtlety of his propaganda will consist of the fact that there will be no propaganda. In short, a very dangerous man." In a speech delivered for him the day before his unexpected death on December 12, 1939, he said, "The Sermon on the Mount is in the long run much stronger than all Hitler's propaganda or Goering's guns or books. It is not for me to tell you what you ought to do. That is entirely for you to decide for yourselves. But it is my business to see that you are informed of the essential facts. Unless you are so informed you cannot form judgments, and I, not you, would be responsible for the consequences."

Lord Lothian's ashes were interred in the National Cemetery at Arlington and his successor as Ambassador was Lord Halifax, who later became Chairman of The Pilgrims of Great Britain. Halifax said that Lord Lothian's work as Ambassador was "one of the outstanding achievements of British diplomatic history." Prime Minister Winston Churchill spoke at a Pilgrim's occasion on January 9, 1941 in honor of Lord Halifax's appointment as Ambassador. Two months later 455 Pilgrims and their guests, including all the cabinet were present at a lunch to welcome John Winant as the new American ambassador. It was a lunch not a dinner because of the blackout and night bombing. The speeches on that occasion were broadcast on the BBC. The Prime Minister spoke first: "Mr. Winant, you come to us at a grand turning point in the world's history. You share our purpose, you will share our dangers, you will share our anxieties, you will share our secrets, and the day will come when the British Empire and the United States will share together the solemn but splendid duties which are the crown of victory." Winant responded, "Today it is the honor and destiny of the British people to man the bridgehead of humanity's hopes. It is their privilege to stand against ruthless and powerful dictators who would destroy the lessons of two thousand years of history. It is your destiny to say to them, 'Here you shall not pass.'" He concluded his speech by saying that the Allies "with the help of God shall build a citadel of freedom so strong that force may never again seek its destruction."

The *Daily Herald* wrote the next day, that Winant was not an orator: "He read, and not too well, every word, looking down at his script. But his words were more than oratory. They were a declaration of faith." The *Evening Standard*'s view was that "the Ambassador had achieved a feat which few orators can equal": 'He spoke after Mr. Churchill with complete success." The *Sunday Times* called it "an extraordinary triumph."

In 1945 Eleanor Roosevelt was the first woman guest of honor at a Pilgrims function in London. On April 12, 1948, three years after his death, she unveiled in Grosvenor Square, London, a statue in memory of her husband, President Roosevelt. A dinner to mark the occasion was described as "the greatest dinner in the history of the Pilgrims" and was attended by more than 900 guests including Princess Elizabeth and the Duke of Edinburgh. Fifty years later British and American Pilgrims gathered to commemorate and rededicate that statue. The cost was estimated to be £40,000 and the British were invited to contribute to the maximum of five shillings per person. "That the target was reached in only five days demonstrated the high regard that the people of Britain had for the late president," wrote Sir Robert Worcester, American-born long-time chairman of the Pilgrims and also former board member of the English-Speaking Union.

In 1947 General Marshall spoke to The Pilgrims, his only speech in England. Earlier in the year he had proposed the Marshall Plan. In his speech he distinguished between a "special relationship" and a "natural relationship" between our two countries. "There is no more natural relationship in international life than that between the United States and the British Commonwealth. This relationship requires no special political initiative; it is not embodied in any formal treaty or pact."

Worcester, an anglophile who was founder of MORI polls, believes that despite efforts by officials of the two nations to play down the "special relationship," the very strength of the Pilgrims, the standing of its members in both countries, the quality of the speakers at its events, all bear witness to the bonds that make the relationship special. "Special" or "natural," he says, "there is no doubt the relationship exists and it is to the furtherance of Anglo-American good fellowship that the Pilgrims is dedicated."

In 1954 Geoffrey Fisher, then Archbishop of Canterbury, spoke at a Pilgrims dinner. He concluded his speech, which was broadcast on the BBC: "So we find the true secret of Anglo-American relationship and friendship. They cannot become like us; their history and their setting is quite different. We could, if we wished, try to imitate them, blowing ourselves out to compete with them, lengthening the small steps of the tubby figure of John Bull in order to keep pace with the long strides of Uncle Sam. But we should be wrong. Our work in the world and for the world can only be done by our proportions, as America must do her work with her proportions. But we need each other greatly for the health of us both, and the world for its preservation desperately needs what our wholehearted trust and co-operation can bring to it. We need America to keep us moving, eager and young for our years and still adventurous. America needs us to keep her patient, sensitive, and aware that if size often shows on a great scale the splendors of God, his deepest secrets are to be found only in the small, simple and domestic."

The Queen is Patron of what she calls "this special organization."

On its centenary occasion she sent her good wishes to The Pilgrims for "its continuing role to ensure the strengthening of the many ties which bind our two nations so closely together." Lord Carrington, who had then been president for eighteen years, wrote in 2001, "In the changed circumstances of today, this relationship is still as important as ever it was; no one can foretell the future or what may happen in a turbulent world. We would do well to maintain our close relationship, based as it is on shared interests and values."

———————————————

Her Majesty is also Patron of the English-Speaking Union (ESU) while the Duke of Edinburgh was its President until he retired in 2012, positions they held for some sixty years. He was succeeded by The Princess Royal in 2013. The ESU was founded in Britain and the USA in 1918 by Sir Evelyn Wrench who believed that maintenance of the close personal and national ties forged during the Great War were necessary for the preservation of peace. It was to be an inclusive organization "founded in no narrow attitude of race pride, in no spirit of hostility to any people". The ESU aimed at "no formal alliance, has nothing to do with government, but is merely an attempt to promote good fellowship among the English-speaking democracies of the world". The first royal visit came in 1932 and a year later the Prince of Wales accepted to become the President of the ESU.

A HARVEST OF FRIENDSHIPS

The first president of the independent American wing of the ESU was the former president of the United States, William Howard Taft. In the autumn of 1963 the American ESU, pondering its choice of a new Chairman, approached the Duke of Edinburgh but received the polite but firm admonition, "It's the American's business," and the honor went to another former U.S. President Dwight D. Eisenhower. In November 1963 after President Kennedy's assassination, Chairman "D.D. Eisenhower" transmitted to the Duke of Edinburgh a resolution by the American ESU board that "in such dark hours, the friendship that unites the English-speaking peoples takes on a deeper significance as we find consolation in the knowledge that others understand and share our grief."

Where the Pilgrim Society in both countries is known for its high caliber functions and speakers, the ESU is perhaps better known for its active branches, thirty-six in Britain and seventy in the United States which is an independent organization. I have spoken to about a third of both, an enjoyable experience. I was reminded of the difference when I offered to speak to the American Pilgrims about the evacuation and received the short message, "Our speakers for next year are already in place and most of our speakers are diplomats and statesmen." The ESU has also a distinct emphasis on young people with Shakespeare and Public Speaking competitions for schools and school exchanges. For sixty years, too, the ESU has sent out debate teams to the United States and many of the young participants have become in later years major contributors to British parliamentary and public life. In recent decades there has also been a remarkable growth in the formation of independent English-Speaking Union organizations in sixty-four countries around the world and counting.

In the U.S. our different ambassadors are often invited to speak to ESU branches. I have sometimes quoted when speaking to them a slightly supercilious diary entry by one of them, Sir Nicholas Henderson, no relation of mine: "I went to New York for the night to address the local branch of the English-Speaking Union. I hope I am getting the right recipe for their audiences: one or two pure and not too subtle jokes, some remarks about local ESU activities and personalities; the dropping of a prominent name or two; and then a shower of unabashed sentiment — links, relations, ties, shores, common language, Shakespeare, Wordsworth, Churchill, the First World War and the Second World War, a tug at every chord short of singing 'Land of hope and glory.'"

I have then followed this up with the comment, "Well, I will dispense with jokes, pure or otherwise, but I make no apologies for bringing in

Lord Carrington *(President of the Pilgrims)*, HM The Queen *(Patron)* and Robert Worcester *(Chairman)* at the Pilgrims reception at St. James's Palace in 1994.

CENTRAL PRESS

The author speaks to the American ESU branch at Palm Beach, Florida in 2005.

sentiment and Churchill and the Second World War and even 'There'll always be an England'. Because I am talking of a time when spirit and links and relations were as crucial as weaponry."

At the outbreak of World War II in September, 1939, Dartmouth House was virtually deserted and its exchange programs had to be ended. Sir Evelyn Wrench, however, urged members to put the House and the Union to work. "The ESU was born twenty-one years ago during the Great War," he said, "and it has an even greater function to play in the present crisis." So Dartmouth House remained open throughout the war. Its windows overlooking Charles Street were boarded up, shuttered and sandbagged while the basement was converted into an air-raid shelter.

Miss Helena Mills John, General Secretary of the English-Speaking Union in a June 13, 1940 letter to Malcolm MacDonald at the Ministry of Health reported that she had received a cable from Frank S. Coan, the General Secretary of the English-Speaking Union of the United States: "Guarantee care hundred children private homes please circularize members." She added, "I would like to say that if any plans are being considered for the evacuation of British children to the United States, the ESU would wish to take part in those activities particularly as it is the largest British-American organization in peace times and also because I believe I am right in thinking that the original suggestion that the United States should offer refuge to British children came from the American English-Speaking Union and their offers of help in this connection have been repeated again and again since September. Through our British and American Schoolboy Scholarships Scheme we have had many years experience with regard to the sending of British boys to live in the United States for a year at American private schools and during the holidays, and should be very glad to cooperate with the Ministry with regard to this new proposal." There was general agreement that the ESU in the UK and the USA would work with the central organizations in the respective countries and not set up separate schemes.

In Britain Evelyn Wrench, in a letter to *The Times* (July 16, 1940) suggested that the ESU assume co-responsibility for the overseas evacuation of British children to America. He wrote that everyone would understand the government's dilemma over the scheme, that unable as they were to spare enough warships to provide escorts they dared not assume direct responsibility for sending thousands of children unconvoyed across the ocean. Many hundreds of parents had deliberately taken responsibility in regard to their own children. Some of these children were poor, for commercial firms and others had made their own group arrangements for sending children abroad; but inevitably most of them were well-to-do, or had well-to-do friends or relatives in the Dominions or in the United States. "It would be deplorable if the suspension of the Government's scheme deprived the poorer parents of the chance to send their children away, taking all the risks with their eyes open. In the interval before it can be resumed the generosity of thousands of English-speaking people in all parts of the world and the organization already set up on this side, should not be allowed to go to waste. Every day lost is lost forever, and the difficulties of evacuation are likely to grow greater, not less. Until the Government are ready to take direct responsibility once more others must step into the breach. As far as I can speak for two organizations — the Overseas League and the English-Speaking Union — and granted the support of the Government Departments in question, I am sure they could undertake to raise the necessary funds and provide the necessary machinery to carry out the scheme."

He would welcome, he wrote, the cooperation of other voluntary organizations interested in overseas settlement work. The Government's cooperation was also essential. "It would be necessary to take over from them the machinery for the selection and inspection for children, the provision of guardians on the voyage, the allocation of shipping space by the Ministry of Shipping, and the contacts required with Dominions and the United States Governments. Since the Government would otherwise be relieved of financial responsibility, it is surely not too much to expect that they would afford assisted passage rates, as under special migration schemes before the war."

This bold and generous suggestion was not taken up — and we know now that it would have been tested with the sinking of the *City of Benares* just two months later — but Dartmouth House was soon involved in other ways, as is described in Gerard Noel's book *The Journey of the English-Speaking Union*.

As the first winter of the war approached supplies of money and clothing began to arrive at Dartmouth House from the United States as a "transatlantic bridge" was created between the ESU North American headquarters and Dartmouth House. Strict neutrality laws governed what might and what might not be sent across the Atlantic. However it seems that sending items as "gifts" provided a legal loophole. Before long, both ambulances and canteens arrived as "gifts" — and even small arms for the Home Guard.

It was to the English-Speaking Union that Gilbert Winant, the new American ambassador who followed Joseph Kennedy made one of his most powerful speeches. It was on May 15, 1940, soon after the House of Commons chamber was destroyed by bombs. He noted that across the street from Parliament and Westminster Abbey there still stood the statue of his hero, Abraham Lincoln. "I am proud that Lincoln was there in all that wreckage as a friend and sentinel…and a reminder that in his own great battle for freedom, he waited quietly for support for those things for which he lived and died." Author Lynne Olson writes, "That veiled comparison of Lincoln to the British people was followed by a somewhat less subtle declaration by the ambassador that he stood firmly with the British — and thought it was time his own country did so, too."

Winant continued, "We have all slept while wicked, evil men plotted destruction. We have all tried to make ourselves believe we are not our brother's keeper. But we are now beginning to realize we need our brothers as much as our brothers need us." As both the *Times of London* and the *New York Times* pointed out, Winant's use of "we" in his speech was aimed at the United States as at Britain.

In February 1941 the Queen visited Dartmouth House, a visit that was filmed by the BBC. She is seen examining the hundreds of clothes and small gifts which had poured across the Atlantic. She was touched by a small boy's letter to an ESU member in the United States who had sent him clothes. He had just been evacuated from London and he wrote to his American friend, "Thank you for the socks and gloves and hat. We have had a lot of snow and they kept me warm. My dad is in the Royal Air Force and a bomb fell on our house but mummy found some knives and forks left. I like the garden here and the rabbits. We didn't have them in London. I am seven." Before leaving the Queen expressed her own gratitude to those on the other side of the Atlantic who had acted in this direct and personal way.

So many gifts came in that a War Relief Department had to be set up and became as the ESU history records, "the hub of a dauntingly logistical exercise run with military precision." Crates of medical equipment, blankets, clothes and toys arrived in the workrooms where they were unpacked, sorted and shelved as appropriate. Ambulances, snack bars and mobile canteens came in from the United States. Emergency calls for aid came in from across the country and crates of supplies were promptly dispatched. "With the fierce intensity of bombing in the Blitz, many of the most disadvantaged people came from London itself. These poor people, some of whom had lost close family members as well as all their possessions, found their way to Dartmouth House. Many must have been in acute distress. The ESU staff and volunteers did their absolute best, under what must often have been in tragic circumstances. Nothing was wasted. Even the wood of the crates went make shelves for the workrooms. When there was enough shelving, it was used by members of the London Fire Brigade to make toys for children who otherwise would have none."

The ESU branches around the country were also active as they changed their role to one of aid work with a particular priority to the distribution of clothing in local areas. Meanwhile, the ESU was keeping an eye on the position of British parents of children in the United States who wished to bear the financial burden of their children's upkeep, but were prevented from doing so by currency restrictions that prevented any money at all. The *English-Speaking World* wrote, "While no one doubts the willingness of their American hosts to look after them, British parents feel it unfair that any such generosity should be demanded for an indefinite period." The newsletter quoted the words of an American woman Member of Parliament, Mrs. Beatrice Rathbone, in a letter to *The Times*: "We all know that most parents are loath to relinquish their financial responsibilities for the children, and however warm-hearted may be the generosity of the American foster parents — nevertheless the first enthusiastic reception might become less fervent as the war lengthens, and the increases incurred by these child-guests increases." Mrs. Rathbone suggested the setting up of a common fund to which parents could make contributions which could for the time being be invested in war savings. At the end of the war this fund could be sent for distribution to the foster parents or presented to various charities in America as "a memorial to the kindness and generosity of Americans today."

This, too, did not happen but the following year the government relaxed restrictions slightly though not enough to cover children's costs.

From the onset of the war Dartmouth House operated an open-door policy towards foreign servicemen and women. Some visitors came for free clothing while others came for free lectures and parties. At the end of 1941 after the United States entered the war the ESU role changed again, this time from aid distribution to that of providing hospitality for American forces in London. Members took a variety of initiatives aimed at further increasing the morale of American service personnel with furloughs and leaves arranged in members' homes. An information center in the present-day Wedgwood Room was opened in July 1942 by Mrs. Winant, the wife of the American Ambassador. Similar ESU centers followed around the country. A year later another house in Charles Street with an extra club room and canteen was opened by Mrs. Churchill, wife of the Prime Minister.

Noel writes, "It is so strange to think of Sir Evelyn Wrench's original conception of the ESU as an instrument of repayment to overseas people — particularly Americas — for their glorious traditions of hospitality. All those years of devoted service during the 1920s and 1930s were rewarded a hundredfold with the volume of gifts pouring through Dartmouth House during the Blitz. And later the generosity to the GIs was rewarded once again." It is estimated that, in 1944 alone, more than 40,000 U.S. service personnel were helped by the various facilities of Dartmouth House.

Today the English-Speaking Union, building on its traditions and its expertise, and benefitting from the universal appeal of the English language, runs a broad variety of charitable activities which bring together and empower people of different languages and cultures. Through their work in public speaking and debating; educational scholarship, and international exchange, the ESU now touches the lives of tens of thousands of people each year.

In 2010 on the initiative of Sir Robert Worcester the Pilgrim Society of Great Britain convened at Dartmouth House an event bringing together former evacuees who were members of the Society to discuss the effect of several thousand young British children spending formative years in the United States. ESU members were also invited. Chairing the occasion was Sir Brian Fall, a Governor of the ESU, Chair of the SeaVac project and a former Minister to the United States and Ambassador to Canada. I was asked to be one of the panel of Pilgrim members who had been evacuees.

Introducing the panel and referring to the special relationship, Sir Brian suggested that the loudmouths at each end of the spectrum inevitably dominate. "Some people say there is a special relationship there, so perfect and so important to the United States that it makes it quite unnecessary for Britain to have any concern at all about the European Union on its doorstep. The other end of the spectrum says that it is a lot of post-imperial, delusive rubbish and there is no substance to that thing at all. Both, I would say, are quite clearly wrong.

'If you want to draw a spectrum of that, I think the post-war hard hats would point to the intelligence and the nuclear deterrent relationship with the United States which is certainly special. Right at the other end of the spectrum in terms of history and perhaps non-hard-hattedness, go for a walk round a cemetery in a small New England town and look at the surnames on the gravestones and they say something which is also quite important. And in between, why does the American Bar Association come over and spend a day in the slightly rural Thames-side Runneymede? There is a huge amount there, and provided we don't follow the fashion

Blitz children write letters to their American benefactors.

The American Ambassador to Britain, Matthew Barzun, addresses the Pilgrims in 2013.

The Pilgrims convene a meeting at Dartmouth House of former evacuees who are members to discuss its effect on their lives. ESU members attended.

of exaggerating either by puffing up or by over knocking down there is something very worthwhile and very special there."

Sir Brian's interest, from service in the United States and having friends who were evacuees, was to ask whether these childhood evacuees were not also one of the special features of that relationship. "You can say what is 3,000 people dealing with a country so enormous as the United States, or indeed as a percentage of the population of the United Kingdom? But if you think about immediate post-war Europe, having those school students becoming young adults who had firsthand knowledge of and appreciation of the United States, there was something a bit special in that, and I am not sure whether the rest of the continent could have produced that added together. And my hunch has been that as these evacuees went through school, on to university some of them, into services, into government service, into the military, into civilian jobs, they produced a cohort of people with that special knowledge and in many cases special appreciation of the United States, and they no doubt passed some of that on to their families as they grew up. So much more important, I think, than the crude statistics might suggest."

The panelists, responding, reported varying experiences having spent the war years in different parts of the United States ranging from Kansas and Minnesota to Massachusetts and New York, some having attended state and some private school, and one who was accompanied by his mother. Depending often on their age, panelists returned in different years, 1943, 1944 and 1945, all with a love of America, and still maintaining their wartime links and friendships. They included Patricia McAlpine, who had lived in New Jersey. Her father, Captain F.W.H. Jeans, had been wounded at Narvik in June 1940 while in command of HMS *Southampton*, her mother was a nurse and starting a farm. As conditions worsened on the European continent the parents decided to send Patricia, thirteen, and her brother, ten, to the safety of the United States for the duration. What affected her most about being in America "was the fact that everyone was so incredibly kind. They couldn't have done more for us." She said that the return home had been a difficult time but the kindness she experienced in America had stayed with her and had given her self-confidence and a motivation for life. "I remained in touch with the family I was with and we visited every year or they visited us. We have been over there this year seeing them and although both sets of parents have died long since, we still have this contact."

David Moller admitted that his stay in New York had made him so unapologetically pro-American that he often embarrassed his American friends. He had also never experienced the criticism which some evacuees had faced when they returned to Britain.

Baroness Williams brought a different perspective. She went with her brother to Minnesota which was populated by people of German and Scandinavian origin who regarded Japan rather than Germany as the principal enemy. She was struck by what she felt was a sense of space which in many ways has equated to a sense of freedom. "It was geographical space but it was the feeling of psychological freedom that went along with it, that I found tremendously attractive, because England has always seemed a tight small country of secret gardens and secret places." It was a very different society from Britain, "a world with far less of a sense of status and almost no sense of class, compared to the England I had known and been brought up in for the first nine years of life. That struck me very forcefully and probably was a shaping factor in the whole of the rest of my life."

In the discussion that followed other evacuees responded from the floor. Norman Moss had become later foreign correspondent of an American radio network and wrote books about America and Britain. Rex Cowan underlined political aspects of the evacuation. Their presence in the United States, he said, was a useful tool because Roosevelt needed as much sympathy for the Allies as he could get. He had returned as a Fulbright Scholar. "I have never left the unfinished business of the United States." Cowan produced the film The Young Ambassadors, which later became in the United States The Orphans of the Storm. Anita Walker said that she had been able to pass on the great love she had for America to all her children. Richard Price had received a good education in the United States which helped him later in running an American company (see last chapter). His relationship with his school in Boston "has been one of the most important relationships I have ever had in my life." He had worked in television for forty years.

In the discussion that followed, the question of the special relationship returned. Denis Brown, who had been evacuated to Kansas City, spoke of his deep and abiding love of America. We might fall out, for instance over the British Petroleum incident, but in the end friends had to make up. "I think we both realize where our interests lie."

Baroness Williams said that she had gone to America probably six times a year for twenty years and taught for many years at Harvard. The special relationship was seen much more as such in Britain than there, particularly in the midwest where she had been evacuated. People there were not politically sympathetic to the idea of besieged Britain. She felt that the relationship might diminish but it could "stand up to a certain amount of frank criticism both ways."

I concluded my remarks by saying that my transatlantic friendships and relationships were not going to be affected by what happened in political life. I quoted words from Winston Churchill at Harvard in 1943. He said: "Whatever form the system of world security may take, nothing will work soundly or for long without the combined effort of the British and American people. I therefore preach continually the doctrine of the fraternal association of our people, not for any purpose of gaining invidious material advantage for either of them, not for territorial aggrandisement, or the vain pomp of earthly domination but for the sake of service to mankind and for the honor that comes to those who faithfully serve great causes."

―――――――――――

In 2013 American Ambassador Matthew Barzun, when talking to his youngest son about the possibility of moving to London, mentioned the 'special relationship.' "He asked me what that meant. Words like 'allies' didn't work. 'Historical bilateral bonds' was met with a blank stare. I thought for a while and then said, 'We're best friends.' That worked." On September 26, following tradition, his first speech in Britain was to The Pilgrims. He said on that occasion: "The relationship is not only alive and well, it's as strong as it has ever been.... As Pilgrims and ambassadors we believe in the value and strength of the Anglo-American alliance. When we are asked to defend if it's alive and if it matters — as we have been recently — we do so. That's a good thing. But as I have listened with great appreciation, to smart defenders from both sides of the Atlantic and to my own attempts, it struck me that we often fall into two traps when trying to defend it. The first tendency is to hark back to history and the triumphs of the past, invoking images of bronze statues, of Churchill, FDR, Eisenhower, the Eagle squadron. These mental images reinforce a sacred quality, as they should, but they also make our relationship feel like a relic. The other trap is to go to the extreme and divert attention to the laundry list of programs and initiatives our governments cooperate in...we cast the special relationship in bronze or paper over it. In both cases it can make this relationship feel remote and restricted."

He summed what it should be as "a real relationship that learns and builds and prospers from our differences as much as from our areas of disagreement. A relationship that is inspired by history but not imprisoned by it. The work for all of us who value strong Anglo-American ties is not simply to address the question of whether the special relationship is alive, and answer yes, and move on. It is to do away with the question altogether by expanding people's understanding of our alliance, to explain that the relationship lives with us in our time and is the business of everyone. Our challenge is to take the special relationship out of the history book and into people's daily lives."

That is a challenge, as Sir Brian intimated, that a large number of wartime evacuees have accepted over the last seventy years. Indeed, we have our own special relationship.

CHAPTER THIRTEEN

NO RIGHT
TO REMAIN
STRANGERS

WAS IT A GOOD THING OR A BAD THING TO BE EVACUATED.... THERE
WERE THE PLUSSES AND THE MINUSES AND YOU ADD THEM ALL UP AND
WHAT DO YOU GET? A CONFUSED EIGHTY-YEAR-OLD. IT'S ALL IN THE
PAST AND I'VE LIVED THE BEST PART OF MY LIFE AND THERE'S NOTHING
TO BE GAINED BY AGONIZING OVER THESE ANCIENT HAPPENINGS. LET
US FORGET ALL THESE WEIGHTY ISSUES. I HAD A HELL OF A GOOD TIME
OVER THERE. IT MAY HAVE CAUSED PROBLEMS BUT WHAT THE HECK I
THOROUGHLY ENJOYED MYSELF, SO THERE.

—Brian Joseph

"I WOULDN'T HAVE HAD AN EMBEDDED FEELING ABOUT EQUALITY IF
I HADN'T BEEN EVACUATED"

—Baroness Williams of Crosby

Looking back more than seventy years, one might be entitled to
come to the conclusion that the evacuation plans for North America were
completely unrealistic, in practice harmful to family life and turned out to
be unnecessary. One might also say with equal accuracy that the evacuation
of children to North America enriched the lives of thousands on both
sides of the Atlantic, broadened the horizons of hosts and evacuees, helped
bring home to Americans Britain's plight, and that consideration of it was
politically necessary.

So generalizations about overseas evacuation are inappropriate. Evacuees
ranged from babies to young teenagers, some went alone and some with
their siblings, a few were accompanied by their mothers, some went to

family members, some were part of a university or company initiative
or the government scheme while many went entirely privately. Some
by upbringing were used to family separation and some were away from
family for the first time. Some fitted in and some didn't, some were
emotionally capable of coping and some felt that their lives were ruined.
Some had 'the time of their lives' and some even now can't bear to talk
about it. Some were made fun of and some were arrogant. Some were less
than two years in North America, most five years and a few even longer. It
is also hard for evacuees to separate their learning experiences in formative
years spent abroad from learning experiences they might have had anyway
if they had stayed at home.

Fault lines run within families with one sister loving her time and
another hating it, one brother benefiting enormously, another scarred for
life. Evacuee Martyn Pease, for instance, takes the view that "the critics have
the better of the argument" and cites the death of the children in the *City
of Benares* tragedy. Whereas his sister, Veronica Pease Farrington, also an
evacuee, thinks it was a fine idea because of the threat of a German invasion.
She loved her host family and the USA, has lived there for many years, and
says, "It completely changed my life."

There were particular circumstances in Britain in 1939 and 1940 that
made overseas evacuation an option that is never liable to be repeated and
one that in many cases is favorably regarded by the participants. They
include the nature of the threat and the fact that travel and communications
had not made the great leap forward of the last part of the twentieth century
and our present century. It should be repeated that in the spring and early
summer of 1940, after the evacuation of troops from Dunkirk, it looked as
if Britain would be invaded and that the Germans might win. If either had
happened most parents would have been glad that their children were out of
danger and today's historians might well be praising their foresight. "There
was the notion that if Britain fell to the Nazis we children would represent
British survivors," writes evacuee Meg Weston Smith, "and of course this
aspect of whether the evacuation was a good idea was never put to the
ultimate test. That was putting a big onus on small shoulders but keeping our
Britishness was never questioned. We took a distinct pride in sticking up for
Britain." I met her and her sister at Christmas 1945 in New Hampshire.

I emailed more than a hundred evacuees to the United States and
Canada: "I would be particularly interested to know whether, with
hindsight, you felt that evacuation was a good idea or a bad mistake and
whether your subsequent life benefited from or was adversely affected by

it, indeed any aspect that hasn't been sufficiently brought out." It was not a very profound question but one that produced a heartfelt ten thousand words from fifty-two of them. These sample responses do not make this chapter a comprehensive picture of the whole but is a good snapshot of the thoughts that remain after all these years.

To ask now whether overseas evacuation was right or wrong is almost pointless. It happened. But there are groups of people whose views would, with every justification, be respected. They are the parents and communities of children who died at sea in the sinking of the *City of Benares*. Several sets of siblings died in the sinking of that liner including the five Grimmond children, and the eleven children from Sunderland who were on board of whom only one was saved. One can only be grateful that the death toll of children on the Atlantic was small. The other would be those who were Jewish and whose parents were acutely aware of what was happening at that time to fellow Jews in the concentration camps across the Channel. Evacuee Lord Janner is sure the evacuation was a good idea. "My father was an outstanding leader of the Jewish community and knew that he was on Hitler's death list." With an invasion expected, his parents decided that his sister and he should be sent to safety. "The problems arose when the ships were sunk. One was just a day ahead of the ship in which I was evacuated to Canada and my parents said that if they had known that there was this risk, they would not have sent me away." One must also surmise the regrets on the part of parents whose children were killed by bombs in Britain where they had turned down the offer of overseas evacuation.

John Bedwell is in no doubt that his father made the right decision. His father had been a German prisoner of war in the Ruhr from 1916 to 1918 and a witness of the food riots as the German economy collapsed. John's mother had died two years earlier and so his father also had to look after three children. So for John the evacuation was "a good thing." The Reverend Alan Jones, who now lives in Australia, says that his father, who was manager of London's Grosvenor House Hotel, where most of us evacuees were processed, had had close contact with Germans prior to the war and "knew more than most how inhuman Hitler's regime was." He felt he was faced with a choice between "having my brother and me subjected to the same merciless thuggery of the SS should Hitler invade, a distinct possibility in May 1940, or go to the comparative haven of his business friend's house in Beverly Hills." But, like many, he says, "There is no simple answer. The deprivation in being separated from mother and father was and still is a gut-wrenching feeling for some. However, we did survive." His wife still cannot come to terms with his parents' decision to have the children go to America.

For June Roper the evacuation was eventually a good idea. She found out what it was like to live in a happy family atmosphere. She had lived with an RCMP family that was not wealthy but treated her well. Coming back to London was for her horrendous and led to some medical problems. "I was twelve when I returned to a grey, bomb-damaged London. I did not really care for my parents but accepted them as I had learnt over the last five years to accept everything. For my mother, though glad I was safe through the war, it must have been hard when I returned and was not the loving seven-year-old who she sent away. She added that nobody was interested in her experience. "When I found *See You After the Duration* and other books it was wonderful to feel I was not alone." Muriel Russ found that "the freezing houses and food rationing" were hard to deal with. But even though she attended seven different schools in five years, which was not good for her formal education, she still values the experience and the happy memories. "By the law of averages," she says, "there are going to be horror stories of children placed in unsuitable homes and one must feel deeply sorry for them."

Most evacuees have a positive view of those years, though practically all recognized the downside, many emphasizing the damage done by separating children from their parents at an early age. Penny Jaques wrote me: "The long-term problems outweighed the immediate benefits." She says that the experience of children evacuated within Britain brought home to professionals that children were happier staying with parents, even if in greater physical danger, than being separated for long periods of time. As a result hundreds of children were returned home. But those sent abroad were stuck. Parents and children could never make up for the lost time and there were serious cultural and loyalty problems. "My special interest is in the long term psychological effects of separation particularly on younger children. It is a trauma to be parted from a loved parent and children have to develop all sorts of emotional strategies to survive a quite overwhelming distress. Many relationship difficulties and some serious mental health problems in later life can be traced to the trauma of evacuation."

Bridie Luis Fuentes finds it significant that many former evacuees went into the caring professions in some way. "Many children did not have the wonderful experience that you and I had." Her mother had been an escort on two of the Atlantic crossings which stopped after the *City of Benares* went down. For Bridie the most traumatic time of her life was returning home from foster parents to parents who were strangers and "having to learn to be someone else's child." She frequently said to her mother, "Aunt Priscilla doesn't do it like that." On the long-term positive side she has become "more understanding of different cultures." The children of her foster parents are like siblings to her and when her daughter was married they responded with a gift to the charity in Boston, The Home for Little Wanderers, where she had been cared for before coming to them. "I also dislike traveling to a degree where I feel ill at the thought of it, especially going abroad. It has become worse with time too, unfortunately. I can only conclude that being taken from a loving family twice has this sort of effect even though they were all good people."

To Margaret Fitter evacuation was generally a good idea and benefited the children involved. If Britain had been invaded and lost the war, even more so. For her late brother, Stephen, and herself, it was the best thing that ever happened to them. In later life they often agreed that it was a "life saver, and it kept their sanity." Her English home had been an unhappy and very violent place. "Spending nearly five years in a peaceful, normal Canadian home was our salvation." Stephen became a child psychiatrist and at his funeral many people came to tell her that he turned their life around when they came under his guidance. "I think you can call this a benefit of the evacuation…the evacuation years brought me nothing but good. They enriched my life and I'm glad they happened."

Gerald and I have never regarded our evacuee experience as a handicap or a setback. It has always been something for which we are grateful. Is that because our experience was different from others or because the course our lives took and the way of life and attitudes we adopted minimized any drawbacks from the experience? But none of the positives should minimize the really sad experiences of some overseas evacuees. Those who were split up, those who were with families that were unsuitable, or were with mothers who had insufficient funds and could not transfer more from England, or those children who had to undergo the humiliating "cattle market" of being chosen out of a group, a more common experience for the internal evacuees. Some evacuees feel that their life was ruined, or that the experience was so traumatic that they don't even want to talk about it. Some felt that they never fitted in when they returned. One evacuee told me of a friend of his, who was also evacuated, who committed suicide. Would he have done it anyway? Lord Lucan's sister even thinks that her brother "went to the bad" because of evacuation. Many seldom ever thought about the evacuation again, but just got on with life. But everyone must have been even unconsciously in some ways affected. It wasn't until a long way into the process of writing and facing the negative experiences of some other evacuees that I began to think, as I mentioned earlier, that perhaps there was a downside for me and for my brother as well in a less close family relationship.

Margaret Smolensky isn't sure that overseas evacuation was such a great idea although it seems to her that it was better thought out than the internal one in 1939 when taking evacuees into one's home was made compulsory. She and other "Corbies" at their reunions were united in the view that if they, or their parents, had known how long they were going to be away, both would have rejected the opportunity and hosts would likewise would have been less likely to volunteer. At the time "most assuredly we older ones looked upon the whole thing as something of an adventure." She confirms that much depended on the hosts who took them in. Her experiences were far from satisfactory, nevertheless she loved Canada, found much to admire in its people and attitudes and now lives there.

One evacuee told me that he felt that his evacuation was a mistake and when he returned to England at age fifteen was "out of place": "Break up of family life is always regrettable. My parents always acted as they thought in our best interests, but looking back, it is probably best to stick together." Pat Jones said she never did come to terms with her time away from home and family.

Helen Macbeth, one of the younger evacuees "…bounced happily through the changes of family. We were extremely lucky, as the three of us siblings were fostered together by a childless couple of great emotional generosity, who, for example, built up in me excitement to go 'home,' which I couldn't even remember." She frequently returns to visit her "foster cousins" and their families.

Evacuees single out particular aspects that they disagreed with. Martin Revis is critical of the Ford Motor Company of Canada scheme because he believes that host families who took children felt under pressure in terms of their future careers. But he adds: "The impact of those five years were profound on many of us and I find that as I get older I think about them more often, but without rancor, although I realize that things would have been much different if I had stayed at home." His life as a reporter in Fleet Street and twelve years in Africa have probably been more interesting than if he had stayed in England: "It has certainly been more restless, and I attribute the difficulties I have had in establishing intimate relations to the lack of affection in those wartime years."

Likewise, Doreen Wright felt the *Boston Transcript* scheme was "seriously wrong" because of the pressure built up by getting communities to compete against each other to see which could take the most evacuees. "My foster father was a mayor and I don't doubt he felt a certain pride in the achievement of the town." There was also mental illness in the family, education was out of joint, it was an artificial life, and on the whole it was a bad thing we went."

Granville Bantock, from the Actors' Orphanage, who was in the United State for two years, writes: "From an education point of view it was a disaster, but I continue to remember it as a wonderful experience." He is still in touch with members of his host family. Looking back he would rather have stayed in Silverlands, the wonderful "country house" that was the home of his English school.

John Bradley, on the other hand, when he returned from Canada as a ten-year-old found himself two years ahead of his fellow students.

Roger Cunliffe has no doubt that the evacuation was a good thing. "We were in an exceptional foster family, and our foster parents were wonderful parenting role-models when I came to have kids. To live in a second culture is to learn, early in life, that there's more than just the 'Best British' way of doing things. And by extension, then third and fourth cultures become more understandable. Cultures tend to be different from each other, rather than better/worse (the Little Englander attitude). I came back knowing very little Latin, but having learnt English as a language rather than as the by-product of Latin translation (at Eton the masters said they could always spot us SeaVacs by our better use of English); and I was well ahead in science, and enjoyment of it (for years afterwards my US foster-father sent me a subscription to the *Scientific American*)." Conversely, at first at school he was a bit of a social pariah, as he didn't know British ways, and had not "been through the war."

Hugo Kindersley feels that his time in New York State was particularly educational as there was mingling with the opposite sex on a scale and in a way that would not be contemplated in England. "I was eleven at the time and when I returned to England I was considerably in advance of my contemporaries." The advantages were somewhat offset by the eighteen-month absence from his parents at an impressionable age, but against this he could offset the independence gained, and his relationship with his parents became very close again on return. "I feel that my time in Canada at that age was beneficial as I have always had an easy relationship with all North Americans ever since. The only factor I found difficult to live with for many years was the feeling that I had been a coward in crossing the Atlantic at a time of crisis."

Ian Jessiman's horizons were widened. He learned French and even began to cook, which he would never have done at home as his family had a cook and a parlor maid. "It has been useful on one's CV from time to time to have spent two years in Canada." Chris Kennington is sure that his time there did him "a power of good." He writes: "I went out a very spoilt and unworldly child; I came back a good deal less spoilt and slightly more in touch with the world." He went on to achieve a first-class degree in engineering at Cambridge University. John Chalmers speaks of the extraordinary kindness of relatives with whom he stayed in Oregon, but was never again as close to his parents. As described earlier his introduction to ornithology created in him a lifelong interest in the subject and to his writing a book about Audubon: "On balance I look back on the episode as positive and am glad to have experienced it."

Barbara Mellor believes she "had the best of both worlds" and "went to the university of life." She was old enough not only to have been adopted by a wonderful American family and have made life-long American friends but to join the Wrens (The Women's Royal Naval Service) and "do my little bit for the war effort."

Diana Lamming wrote: "I benefited especially in my education with four more years in high school that I wouldn't have had if I had stayed in England. I made long-standing friendships and was privileged to have had the opportunity to be sent to safety."

Meg Weston Smith, who became a teacher, says her years in the USA generated many deep and lasting transatlantic friendships. It was an exceptionally happy time and a wonderful adventure quite outside her previously sheltered existence in Oxford. "The net result of my five years was to open up my mind to a 'can-do' attitude, to take a broad view, and to be aware that so-called conventions can be different in different countries and that both can be right in their own contexts." Far from being psychologically damaged she was given "a solid rock foundation."

Betty Corfield: "For the life of me," as she puts it, cannot think of any adverse effects of the whole thing, for it opened up so many new experiences and contacts, and widened her perception of the world, of Britain and of the USA in a wonderful way. "For me personally, being acutely shy, it gave me a lot more confidence having such a 'handle' to talk about. Undoubtedly, those we left took the heartbreak. My mother suffered. She would never go near Euston station afterwards, where we waved our goodbyes."

Felicity Arnott "…wouldn't have missed it for worlds" but if her children at that age had been put in such a position she as a parent would not have sent them away.

Jean Lamb writes: "I have nothing but wonderful thoughts of my time in America 1940–44, but appreciate we were very fortunate. I found it hard when we came home — my grandmother was horrified by my American accent! As a result of my happy memories I got a job at the US embassy when I went to London to work." More than fifty years later she is still in touch with the children and grandchildren of her host family.

Bridget Whyte, like many of us, rather took the experience for granted and hopes that in later life she somehow conveyed a gratitude to them that was never articulated. "I just looked on them as my family."

John Wilkinson was taken in by an excellent family who even invited him and his wife for their honeymoon in 1956. He found it unsettling to go from a strict prep school to the fairly lax regime in America and then back to the discipline of an English public school. He also found it uncomfortable that one could not pay back all the kindness received during one's stay.

"It did me a world of good," says Ann Spokes-Symonds, who was one of the Oxford party and later became the city's lord mayor. Hearing about some evacuees still traumatized from their experiences she says: "One realizes how fortunate so many of the Oxford party were." Many of them, as was the case also with many from the large group from the Actors' Orphanage, went back after the war to live in the USA.

Of particular value to Philippa Russell from her four years in Canada was "to experience the unbelievable kindness and generosity of strangers who, as it turned out, were landed with two girls for far longer than they were expecting." She also valued as a teacher being able to speak to primary school classes who are "doing" World War II about what it was like for young evacuees, the feelings, as she says, behind the facts.

How much the presence of several thousand British children in the United States played a part in bringing home to the American public the reality of the war in Europe? It would be hard to measure. But the links we established have continued to foster the special relationship that is often denigrated. Even those for whom the separation still rankles, expressions of gratitude to North American hosts prevail.

Juliet Boobbyer, who was evacuated to Long Island and whose father, Rennell Rodd, is quoted in chapter 11, says that many people felt that the safety of the United States, even if it mean separation, was better than Nazi Germany. She doesn't believe one should make blanket judgments on a situation that people nowadays cannot conceive of in retrospect. Her father, who moved in government circles, had seen what war meant for children and the effect on their health for the rest of their lives. "He was only too aware how likely it was that Britain would be invaded. Britain could have been starving. The more children that left, more for those that remained. The time overseas gave us all a chance to know America from the inside. Some things were good and some painful. There will always be questions for each individual as to whether their parents made the right decision. It is fashionable nowadays to blame difficult experiences and the things that happened in the past on the way we are now. It is not so common to face those experiences and accept them as part of life and then to let them go, so that they become part of the wisdom and understanding of life that we all carry and share with others."

Four Hutchison sisters from Glasgow spent the war in Canada and are thoughtful about the experience. One of them, Ruth Mackenzie, says that her parents did not honestly know whether to send her and her other sisters, but had tried to do what they felt was right. "It was certainly done for the best. Making the right decisions in a fast-moving war must be even more difficult." Her sister, Anne Mackay, feels she has been left a legacy of friendships lasting to this day; understanding of being cut off from home and family; and valuable insights into living in another country. "Looking back, I think the whole overseas evacuation was probably unnecessary — but who, then, could have known." Ruth recalls that many years later when she was in her twenties, she realized that there was a part of her heart closed up. "The whole evacuee experience came into my mind and I knew that was where it all began." By coincidence, she received a letter from her mother who had also been reliving this period. She wrote of sorrow at her inability to help her over the first difficult months. "I was unhappy, too," she wrote, "but it was war and I felt I should maintain a stiff upper lip! If I had just been honest I might have helped you to say what you really felt. I am so sorry."

"That opened the door to freedom from the past for me, and I know that I need never shut my heart again, no matter what rocks that any of us must climb. No blame; no bitterness. For this I must thank my evacuee experience."

Ellie Vickers writes: "The evacuation offered us all experiences not available to us in any other way at that time. Through it our characters were enriched. I know I learned to be more tolerant, more appreciative, more open, more understanding. I met my future husband and made some lifelong friends. Six years is a long time in a young person's life, and if it hadn't been for the fact of wartime, plus my generously understanding parents, it could have left even deeper scars of separation. I had missed growing up with them and we all knew it. But I think we all accepted it and realize I had also been very lucky. Perhaps there was too much philanthropy and not enough realism in the whole idea of a large scale overseas evacuation. It was short-lived and risky and could only apply to comparatively few anyway. For me it was an enormously beneficial slice of life, though not without human cost."

Tim Phillips finds that his wife of fifty years is not very impressed with his overseas evacuation stories and his "fleeing the country" when she had "to go into an air raid shelter to do lessons and clear shrapnel off the hockey field before she could play." Similarly, Martin Revis thinks that any adverse effects of evacuation were "very small beer in terms of what happened to children in conflict zones or in concentration camps."

Margaret Smolensky says: "When you come to a fork in life you take one path and you'll never know whether or not the other one would have made you happier or sadder."

I personally tend to think that we need to be grateful that, for most of us, the evacuation was a small price to pay and can regard those separated years, as some do, as our war service. One father wrote to the American Committee for the Evacuation of Children which was responsible for my brother and me: "It is a debt we parents can never repay and we should like our good American friends to know how deeply grateful we are to them. Perhaps your greatest recompense will be the love for America that our children all have learned." *Transplanted Children,* the final report of the Committee suggested that the British parents were perhaps the greatest losers from the decision to send their children to America, for they missed a great part of the joyful experiences of watching their children grow and participating in their development. David Dearle had one of the most unusual reasons to look forward to his journey home. In 1940 he had been less than a year old when he was evacuated from Southend-on-Sea to Detroit along with his mother, brother Phil, and sister Enid. Enid went home early to England join the WAAF (Women's Air Force) and in 1945 when peace was declared David and Phil and their mother returned on the Rangatiki to Liverpool. He remembers, "At the top of the gangway stood a tall man wearing a raincoat, and my mother said, 'There is your Daddy, David.' "So I met my father virtually for the first time at the age of five."

CHAPTER FOURTEEN

THE GREATEST REWARD

WE WERE EVIDENCE OF A MARVELOUSLY GENEROUS WAVE OF CONCERN WHICH SWEPT NEW ENGLAND AT THE START OF THE WAR, GETTING CHILDREN OUT OF ENGLAND TO THE SAFETY OF AMERICA, AND LOOKING AFTER THEM ONCE THEY WERE THERE WAS SOMETHING MANY BOSTONIANS COULD DO TO SHOW THEIR PASSIONATE SUPPORT FOR THE BRITISH CAUSE, WHILE THEY WERE FRUSTRATED AT A NATIONAL-POLITICAL LEVEL BY ISOLATIONIST FEELINGS.

—Tim Sturgis

Apart from the larger groups which traveled together, like the children from the Actor's Orphanage and the Hoover and Kodak parties, the greatest concentration of British evacuees was in New England.

The largest group there was the 125 children and twenty-five mothers brought to New Haven by the Yale Faculty Committee for Receiving Oxford and Cambridge Children. At a reunion many years later it was noted that among the party were a future government minister, a lord mayor, a judge, an orchestra conductor, several doctors, assorted dons and that "...it was the greatest adventure of their lives."

They arrived on July 24, 1940. The *New Haven Evening Register* captioned two photos: "Refugees find new haven in land holding promise of peace" and "England's new generation here to live as Americans." Soon all were established in foster homes and most of them of faculty members. Ann Spokes-Symonds, who was one of the evacuees, has assembled the recollections from that time in a book, *Havens across the Sea,* and I write more about the Oxford party in *See You After the Duration.*

It is perhaps not surprising in view of the *Boston Transcript* promotion of the idea of taking in British children that many came to live in Massachusetts. Through daily articles the newspaper appealed for local homes for evacuees. "These children when they return to England," one article stated, "will be bound to take something of America with them, just as they are bound to bring something of England with them to this country." The paper envisaged "a sort of Anglo-American union of youth."

One evacuee who came to Massachusetts as a result of the story in the *Boston Transcript* and found himself in an unusual home was Ian Rose. In Liverpool he and 250 children were seen off on the sixteenth of August, 1940 by the city's Lord Mayor who told them how lucky they were. Ian remembers being upset mainly because nobody knew it was his ninth birthday. He didn't think any of the children understood the war or why their parents were sending them to America. "All we knew was that we were going on an adventure."

He thinks he must have asked at the Grosvenor House interview for young foster parents and to be able to live in the country. For he found himself in Topsfield outside Boston and hosted by Elmer and Caroline Foye who were in their late twenties and had only been married six months. "What generosity of spirit," Ian says. His first words on arriving at their house were: "Am I going to live with a vicar?" For the Foyes were the live-in caretakers of the 1683 Parson Capen House which was to be his home for the next five years. In 1960 this well-preserved example of early colonial architecture was proclaimed a National Historic Landmark.

Ian attended the local Topsfield School for the next four years and then was a year as a weekly boarder at Noble and Greenough School. This latter commuting experience must have given him the flavor for travelling, he says. "I was soon going to double-headers at Fenway Park to see my team, the Boston Red Sox." He went to summer camps and learned to swim, which was necessary in one of them "...as we often took a cake of soap to the Ipswich River for our weekly bath." One year he was part of a radio broadcast made by WBZA from Topsfield, USA, to Toppesfield, in Essex, England. Ian had written regularly to his parents but "...this was the only time my parents heard my voice in five years."

Like John Chalmers (chapter 4) and thanks to host Elmer, Ian became an ardent "birder." "I still remember seeing the first Brown Capped Chickadee in Essex County." He won first prize at school for a list of over a hundred species. In his first year at Camp William Lawrence he identified a black-throated blue warbler. "I did not see another one for sixty years." He has been birding as widely as India and Nepal and in three-quarters of the South and Central American countries. On the World Spotters list he was credited with over 3000 birds. Elmer later became first director of the Audubon Bird Reserve in Topsfield and Elmer's son Richard also took up birding.

For Ian, having to go back to England near the end of the war after having bonded with his American hosts, was a shattering experience. "I only knew I didn't want to leave, and didn't comprehend how my parents must have suffered during the war." He returned home on the escort carrier HMS *Tracker* and docked in Scotland a few days before victory over Japan. He still possesses the book of New England photos given by a local minister friend who inscribed in it: "Ian, you are a bit of old England and a bit of New England. Turn these pages often that you may remember ever New England."

Ian could never forget. He his wife, Janet, and their three children and nine grandchildren, keep alive that link. In 1958 Ian made his first return visit and he and Janet spent three months at Elmer's bird sanctuary. "Elmer and Caroline were wonderful parents," Ian says, "and so much they taught me has remained for life." He wrote me in 2014 about one exchange of letters: "My love for my American friends was so solid that I have corresponded nearly every year since."

Other Boston suburbs, like Milton, hosted many of the evacuees. Indeed, on August 31, 1940 the *Milton Record* could report that Milton "… proved to be one of the leading communities in child welfare work." It was where Gerald and I were beneficiaries of another impressive initiative, which was due to the untiring commitment of forty-seven-year old Sylvia Warren, who ran stables on the edge of Boston at River Bend, Dover. At the beginning of the war she and her circle of friends got in touch with friends in England offering help for their children. Three of those she took in were Martin and Dominick and Oliver Lobkowicz, eleven, nine and six respectively, who had escaped to England from Czechoslovakia. Their father was at that time Ambassador for the Czech Government-in-Exile in London. Martin says, "The reason she took my brothers and me herself was that for many years she had bought her Irish hunters from my great aunt, Edith Somerville of *Irish RM* fame."

The next four years, according to Sylvia's biographer, Margaret Thomas Warren, were "…surely the most important in her life and she wouldn't have had a dull moment in all that time." Her maternal grandfather had been the first U.S. Ambassador to Great Britain and she had been an army nurse in World War I and she "cared passionately about the war and the English people." She ended a letter to Mrs. Lobkowicz in which she described herself and her home: "Believe me, in this country, it

Ian's daughter visits the Parson Capen House where her father lived for five years during the war war and which is now a National Historic Landmark.

Sylvia Warren who ran stables at River Bend, Dover.

CABLEGRAM

-AMERICAN TELEGRAPH Co., LD.   CANADIAN NATIONAL TELEGRAPH AUG 21 AM2 07

AT 22 GREAT WINCHESTER STREET, LONDON, E.C.2. (Tel. No. London Wall 1234.)

FM0544P SANS ORIGIN 38 20

NLT MRS COGHILL   443 CK
CARE ATKINS 49 SLOANEGARDENS
LONDON SW=

PASSED BY CENSOR No. 2420

CHILDREN ARE HERE SAFE AND WELL STOP NURSE SAYS THEY WERE
ANGELS ALL THE WAY STOP I AM ESCORTING THEM TO BOSTON SO
DELIGHTED FOR YOU LOVE=

ISABEL FARLEY.   18.7

Telegram announcing our arrival.

is esteemed the greatest privilege to have the opportunity to contribute a little toward the cause you are fighting for."

Sylvia felt that many families would only entrust their children to go to homes known or recommended to them. Her British friends included Ambrose Coghill, who became Sylvia's London agent. One of her American circle of friends was Harry Cabot, whose mother cabled English cousins offering to take any children of their common ancestor, Russell Sturgis. Seven children came, one of them a great-grandchild, Tim Sturgis. "An amazingly generous offer," he says. It was with the Coghill's children, Toby and Faith, that Gerald and I travelled out on the *Duchess of York*.

The Warren Committee, as it became known, was incorporated on October 9, 1940 so that it would be in a position to receive funds to help the children. Because she had earlier been in touch with so many people in England including Mrs. Coghill, who had an office in London to carry out the work required there, the U.S. Committee gave its sanction to the Warren Committee. Sylvia, together with Henry B. Cabot and James H. Perkins formed the Executive Committee.

Most of the Warren Committee evacuees like us were placed with families who paid the children's full support and expenses. But, when families were unable to do so, the committee made up the difference. Most of the money came from committee members and their friends. Large family groups or groups with mothers were placed in homes run by committee funds. Two such houses were Mr. and Mrs. Donald's house in Milton, opened in September 1940 and the committee's own house in Westwood, opened in August 1941.

Sylvia Warren enlisted the help of Travellers Aid to meet the boats and look after the children. In August she wrote to Mrs. Coghill: "If it is a tremendous satisfaction for you to get little white-faced children off, and I know it is, you can imagine the satisfaction that you should feel when I get the little white-faced children at the train here, holding their hands over their ears if the train whistles, and cringing at first when the passenger planes go overhead." She was working hard to place children in homes that approximated to the background they came from "...not only for success here but for repatriation later on." She was competing for space with the U.S. Committee.

She also wrote: "We are not having the slightest difficulty with any of the children, and they seem to have settled down happily, and foster parents are delighted." Medical expenses, she told Mrs. Coghill, are covered by White Cross and Blue Cross "so you must make British families feel that the schools, the hospitals and doctors, everyone are doing their part for the children who come, so that no very heavy burden falls on individual hosts and hostesses." She added that the children were not perturbed: "It's a mercy, isn't it, to be very young?"

In its final report (August 20, 1944) the Warren Committee stated: "Our records show that since 1940 we have participated in the care of some 1200 cases. Without a long list of figures, difficult to compile and boring to read, it would be impossible to gauge the exact extent of our involvement in each case. Our telephone bill gives some idea of the outgoing calls involved. Sometimes it was only one telephone call; sometimes it included every arrangement from England to the United States and back to England, and a blow-by-blow account of the intervening four years." Sylvia wrote to a British official, "Our hope is that, though the whole evacuation scheme was on too small a scale to be really effective, what scope it had will to some extent create bonds between your country and mine." She herself received a letter from the British Embassy in Washington, D.C. dated May 27, 1947. Signed by H.R.F.Brett of the Honors and Awards Section, it stated: "It is with much pleasure that I inform you that The King has been pleased to award you His Majesty's Medal for Service in the Cause of Freedom, in recognition of the valuable services you rendered to the common cause."

On the whole, evacuees in America tended not to get together with other evacuees and I have found that many did not even know that there were other British children in their town or city. We had a considerable age range and I never met most of the Milton ones. There are few group photographs. But I do have one taken in August 1940 when we first arrived and all came for a party at Sylvia's home. Among those in the picture are the Lobkowicz brothers holding the Warren donkeys, Tim and the other Sturgis children, the Coghills, and my brother, Gerald, and I and also next to us Richard Price (see last chapter).

When the idea of a mass evacuation from Britain was discussed Milton Academy offered to take the boys from Westminster School with which it had had many exchanges over the years. But by July 22, when it was clear that Westminster did not plan an organized removal, Milton Academy said it was open to enquiries from the Milton community. The headmaster, William Field, saw the welcoming of evacuees as "a unique opportunity for a personal contribution to the Allied cause...not only do we feel that your cause is ours, but our admiration for the British resistance is unbounded." A look at the Academy's class lists for 1943 show a total of thirty-one British children in the boys' and girls' and junior school classes.

Milton evacuees have expressed their gratitude and kept their links. Tim Sturgis said at his fifty-year reunion: "Those of us who came were only

ASHFIELD PRESS

In Sylvia's garden.

children, and we took it all very much as it came, amazingly unquestioning. The overwhelming feeling of us all was the unbelievable, open-ended, and endless generosity of our American hosts, so often given without our knowing, in the hope that we would never know. They were memorable years, and a bond had been forged, which has lasted these fifty years."

He feels that he profited enormously from the experience. "Educationally, Milton Academy provided a much more liberal and imaginative an education than I was likely to have had in England. I therefore came back to England a more open and less conventional young man, for which I am grateful. Also it made one far less parochial; things could be done differently, policemen didn't have to have funny hats, you didn't have to drive on the left, there was baseball as well as cricket. So one was able to become far more critical of one's own country, which was, I am sure, good for it and for me. But perhaps the greatest reward was having an American family who had become friends, who visited us in England and whom we visited in America. And this trans-Atlantic social traffic has continued with our children. America is an important and lively factor in the current world, whatever we may feel about its present policies, and the connection with that stimulating country has been able to provide of lifelong interest and benefit."

Geoffrey Roughton, who lived with Milton's Forbes family, described his years as "a fabled existence as the Forbes were in the top echelon of Boston aristocracy." The grandfather of his host, Will Forbes, had backed Alexander Graham Bell and founded and was first president of AT&T. Geoffrey was one of the speakers at Will's funeral. "There was much magic," he says, "about going to America and returning on a British aircraft carrier in a convoy in mid-June in 1944." One of the only downsides, he told me, was that his mother had a strong sense of guilt about sending him to America and when he talked with her about it "the discussion tended to become tearful." Edward Darwin, who was in my brother's class told me: "Decades later my mother said of that time that they had hoped that the Forbes family would have proved good foster parents if things had gone badly wrong."

Also staying with the Forbes family was Barbara Miller. She and her brother Robin had an alarming outward trip across the Atlantic in the *Baltrover*, an armed merchantman built in 1913, arriving as late as November 15. On the second day out their convoy was bombed unsuccessfully. On the fourth day when the weather deteriorated badly and the convoy split up, they were approached by a U-Boat at which their ship's gunners fired two shots. The submarine submerged only to reappear in the evening and they had another unsuccessful shot. Brother Robin writes: "Thank God it was really far too rough for any torpedoing."

Their family, Robin told me, were "colonials" in that his father was a tea planter in Ceylon. They were out there until 1934. His father was due leave in 1939 but didn't get home until 1948. During the intervening period his mother had looked after the four children except when they were at boarding school. So Barbara and he were quite used to parting the family home. "The evacuation was just another adventure although neither of us expected four years of adventure at that time. If he were asked about evacuation he would have nothing but praise for it and "should I have had to consider it for our three I would not have hesitated so long as I thought the arrangements were properly set up." But, he adds, "it must have been hard for those children who had no experience of being away from their parents for any length of time. One comes to expect certain things and to have to handle them as best as possible."

Robin went back in 1995 for the fiftieth reunion of his Milton Academy class. He is remembered for being the captain of the school's unbeaten 43/44 wrestling team. When Robin and his wife visited Boston in 2009 they were met by a grandson and granddaughter of the Converse family who looked after them for four years during the war. They stayed with the grandson and remain in constant email with the family, who has already stayed with them

The *Duchess of York.*

in England. On their last visit to Boston the Millers were shown round the Milton Academy campus by the headmaster. They, like many of us, give to its Alumni funds. The development and alumni offices are naturally happy to have of us on their mailing lists! I personally haven't large sums to contribute but even though I didn't graduate I do so every year so as, in good American style, I can help keep the percentage of my year's Milton class participation high! Robin eventually returned to India as a tea planter. His sister became a physiotherapist and then married a naval officer, John Nelson.

Toby Coghill, who with his sister, Faith, accompanied us on the *Duchess of York*, attended Milton Academy before moving up to Canada. Toby went on to become the much-respected headmaster of Aberdour House, the feeder school for Gordonstoun. Toby, later Sir Toby, became chairman of the board of governors of Aiglon School in Switzerland. An evaluation of his work there in *Aiglon Life* in May 1999 stated that through his four-year period of schooling in the United States and Canada, he was "well placed to be an informed advocate of international schooling with all its attributes: open-mindedness, flexibility, cultural curiosity and concern with global issues — refreshing antidotes to parochialism." His obituary in *The Times* stated: "His own childhood evacuation to America and subsequent schooling at Gordonstoun gave him an indefatigable confidence, and Cambridge Blues for rowing and ice hockey proved his sporting prowess." Toby gave his son the middle name Farley after his American family. In 1991 Faith had a fiftieth

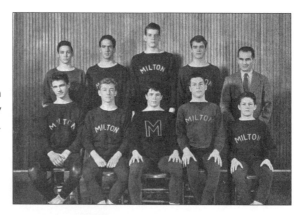

In the middle Robin, captain
of the Milton Academy
unbeaten swimming team.

At camp in New Hampshire,
author seated second from
right and Dominik Lobkowicz
seated center.

ASHFIELD PRESS

Sylvia at home.

Martin Lobkowicz.

reunion in Oxford of seventeen children who had been in Boston. She says: "We never said thank you enough. We took it for granted." Toby, she says, had a particularly happy time. The Farleys had had three daughters "…so they reared Toby as the son they hadn't had."

Jennifer Richards (Clarke) who was an evacuee at the Academy's lower school and a short time at the Girls' School wrote sixty years later that the four years in America were an important and very exciting time of her life and a wonderful opportunity. She is still in touch with friends she made at school. "A lot of Americans were incredibly kind and generous to us English children and I very much appreciate and am grateful to them and to Milton Academy for giving me those years of good education." She agrees with Faith Coghill that they have not been thanked enough.

The end of World War II and then the ending of the Cold War brought dramatic changes to the prospects of the Lobkowicz family. It became clear to Sylvia Warren that the Lobkowicz children, who had lived with her, and the parents who had represented their country in Britain during the war, would not be safe in a Czechoslovakia taken over by the communists. So Sylvia Warren divided her home so that the whole family could live there. As Margaret Thomas Warren puts it, "not only did she work ceaselessly for the Warren Committee but she also took three children into her own home. They became her family forever, and then their parents."

We had no idea at the time of the distinguished pedigree of our friends. The family is known not only as Princes of the Holy Roman Empire but also as patrons of Beethoven, Mozart, Goethe, Haydn and Dvorak. Indeed, Beethoven's third and fifth symphonies were dedicated to Martin's ancestor, Franz Josef Maximilian Lobkowicz, and first performed at the Lobkowicz Palace in Vienna. Maximilian, the father of the three Lobkowicz boys, returned after the war to Czechoslovakia but had to flee two months after the Communist take-over in February, 1948. With the ending of the Cold War, however, the Lobkowicz family, one of the oldest noble families in Bohemia, had nine castles returned to them, although most were in a state of disrepair.

Martin Lobkowicz, a graduate of Milton Academy and Harvard College who served in the Korean war, died in 2014. In an obituary *The New York Times* wrote: "After the Velvet Revolution of 1989 Mr. and Mrs. Lobkowicz and their son William actively participated in a series of restitution laws passed under the inspired leadership of Czech President Vaclav Havel, to recover the family's castles and art collections stolen by the Nazis and then the Communists. Financed privately and especially through charitable donations, the collections were returned and are being restored. Museums have been opened at

Nelahozeves Castle and The Lobkowicz Palace, where scholars and the general public have access to a rich cultural heritage spanning seven centuries."

A history of Milton Academy written in 1948 reported that the school's life had been enriched by the evacuees from Britain. "Not only did they give it an opportunity to serve, they taught Milton much. To this day the faculties of the three schools use the experience they have had of teaching overseas students it sent back across the Atlantic, the records they subsequently made, and above all the friendships so begun."

John Wilkinson came back to Milton on his honeymoon in 1956. In the Milton Graduates' newsletter in 1998 on the school's 200th anniversary he wrote, "My generation was conditioned by the unforgettable events of World War II, and I pray that the deep friendship and alliance between America and Great Britain so vital then will grow ever stronger in the future. I wish Milton Academy every possible success in the future and would declare that a very special possession I have is a gold wristwatch. This was a gift from my foster father, also a Milton graduate, inscribed, 'Dare to be true'" (Milton Academy's motto).

CHAPTER FIFTEEN

AN ONGOING RESPONSIBILITY

"ASIDE FROM MATERIAL COMFORTS, EDUCATIONAL OPPORTUNITIES, AND EXCELLENT MEDICAL AND DENTAL CARE, MOST OF THE CHILDREN WHO CAME TO AMERICA REAPED A RICH HARVEST IN NEW AND DEEP FRIENDSHIPS. WHILE THEIR KNOWLEDGE OF THE WORLD WAS BEING BROADENED BY FIRST-HAND ACQUAINTANCE WITH THE CUSTOMS AND MATTERS OF ANOTHER LAND, THEY EXPERIENCED AN EXCHANGE OF WARMTH AND AFFECTION WHICH ATTESTED TO THE ESSENTIAL HUMANITY OF PEOPLE IN FARAWAY PLACES. THEY HAD AN APPLIED LESSON IN INTERNATIONAL UNDERSTANDING, WHICH, BECAUSE IT CAME TO THEM IN THEIR FORMATIVE, GROWING-UP PERIOD OF THEIR LIVES HAD A CHANCE TO SINK DEEP."

—Transplanted Children, Report of U.S. Committee for the care of European children.

In a 2014 description of her evacuation for her family, Jessie Waterhouse (née Faber) wrote me. "The keeping up of the ties of friendship over three generations (to date) must count as the most important legacy of those years. Also, the chance to experience how things were done in a strange country, to appreciate the differences and yet find that we shared the same values. The kindness and generosity of the American people was and remains beyond price."

In 1940 her parents had received a cable from American friends Munro and Bettie Hubbard urging them to send the children, Jessie, twelve, Michael, eleven, Tessa, nine and Colin, six, across to safety: "just until the threat to London is over."

"My parents eventually agreed." It was a difficult decision for them. She surmises that their duties — her father was running the Home Guard in Kensington and her mother the canteen at St. James' Palace — could be carried out better without the presence of the children. "Nobody asked us if we wanted to go: we would probably have said 'No' to the idea, but it was presented to us as an adventure, probably not a very long one." They embarked in Liverpool on the SS *Britannica* with many other children.

The Hubbards welcomed them with open arms and took them to their home in Pelham Manor, New York. "They couldn't have been kinder or taken more trouble over us." The two younger children were enrolled in the local school and Jessie and Michael were sent to boarding schools in Connecticut, Saint Margaret's and Avon Old Farms, which the Hubbard children had attended.

Soon, however, there was a tragedy. In a terrible car crash Mr. Hubbard and daughter Jane were killed and Mrs. Hubbard badly injured. The children couldn't go back to Pelham Manor and were eventually taken in by the Children's House in Tuxedo Park. Jessie's headmistress and Michael's headmaster offered to keep them at their schools without any payment. After Mrs. Hubbard's accident Jessie spent most of her vacations with families of school friends and she was also in the Connecticut Women's Land Army. "Staying with families who always treated me as an extra daughter," she told me, "cemented our friendships and made the deepest impression."

These acts of "incredible generosity" had a profound influence on her and her brother: "They enabled us to continue our excellent education and to maintain our friendships. Children's House itself was a hugely generous act on the part of Hans Sonne, and I like to remember that when his eldest daughter Fifi came to study in England (and eventually marry a young English Don), she was able to treat my mother's house as a home from home."

After the war it was a great joy for her parents to be able to welcome to their home some of those people who had been so wonderful taking them into their hearts and homes. "And they didn't feel they were meeting as strangers. Many of my school friends came to Europe later as part of their future education, and always stayed with us, and, later still, their children came to stay with my children, and vice versa. I always kept in touch with the school, and some twenty years later when almost the entire senior class came on a post-graduate trip to Europe, my husband and I invited them to our house to look at my mementos and then he arranged for them an eighteenth-century lunch at Dr. Johnson's pub, the Cheshire Cheese He was the architect in charge of the fabric (i.e. to stop it falling down) They had a candle-lit lunch in the cellars with waiters in costume. I had wonderful letters afterwards telling me it was the highlight of their whole trip. Just a little bit of payback that I was able to do.

"The widening of horizons stood me in good stead in my working life, especially when I was at SHAPE (Supreme Headquarters Allied Powers Europe) in Paris with many Americans who had never before been to Europe. I like to think I helped them to acclimatize and appreciate, as I had learned to do, the benefits of other points of view."

Jessie wrote me in 2015, "So many strands came to make up the well of friendships from my American years."

The widening of her horizons in the United States, as Shirley Williams told The Pilgrims (chapter 12), has also been clearly a shaping factor in her life and work. She was a co-founder of Britain's Social Democratic Party in 1981, leader of the Liberal Democrats 2001-2004, a cabinet minister and long time Member of Parliament, and now sits in the House of Lords as Baroness Williams of Crosby. She is also Emeritus Professor of Elective Politics at the Harvard Kennedy School of Government.

She and her brother John, spent the war in the Twin Cities, sent to family friends because their parents were on the Gestapo black list. She recalls how

Shirley Williams as a 12-year-old evacuee.

Shirley Williams on the JFK School of Government's website.

her hosts were astonishingly generous and kind to them but she lived in the State of Minnesota which was "not particularly sympathetic to the idea of besieged little Britain". However, after Pearl Harbor the British became the heroes of the hour and she became the local hero because she was one of the very few British children in the Twin Cities. She took to America, she says, "like a duck to water", enjoyed "freedoms she "had never enjoyed in England" and felt her years there gave her a sense of promise of "a new world where everything is possible." "It was in that simple and heroic time," she writes in her autobiography, *Climbing the Bookshelves*, "a country undivided by class, united by the war effort, a country of flourishing and vibrant communities with a shared sense of its historical destiny." Even at a young age she was conscious of the way different people whether plumbers or doctors or secretaries were not judged by their social background. "There was a sense of the high possibility of a society ready to pull together." She was horrified on her return to Britain, at the extent to which Britain was "mired in class". She says it was one of the things which drove her into politics.

Her biographer, Mark Peel, writes that the vast open spaces of the United States had fuelled her adventurous instincts, and the new world emphasis on open informality and incorrigible optimism blended with her own sunny temperament. "As a young girl growing in the U.S. Shirley Williams became captivated by the life and work of Abraham Lincoln, the greatest of all American presidents. Whether she was influenced by the noble sentiments of his second inaugural address, 'With malice toward none, with charity for all', is unclear, but they certainly incapsulated the spirit in which she has lived her life, and that is no mean epitaph."

MILTON FIRST PARISH CHURCH

Dr. Vivian Pomeroy.

The experiences of Richard Price MBE, a Milton evacuee, are a particularly striking example of the continuing link with America that started with evacuation and goes beyond family friendships. Richard lived for four years with the Pomeroy family. Dr. Vivian Pomeroy was the Unitarian minister in Milton and Richard's father, a Unitarian minister in Leeds, England. Pomeroy had been to Harvard Theological College ten years earlier when Richard's father had won a scholarship to Harvard. They met and became friends and kept in contact as the problems in Europe began to grow. At the time of the Dunkirk evacuation when all the British troops were coming back from the defeat in Europe, Vivian invited his father to send his mother, his sister and him to Milton for the duration of the war.

Richard had one of the more alarming outward journeys for a young boy. Although many children, particularly younger ones were unconscious of the dangers, some children who came through unscathed physically were not untouched by the realities. He was in a convoy, he says, of some forty ships that went via Newfoundland to Halifax. Under attack by submarines the convoy was forced to disperse. In an account lodged with the Imperial War Museum he describes a sinking where he saw people sliding down their sloping deck and asking his mother why they didn't stop to pick them up. They would be "sitting ducks," she replied, and the escorts would come back. Their destroyer escort had already left to shepherd an East-bound convoy. For Richard the evacuation was "a huge plus" but he doubts whether he would have put his family through the danger of an Atlantic crossing in September 1940 if he had known what we now know.

Richard found his four years with his mother and sister in Milton "a hugely memorable time" and the lessons he learned had varied applications. He and his mother, for instance, encouraged his Unitarian father minister to start a children's church as his Milton host had done.

Richard has had more than forty years experience in film and television and has been awarded a fellowship by BAFTA (British Academy of Film and Television Arts) and been decorated by the Queen for services to television. He has co-produced many award-winning programs working with broadcasters, including Disney, PBS, NBC, Channel 7 Australia and NHK Japan.

In 1968 he started RPTA his own international television company. He had previously been the International sales director of Granada TV, one of the big five commercial TV companies in the UK, and one of his motivations was a wish to break into the huge U.S. market. "I had begun to do that with Granada but there were huge barriers including technical problems like not being able to use each other's video recordings as they had different line standards. What I did have was a background of a part U.S. education and I felt, thanks to Milton and my life there for nearly four years, a confidence that at least I had a relaxed feeling about working there, having my own American company for over twenty years."

Richard Price, Chairman of BAFTA, 1990, with guest of honor Princess Anne.

One of the first TV stations he worked with was WGBH in Boston, Thirty years later he had supplied or coproduced many hundreds of hours of TV programs including over 130 hours for their Masterpiece Theatre flagship Sunday night program which was hosted by Alistair Cooke (Letter from America), famous as a broadcaster on both sides of the Atlantic. "We became great friends and I saw him many times in New York where he lived and where I went to work one week in four – out on Sunday night on the last TWA flight and back to London at the end of the week." In 1990 when Richard was Chairman of BAFTA, he presented Alistair with a special BAFTA award for his services to broadcasting.

When in New York Richard would also regularly take the shuttle to Boston to see the station as well as many friends like Dan Pierce and Gertrude Donald who had befriended the Prices in Milton, continuing to do so until she died in 1996 aged 105. He spoke at the eightieth birthday celebration for his sixth-grade teacher Frank Millet and has continued regular contact with Milton Academy including hosting alumni events at his London club. On the fiftieth anniversary of his class year he showed his Emmy award-winning film of Rodgers and Hammerstein's *Oklahoma* at the school, its American premiere, and has developed links between Milton Academy and his own Leeds Grammar School. He told the 2010 meeting

of The Pilgrims, "My involvements in Boston and with Milton Academy
have gone on and on and in two week's time I am back for the sixtieth
anniversary of my graduation and I am going to the ninety-second birthday
of the master who taught me in the sixth grade. The relationship has been
one of the most important relationships I have ever had in my life."

Richard's wartime host, Dr. Pomeroy, was an outspoken advocate of
American families taking in British children. He said in 1940, "We should
all be enthusiastic to see thousands of English schoolchildren gathered here
because not only will they be preserved from damage and death, but they
will grow up to return to their own land with a great love of America in
their hearts, a deep and grateful feeling for the people who saved them; and
thereby they will become a strong ingredient of a better understanding of
America among the English people."

And the other way round, too!

In the opening chapter I quoted a father's anguish at the risk having to
send his four daughters across the dangerous Atlantic waters to the Meem
family in Santa Fé and wrote movingly of his motivation. At the end of the
war he wrote them: "Whatever the future may hold for us all I promise that,
as far as it is in my power, the adventure of the last four years shall not end
at my front door. With the strong emotional bonds which unite your family
and mine we have no right to remain strangers to each other. You must know
how utterly impossible it is to find words adequately to express our gratitude
to you. You must realize how very large is the number of people whose hearts
you have touched by your generosity to the children, and whose faith in the
ultimate decency and kindness of human beings you have restored."

To end on a wider note, all of us who were evacuated to the United
States in World War II were given a little booklet entitled *The Token of
Freedom* and described as "a selection of immortal words by Pericles, Dante,
Shakespeare, Milton, Lincoln, Whitman and others together forming a
spiritual passport fit to accompany the children of the defenders of freedom
who set sail from Great Britain 1940." The booklet was privately printed
for distribution by the Americans in Britain outpost of the Committee for
Defending America by aiding the allies. At the time some of us were too
young to take in its sentiments.

I still have this "spiritual passport" which on the title page states: "This
Token of Freedom was given to me, Michael Douglas Henderson, when I was
eight years old by someone who loved these words and knew what they meant
and knew why I must cherish them and hold them sacred so long as I live."

In a Foreword to the children, signed B.L.W., an American in England, are the words, "When you see the statue of Liberty in New York's harbor, remember why she is holding up a light. It is what any brave mother would do, if her children were travelling a dangerous road in what Chaucer called 'the dark darknesses' of this world. The spirit of Freedom is so dear to the Free People that they have made her image enormous, strong as bronze, beautiful as a proud young Mother. Remember, too, why she is holding fast to written words in a book. Tyrants hate the very words Liberty, *Liberté*, Freedom, and try to destroy the very stones on which they find such words lovingly carved. But your British fathers and mothers are saying No to that. They have said that the name and praise of Freedom shall not be torn down and mocked. They mean what they say. And you are their Messengers. You are going, for a little while, to a country where every child learns by heart at least one of the things in this book: the words of Lincoln at Gettysburg. They are grown-up words about a grown-up Idea. But they are a Token that we Americans, like you, have been dedicated to the great task remaining before us: that we too say that the things your fathers fought for shall not perish from the earth."

There is a lot more for us yet to do together.

THIS TOKEN
OF FREEDOM

WAS GIVEN TO ME,

Michael Douglas Henderson

WHEN I WAS 8 YEARS OLD
BY SOMEONE WHO LOVED THESE WORDS
AND KNEW WHAT THEY MEANT
AND KNEW WHY I MUST CHERISH THEM
AND HOLD THEM SACRED
SO LONG AS I LIVE

AFTERWORD

Previously published as the Foreword to See You After the Duration

I AM HONOURED TO BE ASKED TO WRITE

this foreword to Michael Henderson's book. He and I are among several thousand British children and youngsters who were evacuated to Canada and the United States in 1940.

Millions of children suffered cruelly during the Second World War. More than a million Jewish children were murdered during the Holocaust. A total of 7,736 British children — whom we had left behind, as it were, to face the music — were killed during the relentless German aerial blitz over the British Isles.

Our tribulations in crossing the Atlantic and being taken in by other children's parents were very low down indeed on the scale of suffering. Of the twenty-eight ships in my convoy, eleven were sunk, but all four ships with children onboard got through. Seventy-seven children were drowned when one of the evacuee ships, the *City of Benares*, was sunk: the only child victims of the 1940 sea evacuation, but their deaths brought an end to the evacuation scheme.

The British evacuees were especially fortunate. Many of us, Michael and I included, found the people of the United States (in his case) and Canada (in mine) both welcoming and supportive. We were far from home, and yet, in the main, made to feel at home. We were educated in a far-off land, acquired a strange accent (rapidly lost on return), and learned a great deal about a world that would never otherwise have crossed our ken. Links of Anglo-American and Anglo-Canadian friendship were formed in those days that have lasted to this day, more than sixty years later.

I was one of 727 children who were brought back to Britain in April 1944, in time for D-day and the flying bombs. Michael was sent back, more sensibly, a year later, in time to witness the surrender of a German submarine. On my return I was introduced to my mother with the words, 'This is your mother', and I replied (I was just seven years old), 'How do I

AFTERWORD

know she is my mother?' She was a stranger in my eyes. Similar in intensity are the many vignettes that Michael Henderson presents, not only from his story but from many others that he has assembled.

My passport for the return, which I still have as a precious possession, states that it is 'valid duration war'. No one knew in 1940 how long that duration would be, or indeed if the British would survive the bombing blitz and expected German invasion. This book is the story of that duration. It will bring back vivid images to the minds of all those who were part of the evacuation, memories that hark back now to an age that is long gone, to manners and morals that seem antique today, to simplicities and certainties that no longer exist.

For those who were not part of the saga Michael Henderson so brilliantly recounts, there will be myriad surprises, affectionate vignettes, and warm tributes amid the difficulties and uncertainties of exile.

The memories of individuals can have an unreal, egocentric aspect that does no service to history, only to individual vanity. Michael Henderson avoids this pitfall, producing instead a vivid portrait of the events, moods and atmosphere of a fast-moving, fearful and inspiring era.

One warning to readers of this book: It is a true history of a traumatic period, and there were several occasion when, in spite of myself, I found tears in my eyes. As a little boy, not then four years old, I sang bravely and strongly the song 'There'll always be an England...', and forty years later chose it as my first record on *Roy Plomley's Desert Island Discs* radio programme, and now, sixty-four years later, cried involuntarily as I read its words in this magnificent volume.

Author's note: Sir Martin Gilbert, distinguished British historian, official biographer of Winston Churchill and author of eighty-eight books, was himself an evacuee to Canada. He wrote the foreword to Michael Henderson's earlier book on evacuation, *See You After the Duration*, and spoke at its launch at Dartmouth House, headquarters of the English-Speaking Union, in March 2005. Photographed on that occasion with the author and the then director general of the ESU, Valerie Mitchell. He died in 2015.

— Sir Martin Gilbert

ACKNOWLEDGMENTS

I WOULD LIKE TO THANK THE SEVERAL hundred evacuees who have over the past ten years been in touch with me, sharing their experiences orally or in letters or in emails and allowing me to quote from them. Many of us eighty-year-olds had some fascinating exchanges as we rumbled through our memories. This book would not have been possible without their input and I wish I could have included even more of their experiences and insights. I am glad to be able to finish the book before we, like the veterans of World War II, have all disappeared from the scene.

The evacuees include Dr. Alan Ardouin, Felicity Arnott, Anthony Bailey, Granville Bantock, Malcolm Barlow, David Bateman, John Bedwell, Juliet Boobbyer (Rodd), Ellie Bourdillon (Vickers), John Bradley, Fiona Ross Buchanan, Dr. John Chalmers, Betty Corfield, Rex Cowan, Violet Crane (Warren), Roger Cunliffe, Margaret Fitter, Bridie Luis Fuentes, Bob Hicks, Margot Horn (Nicol), Penny Jaques, Brian Joseph, Hugo Kindersley, Vicki de Kleer (Salamanca), Chris Kennington, Jean Lamb, Sir Christopher Leaver, Jessica Mann, Barbara Mellor, David Moller, Rev. Alan Jones, Pat Jones, Helen Macbeth, Patricia McAlpine, Ruth Mackenzie, Norman Moss, Tim Phillips, Richard Price, Martin Revis, Peggy Robinson (Gibson), Tony Robinson, Geoffrey Roughton, June Roper, Ian Rose, Muriel Russ, Philippa Russell, Valerie Sayers (Goodwin), Jill Sieveking, Margaret Smolensky, Robert Soundy, Ann Spokes-Symonds, Christine Vassar (Tall), Jessie Waterhouse (Faber), Bridget Wakefield (Matthews), Meg Weston Smith, Bridget Whyte, John Wilkinson, Baroness Williams of Crosby, Doreen Wright.

Non-evacuees have also been helpful. They include Robert Ashby of the Actors' Children's Trust, Ambassador Matthew Barzun, Dr. Philip Boobbyer, Sir Brian Fall, Richard Gookin, Lucy Hodgson, Diana Holdsworth, Mary Beth Kreger, Michael Pryke, Hermione Ravenscroft, Martie Sanger, Christian R. Sonne, John Toler, and Sir Robert Worcester.

ACKNOWLEDGMENTS

I am grateful too for all the evacuees who have shared their wartime photos. I have searched widely to discover who has the rights to other photographs from the forties and apologize if I have missed any who should have been acknowledged. In doing so I stumbled across many of my articles which now seem to be owned by somebody else! For the stories of Hoover and Kodak I would like to express my gratitude to Jesse Peers and Kathleen Connor of George Eastman House, Barbara Galosso, and Ann Haines, Operations Coordinator of the Hoover Historical Center for their assistance, and. Dr. Michael Pritchard FRPS and Chris Roberts of Kodak UK. I have also been helped by a thorough description of "The Kodakids" in "Rochester History" Vol LV Fall 1993 by local historian Mary Jo Lanphear Barone and a long article about the Hoover Kids in "The Repository" of 28 August, 2011 by Helen Mannful as well as the autobiographical "Sweet Memories" by Dorothy Warren Mathewson.

I am grateful to *The Sun* for permission to reproduce their dramatic and apposite headline about the "special relationship"; to Paul Holness and Martin Parsons for permission to draw on articles I had written for "Children in War" and a chapter in "Children: the Invisible Victims of War"; to Lady Esther Gilbert for the inclusion in the Appendix of the foreword by her late husband, Sir Martin Gilbert, to "See You After the Duration." The pictures of Sylvia Warren are courtesy of Susan Waine of Ashfield Press and Margaret Thomas Warren, author of "Sylvia Warren, Her People and Their Places."

I am grateful locally for support from Lisa D'Alberti and her team at Northam Library and for constantly needed and patient computer help from Andrew Tregoning as well as from the staff at Complete Computing SW.

My publisher, Ross Hawkins, despite delays has communicated a steady belief in the possibilities of this book, my editor Gloria Martinez has persisted while having to contend with illness and destructive weather storms and fire in her home state of Montana while my designer, Aimee Genter, has once again brought her creative genius to the interior and cover design as she did with a previous book *Forgiveness, Breaking the Chain of Hate.*

I am grateful above all to my patient wife, Erica, who read innumerable drafts and had to contend with delays and uncertainties and my reaction to them.

RESOURCES

Addison, Paul and Jeremy Craig. *Listening to Britain* London:Vintage 2011.

Bailey,Anthony. *England, First and Last* London: Faber and Faber 1985.

---. *America, Lost and Found* New York: Random House 1980.

Bantock, Granville. *Lucky Orphan* 1993 (unpublished).

Barker, Ralph. *City of Benares* London: Methuen 1987.

---. *Children of the Benares* Bebington:Avid Publications 2003.

Barlow, Brian. *Only One Child* Topsham (ME): Just Write 2006.

Bergstrom, Hugo. *An Orphan's War* unpublished.

Bilson, Geoffrey. *The Guest Children* Saskatoon: Fifth House 1988.

Bowen, Sidney. *Dave Dawson with the Air Corps* Akron: Saalfield 1942.

---. *Dave Dawson with the R.A.F.* Akron: Saalfield 1941.

Brittain,Vera. *England's Hour* London: Macmillan 1940.

---. *Testament of Experience* London: Fontana 1957.

Catlin, John. *Family Quartet* London: Hamish Hamilton 1987.

Cave, Patricia. *War Guest* Warminster (Wilts): Adept Services 1995.

Clayton,Tim and Phil Craig. *Finest Hour* London: Hodder and Stoughton 1999.

Collins, Harry. *An Evacuee's Story* Bognor Regis:Woodfield Publishing 2001.

Crosby,Travis L. *The Impact of Civilian Evacuation in the Second World War* London: Croom Helm 1986.

Cull, Nicholas John. *Selling War* New York: Oxford University Press 1995.

Dalgleish,Alice. *Three from Greenways* New York: Scribner's 1940.

Davis, Brian. *I'll Take That One* Privately printed ISBN 978-0-9529151-2-6.

Desforges, Dorothea. *The In-between Years* Yorkshire: Buttercup Press 2001.

RESOURCES

Fethney, Michael. *The Absurd and the Brave* Sussex: The Book Guild 1990.

Gannon, Paul. *Colossus, Bletchley Park's Greatest Secret.*

Gardiner, Juliet. *The Children's War* London: Portrait 2005.

Gillies, Midge. *Waiting for Hitler* London: Hodder and Stoughton 2006.

Grosvenor House – the Inheritance and the People London: James & James 2009.

Harris, Mark, and D. Oppenheimer. *Into the Arms of Strangers* London: Bloomsbury. *2000*

Hempel, Chiu and Sonne, Chris (Eds). *Tuxedo Park: The Historic Houses.*

Henderson, Michael *See You After the Duration* Baltimore: PublishAmerica 2004.

Hobbs, Pam. *Don't Forget to Write* London: Ebury 2009.

Hollingsworth, Hilda. *They Tied a Label on my Coat* London: Virago 1991.

Hirshson, Roberta Star, *There's Always Someone There* Boston: New England Home for Little Wanderers 1989.

Horne, Alistair. *A Bundle from Britain* New York: St. Martin's Press 1994.

Husted, Helen. *Timothy Taylor* New York: Coward McCann 1941.

Huxley, Elspeth. McDonald, Gregory. *Safekeeping* New York: Laurel 1985.

Inglis, Ruth. *The Children's War* London: Collins 1989.

Jackson, Carlton. *Who Will Take Our Children?* London: Methuen 1985.

Johnson, B.S. ed. *The Evacuees* London: Gollancz 1968.

Johnson, Derek E. *Exodus of Children* Clacton-on-Sea: Pennyfarthing Publications 1985.

Kennaway, Susan. *The Yellow Duster Sisters* London: Bloomsbury 2011.

Longmate, Norman, *How We Lived Then* London: Hutchinson 2002.

Lorimer, Jean. *Pilgrim Children* London: Muller 1942.

Magorian, Michelle. *Back Home* New York: Puffin 1987.

Mann, Jessica. *Out of Harm's Way* London: Hodder 2005.

Massey, Victoria. *One Child's War* London: BBC 1978.

Maxtone Graham, Ysenda. *The Real Mrs. Miniver,* London: John Murray 2001.

Menzies, Janet. *Children of the Doomed Voyage* Chichester: Wiley 2005.

Michell, David. *A Boy's War* Singapore: OMF 1988.

Milbourne, Louise. *A Very Different War* Oxford: Isis 2003.

Miller, Alice Duer. *The White Cliffs* London: Methuen 1941.

Montague of Beaulieu, Lord. *Wheels Within Wheels* London: Weidenfeld and Nicholson 2000.

Nagorski, Tom. *Miracles on the Water* New York: Hyperion 2006.

New Yorker Book of War Pieces New York: Schocken Books 1947.

Parsons, Martin. *I'll Take That One* Peterborough: Beckett Karlson 1998.

--- *I'll Take That One Too* Peterborough: DSM 2013.

---. *Waiting to go Home* Peterborough: DSM 1999.

---.and Penny Starns. *The Evacuation* Peterborough: DSM 1999.

Pearson, Kit. *The Sky is Falling* Toronto: Penguin (Canada) 1989.

Peel, Mark, *Shirley Williams: the Biography,* London: Biteback Publishing 2013.

Pelham, Angela. *The Young Ambassadors* London: Andrew Dakers Ltd. 1944.

Raphael, Frederic. *A Spoilt Boy* London: Orion 2003.

Roffey, James. *'Send Them to Safety'* Gringley-on-the- Hill: ERA 2009.

Sanger, M.F.S. *Bittersweet Heiress* Pittsburgh PA: University of Pittsburgh Press 2008.

Sherlock, John and Westheimer, David. *The Most Dangerous Gamble* London: Granada 1982.

Schweitzer, Pam ed. *Goodnight Children Everywhere* London: Exchange Theatre Trust 1990.

Shakespeare, Geoffrey. *Let Candles be Brought* London: Macdonald 1949.

Shead, I.A. *They Sailed by Night* London: Faber and Faber.

Spokes-Symonds, Ann ed. *Havens Across the Sea* Oxford: Mulberry Books 1990.

Statler, Jocelyn comp. *Special Relations* London: Imperial War Museum.

Struther, Ian. *Mrs. Miniver.* New York: Chatto and Windus.

Summers, Julie. *When the Children Came Home* London: Simon and Schuster 2011.

Tall, Christine Vassar, *London War Letters of a Separated Family* 1940-45 Indianapolis: Dog Ear Publishing 2008.

Thorpe, Jeremy. *In my Own Time* London: Politico's Publishing 1999.

RESOURCES

Travers, P.L. *I Go By Sea, I Go By Land* London: Harper and Brothers 1941.

Van de Wiel. *Faces of Fate* Amherst NC: Acadian Printing 2002.

Warren, Margaret. *Sylvia Warren* Ireland: Ashfield Publishing Services 2003.

Werner, Emmy. *Through the Eyes of Innocents* Boulder (CO): Westview 2000.

Wicks, Ben. *No Time to Wave Goodbye* London: Bloomsbury 1988.

Williams, Shirley. *Climbing the Bookshelves,* London: Virago Press 2009.

Winant, J.G. *A Letter from Grosvenor Square* London: Hodder and Stoughton.

www.walsh.edu/hoover-historical-center.com

EVACUEES IN THIS BOOK

Ardouin, Dr. Alan
Arnott, Felicity
Bailey, Anthony
Baker, Janet (Baroness Young)
Bantock, Granville
Barlow (Kempster), Sheila Bohun
Barlow, Brian Bohun
Barlow, Malcolm
Barlow (O'Brien), Susan Bohun
Bateman, David
Baynard-Smith, Jim
Beal (Smolensky) Margaret
Bedwell, John
Bergstroem, Hugo
Bourdillon, (Vickers), Ellie
Bradley, John
Brown, Dennis
Brown, Edna
Brown, Jeffrey
Carnegie, Susan
Carter (Cooper), Eileen
Catlin (Williams) Shirley (Baroness)
Catlin, John
Chalmers, Dr. John
Chalmers, Sheila
Clarke (Richards), Jennifer
Coghill (Garson), Faith
Coghill, Toby (Sir)
Corfield, Betty
Cunliffe, Roger

Curtis, Ronald
Darwin, Edward
De Kleer (Scaramanga), Vicki
Faber (Hope), Tessa
Faber (Waterhouse), Jessie
Faber, Colin
Faber, Michael
Farmborough, Eric
Farmborough, William
Farmborough, Winifred
Fay, Charles
Feasey, Ray
Fitter, Margaret
Fitter, Stephen
Fuentes, Bridie Luis
Gifford, Pete
Gilbert, Sir Martin
Goodwin (Sayers), Valerie
Henderson, Gerald
Henderson, Michael
Hicks, Bob
Home, Alistair
Horn (Nicols), Margaret
Hutchison (Mackay), Anne
Hutchison (Mackenzie), Ruth
Janner, Greville (Lord)
Jaques, Penny
Jeans (McAlpine), Patricia
Jones, Pat
Jones, Rev. Alan

Joseph, Brian
Kennington, Chris
Kindersley, Hugo
Kirwan, Ernest
Kirwan, Peter
Lamb, Jean
Leaver, Chistopher (Sir)
Leaver (Kelly), Gillian
Lobkowicz, Dominik
Lobkowicz, Martin
Lobkowicz, Oliver
Lorden (Bantock), Brenda
MacBeth, Helen
MacNab (Gibson), Joyce
MacNab (McCrae) Yselle
Mann, Jessica
Mellor, Barbara
Miller (Nelson), Barbara
Miller, Robin
Milne (Weston Smith), Meg
Moller, David
Mumford, Bryan
Neame, John
Palmer (Davis), Ruthe
Pease (Farrington), Veronica
Pease, Martyn
Phillips, Tim
Price, (Dr. Peabody) Isabel
Price, Richard
Revis, Martin
Robinson, Fay
Robinson (Gibson), Peggy
Robinson, Philip
Robinson, Tony
Rodd (Boobbyer), Hon. Juliet
Roles, Nicky
Roles, Penelope
Roper, June
Rose, Ian

Ross (Buchanan), Fiona
Ross, Maggie
Ross, Margaret
Ross, Tremayne
Roughton, Geoffrey
Russ, Muriel
Russell, Philippa
Savitski, Tania
Sayers (Love), Pixie
Shuttleworth, Mary-Joy
Sieveking, Jill
Simms, Francis
Simms, Jessie
Soundy, Barry
Soundy, Robert
Stuchbery, (Willcox) Molly
Sturgis, Tim
Spokes-Symonds, Ann
Thomson, Clare
Tinsley, Fred
Travers (Lindsay), Tina
Vassar (Tall), Christine
Wales (Williams), Vina
Walker, Anita
Warren (Crane), Violet
Warren (Mathewson), Dorothy
Watson, Alan (Lord)
Weait, Ursula
Wenham, Charles
Wenham, Ingrid
Wenham, Maud
Wheatly, Ivison
Whyte, Bridget
Wilkinson, John
Wright, Doreen